Praise for *Docker Cookbook*

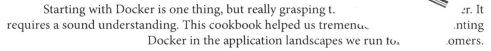

Starting with Docker is one thing, but really grasping t.   ɔr. It
requires a sound understanding. This cookbook helped us tremenɔɔ   nting
Docker in the application landscapes we run toɔ   ɔomers.

—Arjan Eriks, Cloud Computing Services
Director, Schuberg Philis

This is a whirlwind tour of the ever-expanding collection of tools and platforms that work
with Docker, with specific and practical examples. As the core functionality of Docker
becomes even more of an industry standard through the efforts of the Open Container
Initiative, expect to see the this ecosystem continue to expand rapidly. Sébastien's book
can give any practitioner the solid grounding they need to keep up with this
pace of change.

—Chip Childers, Vice President of
Technology, Cloud Foundry Foundation

Sébastien does a terrific job of encapsulating Docker best practices and introductory
material for the novice user across networking, image management, configuration, and
very fast moving orchestration and scheduling ecosystem including Kubernetes and
Mesos/Marathon.

—Patrick Reilly, CEO, Kismatic

See you on the Kubernetes
Slack channel

— Sébastien

Docker Cookbook

Sébastien Goasguen

Beijing · Boston · Farnham · Sebastopol · Tokyo

Docker Cookbook

by Sébastien Goasguen

Printed in the United States of America.

Published by O'Reilly Media, Inc., 1005 Gravenstein Highway North, Sebastopol, CA 95472.

O'Reilly books may be purchased for educational, business, or sales promotional use. Online editions are also available for most titles (*http://safaribooksonline.com*). For more information, contact our corporate/institutional sales department: 800-998-9938 or *corporate@oreilly.com*.

Editor: Brian Anderson
Production Editor: Nicole Shelby
Copyeditor: Sharon Wilkey
Proofreader: Kim Cofer

Indexer: WordCo Indexing Services
Interior Designer: David Futato
Cover Designer: Ellie Volckhausen
Illustrator: Rebecca Demarest

November 2015:   First Edition

Revision History for the First Edition
2015-11-02:   First Release

See *http://oreilly.com/catalog/errata.csp?isbn=9781491919712* for release details.

978-1-491-91971-2

[LSI]

Table of Contents

Preface

Why I Wrote This Book

I have been working on clouds at the IaaS layer for over 10 years. With Amazon AWS, Google GCE, and Microsoft Azure now providing large-scale cloud services for several years, it is fair to say that getting access to a server has never been this easy and this quick. The real value to me has been the availability of an API to access these services. We can now program to create an infrastructure and program to deploy an application. These programmable layers help us reach a higher level of automation, which for a business translates in faster time to market, more innovation, and better user service.

However, application packaging, configuration, and composition of services in a distributed environment has not progressed much despite a lot of work in configuration management and orchestration. Deploying and running a distributed application at scale and in a fault-tolerant manner is still hard.

I was not crazy about Docker until I tried it and understood what it brings to the table. Docker primarily brings a new user experience to Linux containers. It is not about full virtualization versus containers; it is about the ease of packaging and running an application. Once you start using Docker and enjoy this new experience, the side effect is that you will also start thinking automatically about composition and clustering.

Containers help us think more in terms of *functional isolation*, which in turn forces us to decompose our applications before stitching them back together for a distributed world.

How This Book Is Organized

This cookbook contains 10 chapters. Each chapter is composed of *recipes* written in the standard O'Reilly recipe format (Problem, Solution, Discussion). You can read this book from front to back or pick up a specific chapter/recipe. Each recipe is independent of the others, but when concepts from another recipe are needed, appropriate references are provided.

- Chapter 1 goes through several Docker installation scenarios, including using *Docker Machine*. It then presents the basic Docker commands to manage containers, mount data volumes, link containers, and so on. At the end of this chapter, you will have a working Docker host and you will have started multiple containers as well as understood the life cycle of containers.

- Chapter 2 introduces the *Dockerfile* and *Docker Hub* and shows how to build/tag/ commit an image. The chapter also shows how to run your own Docker registry and set up automated builds. At the end of this chapter, you will know how to create Docker images and share them privately or publicly and have a basic foundation to build continuous delivery pipelines.

- Chapter 3 explains the networking mechanisms in Docker. You will learn how to get containers' IP addresses and how to expose a container service on a specific host port. You will also learn about linking containers, and how to use nondefault networking configurations. This chapter contains a few recipes that provide a deeper understanding of networking containers. Concepts such as network namespaces, using an OVS bridge, and GRE tunnels are presented to lay a strong foundation for container networking. Finally, you will also learn about more advanced networking setups and tools, such as Weave, Flannel, and the currently experimental Docker Network feature.

- Chapter 4 goes through configuration of the Docker daemon, especially security settings and remote access to the Docker API. It also covers a few basic problems, like compiling Docker from source, running its test suite, and using a new Docker binary. A few recipes provide better insight on Linux namespaces and their use in containers.

- Chapter 5 introduces the new container management platform from Google. Kubernetes provides a way to deploy multicontainer applications on a distributed cluster. In addition, it provides an automated way to expose services and create replicas of containers. The chapter shows how to deploy Kubernetes on your own infrastructure, starting with a local Vagrant cluster and subsequently on a set of machines started in the cloud. I then present the key aspects of Kubernetes: *pods*, *services*, and *replication controllers*.

- Chapter 6 covers four new Linux distributions that are optimized to run containers: CoreOS (*https://coreos.com*), Project Atomic (*http://www.projectatomic.io*), Ubuntu Core (*http://www.ubuntu.com/cloud/tools/snappy*), and RancherOS (*http://rancher.com/rancher-os/*). These new distributions provide just enough operating system to run and orchestrate Docker containers. Recipes cover installation and access to machines that use these distributions. This chapter also introduces tools that are used with these distributions to ease container orchestration (e.g., `etcd`, `fleet`, `systemd`).

- One of Docker's strengths is its booming ecosystem. Chapter 7 introduces several tools that have been created over the last 18 months and that leverage Docker to ease application deployment, continuous integration, service discovery, and orchestration. As an example, you will find recipes about Docker Compose, Docker Swarm, Mesos, Rancher, and Weavescope.

- The Docker daemon can be installed on a developer local machine. However, with cloud computing providing easy access to on-demand servers, it is fair to say that a lot of container-based applications will be deployed in the cloud. Chapter 8 presents recipes to show how to access a Docker host on Amazon AWS (*http://aws.amazon.com*), Google GCE (*https://cloud.google.com/compute/*), and Microsoft Azure (*http://azure.microsoft.com/en-us/*). The chapter also introduces two new cloud services that use Docker: the AWS Elastic Container Service (ECS (*http://aws.amazon.com/ecs/*)) and the Google Container Engine (*https://cloud.google.com/container-engine/*).

- Chapter 9 addresses concerns about application monitoring when using containers. Monitoring and visibility of the infrastructure and the application have been a huge focus in the DevOps community. As Docker becomes more pervasive as a development and operational mechanism, lessons learned need to be applied to container-based applications.

- Chapter 10 presents end-to-end application deployment scenarios on both single hosts and clusters. While some basic application deployments are presented in earlier chapters, the recipes presented here are closer to a production deployment setup. This is a more in-depth chapter that puts you on the path toward designing more-complex microservices.

Technology You Need to Understand

This intermediate-level book requires a minimum understanding of a few development and system administration concepts. Before diving into the book, you might want to review the following:

Bash (Unix shell)
> This is the default Unix shell on Linux and OS X. Familiarity with the Unix shell, such as editing files, setting file permissions, moving files around the filesystems, user privileges, and some basic shell programming will be beneficial. If you don't know the Linux shell in general, consult books such as Cameron Newham's *Learning the Bash Shell* or Carl Albing, JP Vossen, and Cameron Newham's *Bash Cookbook*, both from O'Reilly.

Package management

The tools in this book often have multiple dependencies that need to be met by installing some packages. Knowledge of the package management on your machine is therefore required. It could be *apt* on Ubuntu/Debian systems, *yum* on CentOS/RHEL systems, *port* or *brew* on OS X. Whatever it is, make sure that you know how to install, upgrade, and remove packages.

Git

Git has established itself as the standard for distributed version control. If you are already familiar with CVS and SVN, but have not yet used Git, you should. *Version Control with Git* by Jon Loeliger and Matthew McCullough (O'Reilly) is a good start. Together with Git, the GitHub (*http://github.com*) website is a great resource to get started with a hosted repository of your own. To learn GitHub, try *http://training.github.com* and the associated interactive tutorial (*http:// try.github.io*).

Python

In addition to programming with C/C++ or Java, I always encourage students to pick up a scripting language of their choice. Perl used to rule the world, while these days, Ruby and Go seem to be prevalent. I use Python. Most examples in this book use Python, but there are a few examples with Ruby, and one even uses Clojure. O'Reilly offers an extensive collection of books on Python, including *Introducing Python* by Bill Lubanovic, *Programming Python* by Mark Lutz, and *Python Cookbook* by David Beazley and Brian K. Jones.

Vagrant

Vagrant has become one of the great tools for DevOps engineers to build and manage their virtual environments. It is best suited for testing and quickly provisioning virtual machines locally, but also has several plug-ins to connect to public cloud providers. This book uses Vagrant to quickly deploy a virtual machine instance that acts as a docker host. You might want to read *Vagrant: Up and Running* from the author of Vagrant itself, Mitchell Hashimoto.

Go

Docker is written in Go. Over the last couple of years, Go has established itself as the new programming language of choice in many start-ups. This cookbook is not about Go programming, but it shows how to compile a few Go projects. Some minimal understanding of how to set up a Go workspace will be handy. If you want to know more, the *"Introduction to Go Programming" video training course* is a good start.

Online Content

Code examples, Vagrantfiles, and other scripts used in this book are available at Git-Hub (*https://github.com/how2dock/docbook*). You can clone this repository, go to the relevant chapter and recipe, and use the code as is. For example, to start an Ubuntu 14.04 virtual machine using Vagrant and install Docker:

```
$ git clone https://github.com/how2dock/docbook.git
$ cd dockbook/ch01/ubuntu14.04/
$ vagrant up
```

 The examples in this repo are not made to represent optimized setups. They give you the basic minimum required to run the examples in the recipes.

Conventions Used in This Book

The following typographical conventions are used in this book:

Italic
Indicates new terms, URLs, email addresses, filenames, and file extensions.

`Constant width`
Used for program listings, as well as within paragraphs to refer to program elements such as variable or function names, databases, data types, environment variables, statements, and keywords.

`Constant width bold`
Shows commands or other text that should be typed literally by the user.

`Constant width italic`
Shows text that should be replaced with user-supplied values or by values determined by context.

 This element signifies a tip or suggestion.

 This element signifies a general note.

This element indicates a warning or caution.

Safari® Books Online

 *Safari Books Online* is an on-demand digital library that delivers expert content in both book and video form from the world's leading authors in technology and business.

Technology professionals, software developers, web designers, and business and creative professionals use Safari Books Online as their primary resource for research, problem solving, learning, and certification training.

Safari Books Online offers a range of plans and pricing for enterprise, government, education, and individuals.

Members have access to thousands of books, training videos, and prepublication manuscripts in one fully searchable database from publishers like O'Reilly Media, Prentice Hall Professional, Addison-Wesley Professional, Microsoft Press, Sams, Que, Peachpit Press, Focal Press, Cisco Press, John Wiley & Sons, Syngress, Morgan Kaufmann, IBM Redbooks, Packt, Adobe Press, FT Press, Apress, Manning, New Riders, McGraw-Hill, Jones & Bartlett, Course Technology, and hundreds more. For more information about Safari Books Online, please visit us online.

How to Contact Us

Please address comments and questions concerning this book to the publisher:

O'Reilly Media, Inc.
1005 Gravenstein Highway North
Sebastopol, CA 95472
800-998-9938 (in the United States or Canada)
707-829-0515 (international or local)
707-829-0104 (fax)

We have a web page for this book, where we list errata, examples, and any additional information. You can access this page at *http://bit.ly/docker-ckbk*.

To comment or ask technical questions about this book, send email to *bookquestions@oreilly.com*.

For more information about our books, courses, conferences, and news, see our website at *http://www.oreilly.com*.

Find us on Facebook: *http://facebook.com/oreilly*

Follow us on Twitter: *http://twitter.com/oreillymedia*

Watch us on YouTube: *http://www.youtube.com/oreillymedia*

Acknowledgments

Writing this book turned out to be an eight-month project. During that time, I read countless blogs and documentation about Docker, and tested everything, and then retested and tested again. Of course, I would like to thank my wife and kids, who gave me time on weekends and at night to write this book. I would also like to thank Brian Anderson, who kept on pushing me, encouraging me, and thanks to regular check-ups, kept me on time and on target. The book would not be complete without additions from Fintan Ryan, Eugene Yakubovich, Joe Beda, and Pini Riznik. Those four guys helped me generate valuable content that will help many readers. Many thanks also go to Patrick Debois and John Willis for their early review of the books, which provided encouragement and valuable feedback to make the book even better. The thorough reviews from Ksenia Burlachenko and Carlos Sanchez helped me fix a good number of issues that will help all readers; many thanks to the two of them. Special thanks to Funs Kessen, who has been a great sounding board on networking and application design and who never turned down my many stupid questions. Finally, many thanks to the early-release readers, especially Olivier Boudry, who were willing to read the book with incomplete content, typos, bad grammar, and a few mistakes; without their corrections and comments, the book would not be what it is now.

## CHAPTER 1

Getting Started with Docker

1.0 Introduction

Getting started with Docker is straightforward. The core of Docker is made of the Docker engine, a single-host software daemon that allows you to create and manage containers. Before diving into using Docker, you need to install the Docker engine on a host, either your desktop, laptop, or a server.

The first recipes in this chapter go through the installation steps to get Docker running in your server. The official Docker documentation covers almost all cases of operating systems. Here we cover Ubuntu 14.04 (Recipe 1.1), CentOS 6.5 (Recipe 1.2) and CentOS 7 (Recipe 1.3). If you want to use Vagrant, Recipe 1.4 is for you.

We also show how to install Docker on Raspberry Pi (Recipe 1.5) to present an installation for ARM processors. For Windows and OS X hosts you can use the Docker toolbox, which packages several Docker utilities in addition to the Docker engine (see Recipe 1.6). The Docker toolbox uses a virtual machine running via VirtualBox to act as a Docker host. This machine is called boot2docker. While using boot2docker is now deprecated in favor of the Docker toolbox, we still present a Docker installation using boot2docker in Recipe 1.7.

To round up the installation recipes, we introduce `docker-machine`, a Docker utility that lets you starts a machine in the public cloud of your choice and automatically configures it to be used with your local Docker client. Recipe 1.9 shows you how to do it with the Digital Ocean cloud.

Once you have installed Docker on your favorite target, you are ready to explore the basic commands necessary to create and manage containers. Recipe 1.11 shows you the first steps to run a container, while Recipe 1.13 walks you through the standard life cycle of a container, creating, starting, stopping, killing, and removing containers.

With those first concepts covered, we dive straight into introducing the *Dockerfile* (Recipe 1.14). A *Dockerfile* is a manifest that describes how to build a container image. This is a core concept in Docker and while Chapter 2 will expand much further on the topic, we cover it here in its most simple form. This allows us to introduce a much more complex example right away, running WordPress.

First we do it in a single container by building a Docker image from scratch and running multiple processes in the container (Recipe 1.15). Docker makes you change your application designer mindset from packaging everything together to creating multiple independent services that can then be interconnected. However, it does not mean that you cannot run multiple services in a single container. Using *supervisord* you can, and Recipe 1.15 shows you how. But the strength of Docker comes with the ease of composing services to run your application. Therefore in Recipe 1.16 we show you how to split the single container example into two containers using container linking. This is your first example of a distributed application, even though it runs on a single host.

The last concept that we introduce in this chapter is data management. Making data accessible in a container is a critical component. You might use it to load configuration variables or datasets, or to share data between containers. We use the WordPress example again and show you how to back up your database (Recipe 1.17), how to mount data in your host into your containers (Recipe 1.18), and also how to create so-called data-containers (Recipe 1.19).

In summary, in this chapter you will go from installing the Docker engine on a host to running a two-container WordPress site in a flash.

1.1 Installing Docker on Ubuntu 14.04

Problem

You want to use Docker on Ubuntu 14.04.

Solution

On Ubuntu 14.04, installing Docker is achieved in three lines of bash commands at most. The recommended installation by the Docker project uses a bash script that is available on the Internet. Be careful, because a preexisting *docker* package is included in the Ubuntu repositories that is not related to Docker (*http://www.docker.com*). Perform the recommended installation:

```
$ sudo apt-get update
$ sudo apt-get install -y wget
$ sudo wget -qO- https://get.docker.com/ | sh
```

You can test that the installation worked fine by checking the version of Docker:

```
$ sudo docker --version
Docker version 1.7.1, build 786b29d
```

You can stop, start, and restart the service. For example, to restart it:

```
$ sudo service docker restart
```

 If you want to use docker from a nonroot user, add the user account to the docker group:

```
$ sudo gpasswd -a <user> docker
```

Exit the current shell and log in again or start a new shell for the change to take effect.

Discussion

You can look at the installation script available at *https://get.docker.com* to perform the installation step by step and customize it to your liking. On Ubuntu 14.04 (*trusty* release), at a minimum you would do the following:

```
$ sudo apt-get update
$ sudo apt-get install -y linux-image-extra-$(uname -r) linux-image-extra-virtual
$ sudo apt-key adv --keyserver hkp://p80.pool.sks-keyservers.net:80
                --recv-keys 58118E89F3A912897C070ADBF76221572C52609D
$ sudo su
# echo deb https://apt.dockerproject.org/repo ubuntu-trusty main > \
/etc/apt/sources.list.d/docker.list
# apt-get -y install docker-engine
```

See Also

- For installation of Docker on other operating systems, see the official installation documentation (*https://docs.docker.com/docker/installation/*).

1.2 Installing Docker on CentOS 6.5

Problem

You want to use Docker on CentOS 6.5.

Solution

On CentOS 6.5, getting Docker is achieved by installing the docker-io package from the Extra Packages for Enterprise Linux (EPEL) repository:

```
$ sudo yum -y update
$ sudo yum -y install epel-release
```

```
$ sudo yum -y install docker-io
$ sudo service docker start
$ sudo chkconfig docker on
```

On CentOS 6.5, it installs version 1.6.2:

```
# docker --version
Docker version 1.6.2, build 7c8fca2/1.6.2
```

Discussion

CentOS 6.*x* is no longer supported by Docker. Instead, CentOS 7 should be used if you want the latest version of Docker (see Recipe 1.3).

1.3 Installing Docker on CentOS 7

Problem

You want to use Docker on CentOS 7.

Solution

Install the Docker package by using the *yum* package manager. CentOS uses *systemd*, so to manage the *docker* service, you can use the `systemctl` command:

```
$ sudo yum update
$ sudo yum -y install docker
$ sudo systemctl start docker
```

You can also use the official Docker installation script, which will use packages from the Docker repository:

```
$ sudo yum update
$ sudo curl -sSL https://get.docker.com/ | sh
```

1.4 Setting Up a Local Docker Host by Using Vagrant

Problem

The operating system of your local machine is different from the operating system you want to use Docker on. For example, you are running OS X and want to try Docker on Ubuntu.

Solution

Use Vagrant (*http://vagrantup.com*) to start a virtual machine (VM) locally and bootstrap the VM by using a shell provisioner in the Vagrantfile.

With a working VirtualBox (*http://virtualbox.org*) and Vagrant (*http://vagrantup.com*) installation, create a text file called *Vagrantfile* that contains the following:

```
VAGRANTFILE_API_VERSION = "2"

$bootstrap=<<SCRIPT
apt-get update
apt-get -y install wget
wget -qO- https://get.docker.com/ | sh
gpasswd -a vagrant docker
service docker restart
SCRIPT

Vagrant.configure(VAGRANTFILE_API_VERSION) do |config|
  config.vm.box = "ubuntu/trusty64"

  config.vm.network "private_network", ip: "192.168.33.10"

  config.vm.provider "virtualbox" do |vb|
     vb.customize ["modifyvm", :id, "--memory", "1024"]
  end

  config.vm.provision :shell, inline: $bootstrap

end
```

You can then bring up the virtual machine. Vagrant will download the *ubuntu/trusty64* box from the Vagrant cloud (*http://vagrantcloud.com*) (now part of Atlas (*https://atlas.hashicorp.com*)), start an instance of it using VirtualBox, and run the bootstrap script in the instance. The instance will have 1GB of RAM and two network interfaces: a Network Address Translation (NAT) interface that will be used for outbound traffic to the public Internet and a host-only interface *192.168.33.10*. You will then be able to ssh to the instance and use Docker:

```
$ vagrant up
$ vagrant ssh
vagrant@vagrant-ubuntu-trusty-64:~$ docker ps
CONTAINER ID    IMAGE    COMMAND    CREATED    STATUS    PORTS    NAMES
```

 In this Vagrant setup, the vagrant user was added to the Docker group. Hence Docker commands can be issued even if you are not root. You can get these scripts from the how2dock repository (*https://github.com/how2dock/docbook.git*) in the *ch01* directory.

Discussion

If you have never used Vagrant, you will need to install it. The download page on the Vagrant website (*https://www.vagrantup.com/downloads*) lists all major package families. For example, on Debian-based systems, grab the *.deb* package and install it like so:

```
$ wget https://dl.bintray.com/mitchellh/vagrant/vagrant_1.7.4_x86_64.deb
$ sudo dpkg -i vagrant_1.7.4_x86_64.deb
$ sudo vagrant --version
Vagrant 1.7.4
```

1.5 Installing Docker on a Raspberry Pi

Problem

You use Raspberry Pi (*https://www.raspberrypi.org*) a lot at your company or you are a hobbyist who enjoys hacking with Raspberry Pi. In either case, you would like to know how to install Docker on your device.

Solution

Use the preconfigured Secure Digital (SD) card image from Hypriot (*http://blog.hypriot.com*). You need to follow these steps:

1. Download the SD card image (*http://blog.hypriot.com/downloads*).
2. Transfer it to your SD card.
3. Install the SD card on your Raspberry Pi and boot it.
4. Log in to your Raspberry Pi and use Docker.

Discussion

For example, on an OS X host, you can follow the instructions (*http://bit.ly/hypriot-docker*) from Hypriot.

Download and unzip the SD image:

```
$ curl -sOL http://downloads.hypriot.com/hypriot-rpi-20150416-201537.img.zip
$ unzip hypriot-rpi-20150416-201537.img.zip
```

Now insert your SD card in your host card reader; list the available disks to find out which one the SD card is. Unmount this disk and transfer the image onto it by using dd. Assuming the disk is disk1:

```
$ diskutil list
...
$ diskutil unmountdisk /dev/disk1
$ sudo dd if=hypriot-rpi-20150416-201537.img of=/dev/rdisk1 bs=1m
$ diskutil unmountdisk /dev/disk1
```

Once the image has been transferred, you can *eject* the disk cleanly, remove the SD card from the card reader, and put it in your Raspberry Pi. You will need to find the IP address of your Raspberry Pi, and then you can `ssh` to it and use `hypriot` as the password like so:

```
$ ssh root@<IP_OF_RPI>
...
HypriotOS: root@black-pearl in ~
$ docker ps
CONTAINER ID    IMAGE    COMMAND    CREATED    STATUS    PORTS    NAMES
HypriotOS: root@black-pearl in ~
$ uname -a
Linux black-pearl 3.18.11-hypriotos-v7+ #2 SMP PREEMPT Sun Apr 12 16:34:20 UTC \
2015 armv7l GNU/Linux
HypriotOS: root@black-pearl in ~
```

You will have a functioning Docker on ARM.

Because containers use the same kernel as the Docker host, you will need to pull images that have been prepared for an ARM-based architecture. Go to the Docker Hub and look for ARM-based images; the ones from *Hyperiot* are a good start.

See Also

- Windows instructions (*http://bit.ly/hypriot-windows*)
- Linux instructions (*http://bit.ly/hypriot-linux*)

1.6 Installing Docker on OS X Using Docker Toolbox

Problem

The Docker daemon is not supported on OS X, but you want to use Docker on OS X.

Solution

Use Docker Toolbox (*https://https://www.docker.com/toolbox*), an installer that contains the Docker Client, Docker Machine, Docker Compose, Docker Kitematic, and VirtualBox. Docker Toolbox allows you to start a tiny virtual machine in VirtualBox that runs the Docker daemon. The Docker client installed on your OS X machine is configured to connect to this Docker daemon. Docker Machine (see Recipe 1.9), Docker Compose (see Recipe 7.1), and Kitematic (see Recipe 7.5) are also installed.

Download the installer from the download page (*https://https://www.docker.com/toolbox*). Once the download is complete (see Figure 1-1), open the installer and go through the steps in the wizard. Once the installation is complete, the finder will open and you will see a link to the *Docker quickstart terminal*. Click it to open a terminal and automatically start a virtual machine in VirtualBox. The Docker client will be automatically configured to communicate with this Docker daemon.

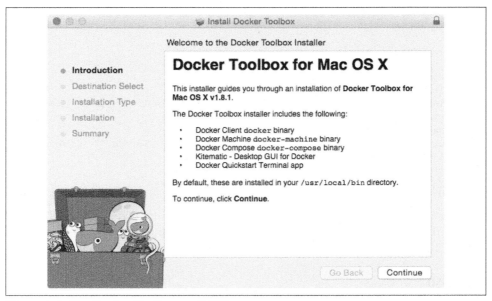

Figure 1-1. The Docker Toolbox on OS X

The Toolbox terminal shows you that the Docker client is configured to use the *default* machine. Try a few docker commands as shown here:

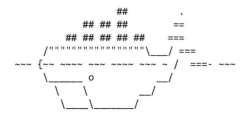

```
docker is configured to use the default machine with IP 192.168.99.100
For help getting started, check out the docs at https://docs.docker.com

bash-4.3$ docker ps
CONTAINER ID        IMAGE       COMMAND       CREATED       STATUS       PORTS       NAMES
bash-4.3$ docker images
REPOSITORY              TAG       IMAGE ID       CREATED       VIRTUAL SIZE
bash-4.3$ docker
docker          docker-compose  docker-machine
```

You see that the docker-machine and docker-compose binaries are also available to you.

Discussion

The Docker Toolbox was introduced in Docker 1.8 and should be the default installation method on OS X and Windows hosts. Prior to the Docker Toolbox, you could use *Boot2Docker* (see Recipe 1.7 and Recipe 1.8). Recipes for *Boot2Docker* are also in this book, but Docker Toolbox should be used. In fact, *Boot2Docker* is still used in Toolbox, as it is the image of the virtual machine started by the Toolbox. You can see this by using the `docker-machine ssh` command to log in to the VM as shown here:

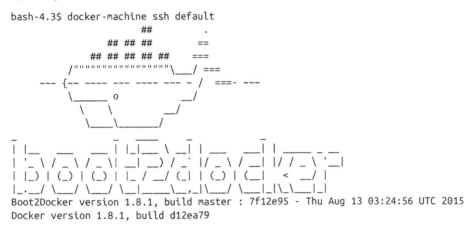

```
Boot2Docker version 1.8.1, build master : 7f12e95 - Thu Aug 13 03:24:56 UTC 2015
Docker version 1.8.1, build d12ea79
```

1.7 Using Boot2Docker to Get a Docker Host on OS X

Problem

The Docker daemon is not supported on OS X, but you want to use the Docker client seamlessly on your OS X host.

Solution

Use the Boot2Docker (*http://boot2docker.io*) lightweight Linux distribution. Boot2Docker is based on Tiny Core Linux and configured specifically to act as a Docker host. After installation, a `boot2docker` command will be available to you. You will use it to interact with a virtual machine started through VirtualBox that will act as a Docker host. The Docker client—which runs on OS X, unlike the daemon—will be set up on your local OS X machine.

Let's start by downloading and installing Boot2Docker. Go to the site (*http://boot2docker.io*) where you will find several download links. From the release page (*https://github.com/boot2docker/osx-installer/releases*), grab the latest release. Once the download is finished, launch the installer shown in Figure 1-2.

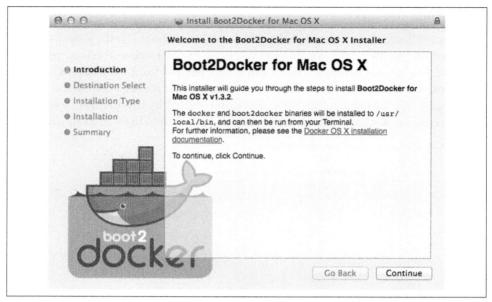

Figure 1-2. Boot2Docker installer wizard

Once the installation is finished (Figure 1-3), you are ready to use Boot2Docker.

In a terminal window, type **boot2docker** at the prompt, and you should see the usage options. You can also check the version number that you installed:

```
$ boot2docker
Usage: boot2docker [<options>] {help|init|up|ssh|save|down|poweroff|reset|
                                restart|config|status|info|ip|shellinit|delete|
                                download|upgrade|version} [<args>]
$ boot2docker version
Boot2Docker-cli version: v1.3.2
Git commit: e41a9ae
```

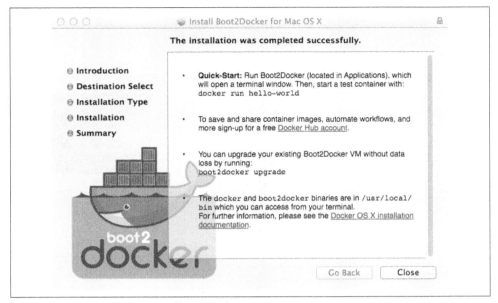

Figure 1-3. Boot2Docker installer completion

With Boot2Docker installed, the first step is to initialize it. If you have not downloaded the Boot2Docker ISO, this step will do so and create the virtual machine in VirtualBox:

```
$ boot2docker init
Latest release for boot2docker/boot2docker is v1.3.2
Downloading boot2docker ISO image...
Success:
    downloaded https://github.com/boot2docker/boot2docker/releases/download/\
    v1.3.2/boot2docker.iso
    to /Users/sebgoa/.boot2docker/boot2docker.iso
```

As you can see, the ISO will be located in your home directory under *.boot2docker/ boot2docker.iso*. When you open the VirtualBox UI, you will see the boot2docker VM in a powered-off state (see Figure 1-4).

Figure 1-4. boot2docker VirtualBox VM

 You do not need to have the VirtualBox UI open; the snapshots are here only for illustration. Boot2Docker uses the VBoxManage commands to manage the boot2docker VM in the background.

You are now ready to start Boot2Docker. This will run the VM and return some instructions to set environment variables for properly connecting to the Docker daemon running in the VM:

```
$ boot2docker start
Waiting for VM and Docker daemon to start...
.......................oooooooooooooooooooooo
Started.
Writing /Users/sebgoa/.boot2docker/certs/boot2docker-vm/ca.pem
Writing /Users/sebgoa/.boot2docker/certs/boot2docker-vm/cert.pem
Writing /Users/sebgoa/.boot2docker/certs/boot2docker-vm/key.pem

To connect the Docker client to the Docker daemon, please set:
    export DOCKER_CERT_PATH=/Users/sebgoa/.boot2docker/certs/boot2docker-vm
    export DOCKER_TLS_VERIFY=1
    export DOCKER_HOST=tcp://192.168.59.103:2376
```

Although you can set the environment variables by hand, Boot2Docker provides a handy command: shellinit. Use it to configure the Transport Layer Security (TLS) connection to the Docker daemon, and you will have access to the Docker host from your local OS X machine:

```
$ $(boot2docker shellinit)
Writing /Users/sebgoa/.boot2docker/certs/boot2docker-vm/ca.pem
Writing /Users/sebgoa/.boot2docker/certs/boot2docker-vm/cert.pem
Writing /Users/sebgoa/.boot2docker/certs/boot2docker-vm/key.pem
$ docker ps
CONTAINER ID    IMAGE    COMMAND    CREATED    STATUS    PORTS    NAMES
```

Discussion

When a new version of Boot2Docker is available, you can upgrade easily by downloading the new Boot2Docker installer and downloading a new ISO image with the download command.

Make sure that you stop the current boot2docker VM with $ boot2docker stop before running the installer script:

```
$ boot2docker stop
$ boot2docker upgrade
$ boot2docker start
```

1.8 Running Boot2Docker on Windows 8.1 Desktop

Problem

You have a Windows 8.1 desktop and would like to use Boot2Docker to test Docker.

Solution

Use the Boot2Docker windows installer (*http://bit.ly/gh-boot2docker*), shown in Figure 1-5.

After downloading the latest version of the Windows installer (an *.exe* binary), run it through the command prompt or through your file explorer (see Figure 1-5). It will automatically install VirtualBox, MSysGit, and the Boot2Docker ISO. MSysGit is necessary to get the *ssk-keygen* binary on your Windows machine. Going through the installer wizard, you will need to accept a couple of VirtualBox licenses from Oracle. The installer can create shortcuts on your desktop for VirtualBox and to start Boot2Docker.

Figure 1-5. Boot2Docker Windows 8.1 installer

Once the installation is finished, double-click the shortcut for Boot2Docker. This will launch the VM in VirtualBox, and you will get a command prompt inside it (see Figure 1-6). You can now use Docker on your Windows desktop.

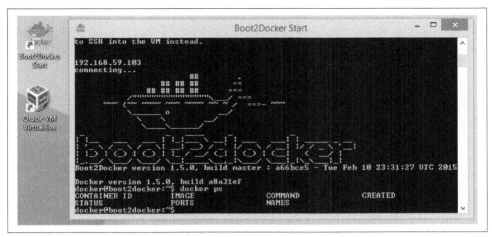

Figure 1-6. Boot2Docker Windows 8.1 command

Discussion

Docker Machine (see Recipe 1.9) also comes with a Hyper-V driver. If you set up Hyper-V on your desktop, you could start a Boot2Docker instance with Docker Machine instead.

See Also

- Boot2Docker for Windows official Docker documentation (*https://docs.docker.com/installation/windows/*)

1.9 Starting a Docker Host in the Cloud by Using Docker Machine

Problem

You do not want to install the Docker daemon locally using Vagrant (Recipe 1.4) or Boot2Docker (Recipe 1.7). Instead, you would like to use a Docker host in the cloud (e.g., AWS, DigitalOcean, Azure, or Google Compute Engine) and connect to it seamlessly using the local Docker client.

Solution

Use *Docker Machine* to start a cloud instance in your public cloud of choice. *Docker Machine* is client-side tool that you run on your local host and that allows you to start a server in a remote public cloud and use it as a Docker host as if it were local.

Machine will automatically install Docker and set up TLS for secure communication. You will then be able to use the cloud instance as your Docker host and use it from a local Docker client. See Chapter 8 for more recipes dedicated to using Docker in the cloud.

 Docker Machine beta was announced (*http://blog.docker.com/ 2015/02/announcing-docker-machine-beta/*) on February 26, 2015. Official documentation (*https://docs.docker.com/machine/*) is now available on the Docker website. The source code is available on GitHub (*https://github.com/docker/machine*).

Let's get started. *Machine* currently supports VirtualBox, DigitalOcean (*https:// www.digitalocean.com*), Amazon Web Services (*https://aws.amazon.com*), Azure (*https://azure.microsoft.com*), Google Compute Engine (GCE) (*http:// cloud.google.com*), and a few other providers. Several drivers are under development or review (*https://github.com/docker/machine/pulls*), so we should definitely expect much more soon. This recipe uses DigitalOcean, so if you want to follow along step by step, you will need an account on DigitalOcean (*https://cloud.digitalocean.com/ registrations/new*).

Once you have an account, do not create a droplet through the DigitalOcean UI. Instead, generate an API access token for using Docker Machine. This token will need to be both a *read* and a *write* token so that Machine can upload a public SSH key (Figure 1-7). Set an environment variable `DIGITALOCEAN_ACCESS_TOKEN` in your local computer shell that defines the token you created.

 Machine will upload an SSH key to your cloud account. Make sure that your access tokens or API keys give you the privileges necessary to create a key.

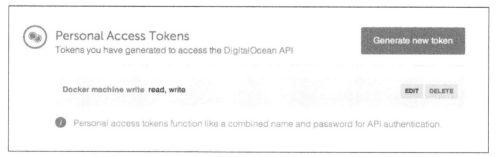

Figure 1-7. DigitalOcean access token for Machine

You are almost set. You just need to download the *docker-machine* binary. Go to the documentation site (*https://docs.docker.com/machine/*) and choose the correct binary for your local computer architecture. For example, on OS X:

```
$ curl -sOL https://github.com/docker/machine/releases/download/v0.3.0/ \
docker-machine_darwin-amd64
$ mv docker-machine_darwin-amd64 docker-machine
$ chmod +x docker-machine
$ ./docker-machine --version
docker-machine version 0.3.0
```

With the environment variable DIGITALOCEAN_ACCESS_TOKEN set, you can create your remote Docker host:

```
$ ./docker-machine create -d digitalocean foobar
Creating SSH key...
Creating Digital Ocean droplet...
To see how to connect Docker to this machine, run: docker-machine env foobar
```

If you go back to your DigitalOcean dashboard, you will see that an SSH key has been created, as well as a new droplet (see Figures 1-8 and 1-9).

Figure 1-8. DigitalOcean SSH keys generated by Machine

Figure 1-9. DigitalOcean droplet created by Machine

To configure your local Docker client to use this remote Docker host, you execute the command that was listed in the output of creating the machine:

```
$ ./docker-machine env foobar
export DOCKER_TLS_VERIFY="1"
export DOCKER_HOST="tcp://104.131.92.15:2376"
export DOCKER_CERT_PATH="/Users/sebastiengoasguen/.docker/machine/machines/foobar"
```

```
export DOCKER_MACHINE_NAME="foobar"
# Run this command to configure your shell:
# eval "$(docker-machine env foobar)"
$ eval "$(./docker-machine env foobar)"
$ docker ps
CONTAINER ID    IMAGE    COMMAND    CREATED    STATUS    PORTS    NAMES
```

Enjoy Docker running remotely on a DigitalOcean droplet created with Docker Machine.

Discussion

 If not specified at the command line, Machine will look for DIGI TALOCEAN_IMAGE, DIGITALOCEAN_REGION, and DIGITALOCEAN_SIZE environment variables. By default, they are set to *docker*, *nyc3*, and *512mb*, respectively.

The *docker-machine* binary lets you create multiple machines, on multiple providers. You also have the basic management capabilities: start, stop, rm, and so forth:

```
$ ./docker-machine
...
COMMANDS:
    active Get or set the active machine
    create Create a machine
    config Print the connection config for machine
    inspect  Inspect information about a machine
    ip   Get the IP address of a machine
    kill    Kill a machine
    ls    List machines
    restart  Restart a machine
    rm    Remove a machine
    env    Display the commands to set up the environment for the Docker client
    ssh    Log into or run a command on a machine with SSH
    start   Start a machine
    stop    Stop a machine
    upgrade  Upgrade a machine to the latest version of Docker
    url    Get the URL of a machine
    help, h  Shows a list of commands or help for one command
```

For instance, you can list the machine you created previously, obtain its IP address, and even connect to it via SSH:

```
$ ./docker-machine ls
NAME      ACTIVE    DRIVER       STATE      URL                          SWARM
foobar    *         digitalocean  Running    tcp://104.131.92.15:2376
$ ./docker-machine ip foobar
104.131.92.15
$ ./docker-machine ssh foobar
Welcome to Ubuntu 14.04.2 LTS (GNU/Linux 3.13.0-57-generic x86_64)
```

```
...
Last login: Mon Mar 16 09:02:13 2015 from ...
root@foobar:~#
```

Before you are finished with this recipe, do not forget to delete the machine you created:

```
$ ./docker-machine rm foobar
```

See Also

- Official documentation (*https://docs.docker.com/machine/*)

1.10 Using Docker Experimental Binaries

Problem

You want to use an experimental feature or a patch that was contributed to the Docker upstream code.

Solution

Use the Docker experimental binaries. You can download the binaries or use the experimental channel that is updated nightly.

Get the nightly builds of Docker in the form of Linux distribution packages:

```
$ wget -qO- https://experimental.docker.com/ | sh
$ docker version | grep Version
 Version:        1.8.0-dev
 Version:        1.8.0-dev
```

Or you can grab the nightly built binaries directly; for example on 64-bit systems:

```
$ wget https://experimental.docker.com/builds/Linux/x86_64/docker-latest
$ chmod +x docker-latest
$ ./docker-latest version | grep Version
 Version:        1.8.0-dev
 Version:        1.8.0-dev
```

If you want to use this binary by default, follow Recipe 4.4.

See Also

- Docker experimental channel (*https://blog.docker.com/2015/06/experimental-binary/*) announced recently

- Running experimental docker binaries (*http://bit.ly/install-binary*)

1.11 Running Hello World in Docker

Problem

You have access to a Docker host and want to run your first container. You want to learn the various life cycles of a container. As an example, you want to run a container and echo `Hello World` in it.

Solution

Typing `docker` at the prompt returns the usage of the `docker` command:

```
$ docker
Usage: docker [OPTIONS] COMMAND [arg...]

A self-sufficient runtime for linux containers.

...

Commands:
    attach    Attach to a running container
    build     Build an image from a Dockerfile
    commit    Create a new image from a container's changes
...
    rm        Remove one or more containers
    rmi       Remove one or more images
    run       Run a command in a new container
    save      Save an image to a tar archive
    search    Search for an image on the Docker Hub
    start     Start a stopped container
    stop      Stop a running container
    tag       Tag an image into a repository
    top       Lookup the running processes of a container
    unpause   Unpause a paused container
    version   Show the Docker version information
    wait      Block until a container stops, then print its exit code
```

You have already seen the `docker ps` command, which lists all running containers. You'll explore many more commands in other recipes of this book. To get started, you want to run a container. Let's get straight to it and use `docker run`:

```
$ docker run busybox echo hello world
Unable to find image 'busybox' locally
busybox:latest: The image you are pulling has been verified
511136ea3c5a: Pull complete
df7546f9f060: Pull complete
e433a6c5b276: Pull complete
```

```
e72ac664f4f0: Pull complete
Status: Downloaded newer image for busybox:latest
hello world
```

Containers are based on images. An image needs to be passed to the `docker run` command. In the preceding example, you specify an image called *busybox*. Docker does not have this image locally and *pulls* it from a public registry. A *registry* is a catalog of Docker images that the Docker client can communicate with and download images from. Once the image is pulled, Docker starts a container and executes the `echo hello world` command. Congratulations—you ran your first container.

Discussion

If you list the running containers, you will see that none are running. That's because as soon as the container did its job (echoing hello world) it stopped. However, it is not totally gone, and you can see it with the `docker ps -a` command:

```
$ docker ps
CONTAINER ID    IMAGE       COMMAND       CREATED    STATUS    PORTS     NAMES
$ docker ps -a
CONTAINER ID    IMAGE             COMMAND            ...    PORTS    NAMES
8f7089b187e8    busybox:latest    "echo hello world" ...            thirsty_morse
```

You see that the container has an ID (8f7089b187e8) and an image (*busybox:latest*) as well as a name, and you see the command that it ran. You can permanently remove this container with `docker rm 8f7089b187e8`. The image that you used was downloaded locally, and `docker images` returns it:

```
$ docker images
REPOSITORY      TAG          IMAGE ID          CREATED       VIRTUAL SIZE
busybox         latest       e72ac664f4f0      9 weeks ago   2.433 MB
```

If no running or stopped containers are using this image, you can remove it with `docker rmi busybox`.

Running echo is fun but getting a terminal session within a container is even better. Try to run a container that executes `/bin/bash`. You will need to use the `-t` and `-i` options to get a proper interactive session and while we are at it, let's use an Ubuntu image:

```
$ docker run -t -i ubuntu:14.04 /bin/bash
Unable to find image 'ubuntu:14.04' locally
ubuntu:14.04: The image you are pulling has been verified
01bf15a18638: Pull complete
30541f8f3062: Pull complete
e1cdf371fbde: Pull complete
9bd07e480c5b: Pull complete
511136ea3c5a: Already exists
Status: Downloaded newer image for ubuntu:14.04
root@6f1050d21b41:/#
```

You see that Docker pulled the *Ubuntu:14.04* image composed of several layers, and you got a session as root within a container. The prompt gives you the ID of the container. As soon as you exit this terminal, the container will stop running just like our first *hello world* example.

 If you skipped the first few recipes on installing Docker, you should try the web emulator (*https://www.docker.com/tryit/*). It will give you a 10-minute tour of Docker, and you will get your first practice with it.

1.12 Running a Docker Container in Detached Mode

Problem

You know how to run a container interactively but would like to run a service in the background.

Solution

Use the -d option of docker run.

To try this, you will run a simple HTTP server with Python in a *python:2.7* Docker image pulled from Docker Hub (*https://registry.hub.docker.com/_/python/*) (see also Recipe 2.9):

```
$ docker run -d -p 1234:1234 python:2.7 python -m SimpleHTTPServer 1234
$ docker ps
CONTAINER ID  IMAGE       COMMAND          ...   NAMES
0fae2d2e8674  python:2.7  "python -m SimpleHTT  ...   suspicious_pike
```

If you open your browser at the IP of your Docker host on port 1234, you will see the listing of the root directory inside your container. Docker automatically creates a correct port mapping between the container and host port 1234, thanks to the -p 1234:1234 option. In Recipe 3.2, you will learn more about this networking behavior.

Discussion

The -d option makes the container run in the background. You can connect to the container by using the exec command and running a bash shell:

```
$ docker exec -ti 9d7cebd75dcf /bin/bash
root@9d7cebd75dcf:/# ps -ef | grep python
root          1      0  0 15:42 ?        00:00:00 python -m SimpleHTTPServer 1234
```

Lots of other options are available (*https://docs.docker.com/reference/run/*) for `docker run`. Experiment by specifying a name for the container, changing the working directory of the container, setting an environment variable, and so on.

See Also

- Docker run reference (*https://docs.docker.com/reference/run/*)

1.13 Creating, Starting, Stopping, and Removing Containers

Problem

You know how to start containers and to run them in detached mode. You would like to learn the basic commands to manage the entire life cycle of a container.

Solution

Use the `create`, `start`, `stop`, `kill`, and `rm` commands of the Docker CLI. Find the appropriate usage of each command with the `-h` or `--h` option or by typing the command with no arguments (e.g., `docker create`).

Discussion

In Recipe 1.12, you started a container automatically with `docker run`. You can also stage a container with the `docker create` command. Using the same example of running a simple HTTP server, the only difference will be that you will not specify the `-d` option. Once staged, the container will need to be started with `docker start`:

```
$ docker create -P --expose=1234 python:2.7 python -m SimpleHTTPServer 1234
a842945e2414132011ae704b0c4a4184acc4016d199dfd4e7181c9b89092de13
$ docker ps -a
CONTAINER ID  IMAGE      COMMAND               CREATED      ... NAMES
a842945e2414  python:2.7 "python -m SimpleHTT 8 seconds ago ... fervent_hodgkin
$ docker start a842945e2414
a842945e2414
$ docker ps
CONTAINER ID  IMAGE      COMMAND              ...   NAMES
a842945e2414  python:2.7 "python -m SimpleHTT ...   fervent_hodgkin
```

To stop a running container, you have a choice between `docker kill` (which will send a `SIGKILL` signal to the container) or `docker stop` (which will send a `SIGTERM` and after a grace period will send a `SIGKILL`). The end result will be that the container is stopped and is not listed in the list of running containers returned by `docker ps`.

However, the container has not yet disappeared (i.e., the filesystem of the container is still there); you could restart it with `docker restart` or remove it forever with `docker rm`:

```
$ docker restart a842945e2414
a842945e2414
$ docker ps
CONTAINER ID      IMAGE       COMMAND              ...    NAMES
a842945e2414      python:2.7  "python -m SimpleHTT ...    fervent_hodgkin
$ docker kill a842945e2414
a842945e2414
$ docker rm a842945e2414
a842945e2414
$ docker ps -a
CONTAINER ID      IMAGE       COMMAND      CREATED    STATUS    PORTS    NAMES
```

 If you have a lot of stopped containers that you would like to remove, use a subshell to do it in one command. The `-q` option of `docker ps` will return only the containers' IDs:

```
$ docker rm $(docker ps -a -q)
```

1.14 Building a Docker Image with a Dockerfile

Problem

You understand how to download images from a publicly available Docker registry but you would like to build your own Docker images.

Solution

Use a Dockerfile. A *Dockerfile* is a text file that describes the steps that Docker needs to take to prepare an image—including installing packages, creating directories, and defining environment variables, among other things. In Chapter 2, we will expand much further about Dockerfiles and image creation. This recipe covers the basic concept of building an image.

As a toy example, let's say you want to create an image based on the *busybox* image but that you want to define an environment variable. The *busybox* image is a Docker image that contains the *busybox* (*http://www.busybox.net/about.html*) binary, which combines most Unix utilities in a single binary. Create the following text file named *Dockerfile* in an empty working directory:

```
FROM busybox

ENV foo=bar
```

Then to build a new image called *busybox2*, you use the docker build command like
so:

```
$ docker build -t busybox2 .
Sending build context to Docker daemon 2.048 kB
Step 0 : FROM busybox
latest: Pulling from library/busybox
cf2616975b4a: Pull complete
6ce2e90b0bc7: Pull complete
8c2e06607696: Pull complete
Digest: sha256:df9e13f36d2d5b30c16bfbf2a6110c45ebed0bfa1ea42d357651bc6c736d5322
Status: Downloaded newer image for busybox:latest
 ---> 8c2e06607696
Step 1 : ENV foo bar
 ---> Running in f46c59e9bdd6
 ---> 582bacbe7aaa
```

Once the build completes, you can see the new images returned by docker images
and you can launch a container based on it to check that the container has the environment variable foo set to bar:

```
$ docker images
REPOSITORY        TAG        IMAGE ID         CREATED          VIRTUAL SIZE
busybox2          latest     582bacbe7aaa     6 seconds ago    2.433 MB
busybox           latest     8c2e06607696     3 months ago     2.433 MB
$ docker run busybox2 env | grep foo
foo=bar
```

See Also

- Dockerfile reference (*https://docs.docker.com/reference/builder/*)
- Chapter 2, which covers image creation and sharing

1.15 Using Supervisor to Run WordPress in a Single Container

Problem

You know how to link containers together (see Recipe 1.16), and would like to run all
services needed for your application in a single container. Specifically for running
WordPress, you would like to run MySQL and HTTPD at the same time in a container. Because Docker executes foreground processes, you need to figure out a way
to run multiple "foreground" processes simultaneously.

Solution

Use Supervisor (*http://supervisord.org/index.html*) to monitor and run both MySQL and HTTPD. Supervisor is not an init system, but is meant to control multiple processes and is run like any other program.

 This recipe is an example of using Supervisor to run multiple processes in a container. It can be used as the basis to run any number of services via a single Docker image (e.g., SSH, Nginx). The WordPress setup detailed in this recipe is a minimum viable setup, not meant for production use.

The example files can be found on GitHub (*http://bit.ly/doc-supervisor*). They include a Vagrantfile to start a virtual machine that runs Docker, a Dockerfile that defines the image being created, a Supervisor configuration file (*supervisord.conf*), and a Word-Press configuration file (*wp-config.php*).

 If you do not want to use Vagrant, you can take the Dockerfile, `supervisord`, and WordPress configuration files and set things up on your own Docker host.

To run WordPress, you will need to install MySQL, Apache 2 (i.e., `httpd`), and PHP, and grab the latest WordPress release. You will need to create a database for Word-Press. In the configuration file used in this recipe, the WordPress database user is `root`, its password is `root`, and the database is `wordpress`. Change these settings to your liking in the *wp-config.php* file and edit the Dockerfile accordingly.

A Dockerfile, a manifest that describes how a Docker image is built, is described in detail in the following chapters. If this is your first use of a Dockerfile, you can use it as is and come back to it later (see Recipe 2.3 for an introduction to Dockerfiles):

```
FROM ubuntu:14.04

RUN apt-get update && apt-get -y install \
    apache2 \
    php5 \
    php5-mysql \
    supervisor \
    wget

RUN echo 'mysql-server mysql-server/root_password password root' | \
    debconf-set-selections && \
    echo 'mysql-server mysql-server/root_password_again password root' | \
    debconf-set-selections
```

```
RUN apt-get install -qqy mysql-server

RUN wget http://wordpress.org/latest.tar.gz && \
    tar xzvf latest.tar.gz && \
    cp -R ./wordpress/* /var/www/html && \
    rm /var/www/html/index.html

RUN (/usr/bin/mysqld_safe &); sleep 5; mysqladmin -u root -proot create wordpress

COPY wp-config.php /var/www/html/wp-config.php
COPY supervisord.conf /etc/supervisor/conf.d/supervisord.conf

EXPOSE 80

CMD ["/usr/bin/supervisord"]
```

Supervisor is configured via the *supervisord.conf* file like so:

```
[supervisord]
nodaemon=true

[program:mysqld]
command=/usr/bin/mysqld_safe
autostart=true
autorestart=true
user=root

[program:httpd]
command=/bin/bash -c "rm -rf /run/httpd/* && /usr/sbin/apachectl -D FOREGROUND"
```

Two programs are defined to be run and monitored: mysqld and httpd. Each program can use various options like autorestart and autostart. The most important directive is command, which defines how to run each program. With this configuration, a Docker container needs to run only a single foreground process: supervisord. Hence the line in the Dockerfile, CMD ["/usr/bin/supervisord"].

On your Docker host, build the image and start a background container off of it. If you are using the Vagrant virtual machine started via the example files, do this:

```
$ cd /vagrant
$ docker build -t wordpress .
$ docker run -d -p 80:80 wordpress
```

Port forwarding will be set up between your host and the Docker container for port 80. You will just need to open your browser to *http://<IP_OF_DOCKER_HOST>* and configure WordPress.

Discussion

Although using Supervisor to run multiple application services in a single container works perfectly, it is better to use multiple containers. It promotes the isolation of concerns using containers and helps create a microservices-based design for your application (see *Building Microservices* (*http://bit.ly/building-microservices*)). Ultimately, this will help with scale and resiliency.

See Also

- Supervisor documentation (*http://supervisord.org/index.html*)
- Docker Supervisor article (*https://docs.docker.com/articles/using_supervisord/*)

1.16 Running a WordPress Blog Using Two Linked Containers

Problem

You want to run a WordPress (*http://wordpress.com*) site with containers, but you do not want to run the MySQL database in the same container as WordPress. You want to keep the concept of separation of concerns in mind and decouple the various components of an application as much as possible.

Solution

You start two containers: one running WordPress using the official image from the Docker Hub (*http://hub.docker.com*), and one running the MySQL database. The two containers are linked using the `--link` option of the Docker CLI.

Start by pulling the latest images for WordPress (*https://hub.docker.com/_/wordpress/*) and MySQL (*https://.hub.docker.com/_/mysql/*):

```
$ docker pull wordpress:latest
$ docker pull mysql:latest
$ docker images
REPOSITORY       TAG          IMAGE ID        CREATED        VIRTUAL SIZE
mysql            latest       9def920de0a2    4 days ago     282.9 MB
wordpress        latest       93acfaf85c71    8 days ago     472.8 MB
```

Start a MySQL container, give it a name via the `--name` CLI option, and set the `MYSQL_ROOT_PASSWORD` via an environment variable:

```
$ docker run --name mysqlwp -e MYSQL_ROOT_PASSWORD=wordpressdocker -d mysql
```

By not specifying the tag for the *mysql* image, Docker automatically chose the `latest` tag, which is the one you downloaded specifically. The container was daemonized with the `-d` option.

You can now run a WordPress container based on the *wordpress:latest* image. It will be *linked* to the MySQL container using the `--link` option, which means that Docker will automatically set up the networking so that the ports exposed by the MySQL container are reachable inside the WordPress container:

```
$ docker run --name wordpress --link mysqlwp:mysql -p 80:80 -d wordpress
```

Both containers should be running in the background, with port 80 of the WordPress container mapped to port 80 of the host:

```
$ docker ps
CONTAINER ID    IMAGE               COMMAND             CREATED           ...
e1593e7a20df    wordpress:latest    "/entrypoint.sh apac   About a minute ago   ...
d4be18e33153    mysql:latest        "/entrypoint.sh mysq   5 minutes ago        ...

...             STATUS              PORTS               NAMES
...             Up About a minute   0.0.0.0:80->80/tcp  wordpress
...             Up 5 minutes        3306/tcp            mysqlwp
```

Open a browser at *http://<ip_of_host>* and it should show the WordPress installation screen with the language selection window, as shown in Figure 1-10. If you go through the WordPress setup, you will then have a fully functional WordPress site running with two linked containers.

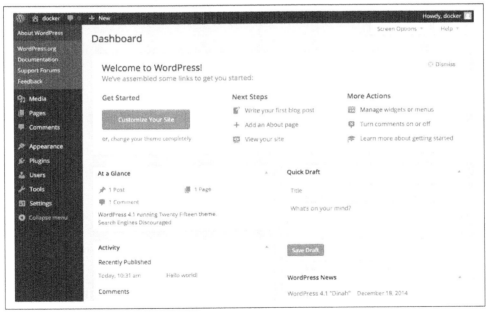

Figure 1-10. Working WordPress site within containers

Discussion

The two images for WordPress and MySQL are official images maintained by the WordPress and MySQL communities. Each page on the Docker Hub provides additional documentation for configuration of containers started with those images.

Do not forget to read the WordPress image documentation (*https://hub.docker.com/_/wordpress/*) and the MySQL image documentation (*https://hub.docker.com/_/mysql/*).

Of interest is that you can create a database and a user with appropriate privileges to manipulate that database by using a few environment variables: MYSQL_DATABASE, MYSQL_USER, and MYSQL_PASSWORD. In the preceding example, WordPress is run as the *root* MySQL user and this is far from best practice. It would be better to create a word press database and a user for it, like so:

```
$ docker run --name mysqlwp -e MYSQL_ROOT_PASSWORD=wordpressdocker \
                            -e MYSQL_DATABASE=wordpress \
                            -e MYSQL_USER=wordpress \
                            -e MYSQL_PASSWORD=wordpresspwd \
                            -d mysql
```

If you need to remove all existing containers, you can use a shortcut making use of a subshell command:

```
$ docker stop $(docker ps -q)
$ docker rm -v $(docker ps -aq)
```

The -v option of docker rm removes the volume defined by the MySQL image.

Once the database container is running, you run the WordPress container and specify the database tables you defined:

```
$ docker run --name wordpress --link mysqlwp:mysql -p 80:80 \
                             -e WORDPRESS_DB_NAME=wordpress \
                             -e WORDPRESS_DB_USER=wordpress \
                             -e WORDPRESS_DB_PASSWORD=wordpresspwd \
                             -d wordpress
```

1.17 Backing Up a Database Running in a Container

Problem

You are using a MySQL image to provide a database service. You need to back up this database for data persistency.

Solution

Several backup strategies are possible alone or in combination. The two main concepts with containers are that you can execute a command inside a container running in the background and that you can also mount a host volume (i.e., a single accessible storage area in your host filesystem) into the container. In this recipe, you will see how to do the following:

- Mount a volume from the Docker host into the MySQL container
- Use the `docker exec` command to call `mysqldump`

Starting from the Recipe 1.16, where you set up a WordPress site by using two linked containers, you are going to modify the way you start the MySQL container. Once the containers are started and you have a fully functional WordPress site, you can stop the containers, which stops your application. At that point, the containers have not been removed entirely yet and the data in the database is still accessible. However, as soon as you remove the containers (`docker rm $(docker ps -aq)`), all data will be lost.

A way to keep the data, even when containers are removed with the `docker rm -v` command, is to mount a volume from your Docker host inside a container. If you were to delete the MySQL container with only the `docker rm` command, the volume defined by the image would still persist even if you delete the container. If you look at the Dockerfile (*http://bit.ly/mysql-dockerfile*) used to build the MySQL image, you sill see a reference to `VOLUME /var/lib/mysql`. This means that when you start a container based on this image, you can bind mount a host directory to this mount point inside the container. Let's do it:

```
$ docker run --name mysqlwp -e MYSQL_ROOT_PASSWORD=wordpressdocker \
                            -e MYSQL_DATABASE=wordpress \
                            -e MYSQL_USER=wordpress \
                            -e MYSQL_PASSWORD=wordpresspwd \
                            -v /home/docker/mysql:/var/lib/mysql \
                            -d mysql
```

Note the `-v /home/docker/mysql:/var/lib/mysql` line that performs this mount. After doing the WordPress configuration, the *home/docker/mysql* directory on the host is populated:

```
$ ls mysql/
auto.cnf  ibdata1  ib_logfile0  ib_logfile1  mysql  performance_schema  wordpress
```

To get a dump of the entire MySQL database, use the `docker exec` command to run `mysqldump` inside the container:

```
$ docker exec mysqlwp mysqldump --all-databases \
                                --password=wordpressdocker > wordpress.backup
```

You can then use the traditional techniques for backup and recovery of the database. For instance, in the cloud, you might want to use an Elastic Block Store (e.g., AWS EBS) mounted on an instance and then mounted inside a container. You can also keep your MySQL dumps inside an Elastic Storage (e.g., AWS S3).

Discussion

Although this recipe uses MySQL, the same techniques are valid for Postgres and other databases. If you use the Postgres (*https://registry.hub.docker.com/_/postgres/*) image from Docker Hub, you can also see in the Dockerfile (*http://bit.ly/postgres-dockerfile*) that a volume is created (VOLUME /var/lib/postgresql/data).

1.18 Sharing Data in Your Docker Host with Containers

Problem

You have data on your host that you would like to make available in a container.

Solution

Use the -v option of docker run to mount a host volume into a container.

For example, to share the working directory of your host within a */cookbook* directory in a container, do this:

```
$ ls
data
$ docker run -ti -v "$PWD":/cookbook ubuntu:14.04 /bin/bash
root@11769701f6f7:/# ls /cookbook
data
```

In this example, you mount the working directory in the host into the */cookbook* directory in the container. If you create files or directories within the container, the changes will be written directly to the host working directory, as shown here:

```
$ docker run -ti -v "$PWD":/cookbook ubuntu:14.04 /bin/bash
root@44d71a605b5b:/# touch /cookbook/foobar
root@44d71a605b5b:/# exit
exit
$ ls -l foobar
-rw-r--r-- 1 root root 0 Mar 11 11:42 foobar
```

By default, Docker mounts the volume in read-write mode. If you want to mount it in read-only mode, you can specify it after the name of the volume, using a colon. For example, to mount the previous working directory to */cookbook* as read-only, you would use -v "$PWD":/cookbook:ro. You can inspect your mount mapping with the docker inspect command. See Recipe 9.1 for more information about inspect.

```
$ docker inspect -f {{.Mounts}} 44d71a605b5b
[{ /Users/sebastiengoasguen/Desktop /cookbook   true}]
```

See Also

- Managing data in containers (*https://docs.docker.com/userguide/dockervolumes/*)

- Understanding volumes (*http://container-solutions.com/2014/12/understanding-volumes-docker/*)

- Data container (*http://container42.com/2014/11/18/data-only-container-madness/*)

- Docker volumes (*http://container42.com/2014/11/03/docker-indepth-volumes/*)

1.19 Sharing Data Between Containers

Problem

You know how to mount a host volume into a running container, but you would like to share a volume defined in a container with other containers. This would have the benefit of letting Docker manage the volumes and support the principle of single responsibility.

Solution

Use data containers. In Recipe 1.18, you saw how to mount a host volume into a container. You used the `-v` option of `docker run`, specifying a host volume and a path within a container to mount that volume to. If the host path is omitted, you create a *data container*. The volume specified is created inside the container as a read-write filesystem not layered on top of the read-only layers used to create the container image. Docker manages that filesystem, but you can read and write to it from the host. Let's illustrate this (with a truncated ID of the volumes for brevity):

```
$ docker run -ti -v /cookbook ubuntu:14.04 /bin/bash
root@b5835d2b951e:/# touch /cookbook/foobar
root@b5835d2b951e:/# ls cookbook/
foobar
root@b5835d2b951e:/# exit
exit
bash-4.3$ docker inspect -f {{.Mounts}} b5835d2b951e
[{dbba7caf8d07b862b61b39... /var/lib/docker/volumes/dbba7caf8d07b862b61b39... \
/_data /cookbook local  true}]
$ sudo ls /var/lib/docker/volumes/dbba7caf8d07b862b61b39...
foobar
```

The directory created by the Docker engine to store the data in the volume defined resides on the Docker host. If you are using Docker Machine to set up a remote Docker host, you will need to connect to this remote Docker host to see the data path of the Docker volumes.

When the container is started, Docker creates the */cookbook* directory. From within the container, you can read and write to this directory. Once you exit the container, you can use `inspect` (see Recipe 9.1) to know where the volume has been created on the host. Docker created it under */var/lib/docker/volumes/*. From the host you can read and write to it. Changes will persist and be available if you restart the container:

```
$ sudo touch /var/lib/docker/volumes/dbba7caf8d07b862b61b39.../foobar2
$ docker start b5835d2b951e
$ docker exec -ti b5835d2b951e /bin/bash
root@b5835d2b951e:/# ls /cookbook
foobar  foobar2
```

To share this data volume with other containers, use the `--volumes-from` option. Let's start fresh and create a data container, and then start another container that will mount the volume from this source data container:

```
$ docker run -v /data --name data ubuntu:14.04
$ docker ps
CONTAINER ID    IMAGE    COMMAND    CREATED    STATUS    PORTS    NAMES
$ docker inspect -f {{.Mounts}} data
[{4ee1d9e3d453e843819c6ff... /var/lib/docker/volumes/4ee1d9e3d453e843819c6ff... \
/_data /data local true]
```

 The data container is not running. Still, the volume mapping exists and the volume has persisted in */var/lib/docker/vfs/dir*. You can remove the container and the volume only with `docker rm -v data`. If you do not use the `rm -v` option to delete containers and their volumes, you will end up with lots of orphaned volumes.

Even though the data container is not running, you can mount the volume from it with the `--volumes-from` option:

```
$ docker run -ti --volumes-from data ubuntu:14.04 /bin/bash
root@b94a006377c1:/# touch /data/foobar
root@b94a006377c1:/# exit
exit
$ sudo ls /var/lib/docker/volumes/4ee1d9e3d453e843819c6ff...
foobar
```

See Also

- Understanding (*http://container-solutions.com/2014/12/understanding-volumes-docker/*) volumes
- Data container (*http://container42.com/2014/11/18/data-only-container-madness/*)
- Docker volumes (*http://container42.com/2014/11/03/docker-indepth-volumes/*)
- Official Docker documentation (*https://docs.docker.com/userguide/dockervolumes/*)
- The aha moment of Docker volumes (*http://bit.ly/docker-aha*)

1.20 Copying Data to and from Containers

Problem

You have a running container started without any volume configuration, but you would like to copy files in and out of the container.

Solution

Use the docker cp command to copy files from a running container to the Docker host. The docker cp command allows you to copy files to and from the host to a container. The usage is as follows and is straightforward:

```
$ docker cp
docker: "cp" requires 2 arguments.
See 'docker cp --help'.

Usage:  docker cp [OPTIONS] CONTAINER:PATH LOCALPATH|-
    docker cp [OPTIONS] LOCALPATH|- CONTAINER:PATH

Copy files/folders between a container and your host.
...
```

Let's illustrate this by first starting a container that will just sleep. You can enter the container and create a file manually:

```
$ docker run -d --name testcopy ubuntu:14.04 sleep 360
$ docker exec -ti testcopy /bin/bash
root@b81793e9eb3e:/# cd /root
root@b81793e9eb3e:~# echo 'I am in the container' > file.txt
root@b81793e9eb3e:~# exit
```

Now to get the file that you just created in the container back in the host, docker cp does the work:

```
$ docker cp testcopy:/root/file.txt .
$ cat file.txt
I am in the container
```

To copy from the host to the container, use `docker cp` again but the other way around:

```
$ echo 'I am in the host' > host.txt
$ docker cp host.txt testcopy:/root/host.txt
```

A nice use case is to copy from one container to another container, which is a matter of combining the two methods by temporarily saving the files on the host. For example, if you want to transfer *root/file.txt* from two running containers with the names *c1* and *c2*, use the following:

```
$ docker cp c1:/root/file.txt .
$ docker file.txt c2:/root/file.txt
```

Discussion

Prior to Docker 1.8, `docker cp` did not support copying files from the host to a container. However, you could do it with a combination of `docker exec` and some shell redirection:

```
$ echo 'I am in the host' > host.txt
$ docker exec -i testcopy sh -c 'cat > /root/host.txt' < host.txt
$ docker exec -i testcopy sh -c 'cat /root/host.txt'
I am in the host
```

This is not needed anymore but is a good showcase of the power of the `docker exec` command.

See Also

- The original idea for this recipe from Grigoriy Chudnov (*http://bit.ly/chudnov*)

Image Creation and Sharing

2.0 Introduction

Quickly after discovering the basic principles of using Docker, you will want to create your own container images. Maybe you will want to package an existing application or you will want to build a new one from scratch leveraging Docker. This chapter is about creating container images and sharing them with others.

The first concept around creating images is that you can start a container using a base image and interactively make changes to it. Docker lets you keep those changes by *committing* them into a new image (see Recipe 2.1). Under the covers, Docker keeps track of the difference between your base image and your new image by creating a new image layer using the union filesystem being used. Sharing this new image is as easy as exporting it to a tar file and giving this tar file to others (see Recipe 2.2).

But making changes to a container manually and committing them to a new images is not highly reproducible and not automated. A better solution is to create a Dockerfile that will let Docker build the image automatically (see Recipe 2.3). You can go through creating a Dockerfile for a simple Python-based Flask application in Recipe 2.4, and in Recipe 2.5 you will learn the best practices to optimize this Dockerfile.

If you have used Vagrant and Packer before you will want to go through Recipe 2.7 and Recipe 2.8; this will help you embrace Docker and build Docker images by re-using your existing configuration management recipes.

Sharing images using the export and import feature works fine, but to share your images with others and integrate Docker into a continuous integration pipeline you can leverage the Docker Hub. The Docker Hub (see Recipe 2.9) is nothing else than an application store. Images on Docker Hub can be shared publicly, and they can also be built automatically through integration with code hosting services like GitHub and Bitbucket (see Recipe 2.12).

Finally, if you do not want to use the Docker Hub, you can deploy your own Docker images registry (Recipe 2.11) and set up your own automated build (Recipe 2.13).

At the end of this chapter you will be able to write Dockerfiles for your various application services and share them through a hosted service like the Docker Hub or through your own Docker registry. This will put you on a quick path toward developing continuous integration and deployment pipelines.

2.1 Keeping Changes Made to a Container by Committing to an Image

Problem

After making some changes inside a container, you decide that you would like to keep those changes. You do not want to lose those changes after you exit or stop the container, and you would like to reuse this type of container as a basis for others.

Solution

Commit the changes that you made by using the docker commit command and define a new image.

Let's start a container with an interactive bash shell and update the packages in it:

```
$ docker run -t -i ubuntu:14.04 /bin/bash
root@69079aaaaab1:/# apt-get update
```

When you exit the container, it stops running, but it is still available to you until you remove it entirely with docker rm. So before you do this, you can commit the changes made to the container and create a new image, *ubuntu:update*. The name of the image is *ubuntu*, and you add the tag update (see Recipe 2.6) to mark the difference from the *ubuntu:latest* image:

```
$ docker commit 69079aaaaab1 ubuntu:update
13132d42da3cc40e8d8b4601a7e2f4dbf198e9d72e37e19ee1986c280ffcb97c
$ docker images
REPOSITORY          TAG            IMAGE ID        CREATED         VIRTUAL SIZE
ubuntu              update         13132d42da3c    5 days ago      213 MB
...
```

You can now safely remove the stopped container and you will be able to start new ones based on the *ubuntu:update* image.

Discussion

You can inspect the changes that have been made inside this container with the
`docker diff` command:

```
$ docker diff 69079aaaaab1
C /root
A /root/.bash_history
C /tmp
C /var
C /var/cache
C /var/cache/apt
D /var/cache/apt/pkgcache.bin
D /var/cache/apt/srcpkgcache.bin
C /var/lib
C /var/lib/apt
C /var/lib/apt/lists
...
```

A means that the file or directory listed was added, C means that there was a change
made, and D means that it was deleted.

See Also

- `docker commit` reference (*https://docs.docker.com/reference/commandline/cli/#commit*)
- `docker diff` reference (*https://docs.docker.com/reference/commandline/cli/#diff*)

2.2 Saving Images and Containers as Tar Files for Sharing

Problem

You have created images or have containers that you would like to keep and share
with your collaborators.

Solution

Use the Docker CLI `save` and `load` commands to create a tarball from a previously
created image, or use the Docker CLI `import` and `export` commands for containers.

Let's start with a stop container and export it to a new tarball:

```
$ docker ps -a
CONTAINER ID    IMAGE          COMMAND       CREATED         ...    NAMES
77d9619a7a71    ubuntu:14.04   "/bin/bash"   10 seconds ago  ...    high_shockley
$ docker export 77d9619a7a71 > update.tar
```

```
$ ls
update.tar
```

You could commit this container as a new image (see Recipe 2.1) locally, but you could also use the Docker `import` command:

```
$ docker import - update < update.tar
157bcbb5fdfce0e7c10ef67ebdba737a491214708a5f266a3c74aa6b0cfde078
$ docker images
REPOSITORY          TAG               IMAGE ID        ...   VIRTUAL SIZE
update              latest            157bcbb5fdfc     ...   188.1 MB
```

If you wanted to share this image with one of your collaborators, you could upload the tar file on a web server and let your collaborator download it and use the `import` command on his Docker host.

If you would rather deal with images that you have already committed, you can use the `load` and `save` commands:

```
$ docker save -o update1.tar update
$ ls -l
total 385168
-rw-rw-r-- 1 vagrant vagrant 197206528 Jan 13 14:13 update1.tar
-rw-rw-r-- 1 vagrant vagrant 197200896 Jan 13 14:05 update.tar
$ docker rmi update
Untagged: update:latest
Deleted: 157bcbb5fdfce0e7c10ef67ebdba737a491214708a5f266a3c74aa6b0cfde078
$ docker load < update1.tar
$ docker images
REPOSITORY          TAG          IMAGE ID          CREATED          VIRTUAL SIZE
update              latest       157bcbb5fdfc      5 minutes ago    188.1 MB
ubuntu              14.04        8eaa4ff06b53      12 days ago      192.7 MB
```

Discussion

The two methods are similar; the difference is that saving an image will keep its history, and exporting a container will squash its history.

2.3 Writing Your First Dockerfile

Problem

Running a container in interactive mode, making changes to it, and then committing these changes to create a new image works well (see Recipe 2.1). However, you want to automate building your image and share your build steps with others.

Solution

To automate building a Docker image, you describe the building steps in a Docker manifesto called the Dockerfile. This text file uses a set of instructions to describe which base image the new container is based on, what steps need to be taken to install various dependencies and applications, what files need to be present in the image, how they are made available to a container, what ports should be exposed, and what command should run when a container starts, as well as a few other things.

To illustrate this, let's write our first Dockerfile. The resulting image will allow you to create a container that executes the /bin/echo command. Create a text file called *Dockerfile* in your working directory and write the following content in it:

```
FROM ubuntu:14.04

ENTRYPOINT ["/bin/echo"]
```

The FROM instruction tells you which image to base the new image off of. Here you choose the *ubuntu:14.04* image from the Official Ubuntu repository (*https://regis try.hub.docker.com/_/ubuntu/*) in Docker Hub. The ENTRYPOINT instruction tells you which command to run when a container based on this image is started. To build the image, issue a docker build . at the prompt like so:

```
$ docker build .
Sending build context to Docker daemon  2.56 kB
Sending build context to Docker daemon
Step 0 : FROM ubuntu:14.04
 ---> 9bd07e480c5b
Step 1 : ENTRYPOINT /bin/echo
 ---> Running in da3fa01c973a
 ---> e778362ca7cf
Removing intermediate container da3fa01c973a
Successfully built e778362ca7cf
$ docker images
REPOSITORY         TAG        IMAGE ID        ...    VIRTUAL SIZE
<none>             <none>     e778362ca7cf    ...    192.7 MB
ubuntu             14.04      9bd07e480c5b    ...    192.7 MB
```

You are now ready to run this container, specifying the image ID of the freshly built image and passing an argument to it (i.e., Hi Docker !):

```
$ docker run e778362ca7cf Hi Docker !
Hi Docker !
```

Amazing—you ran echo in a container! A container was started using the image that you built from this two-line Dockerfile. The container ran and executed the command defined by the ENTRYPOINT instruction. Once this command was finished, the container job was done and it exited. If you run it again without passing an argument, nothing is echoed:

```
$ docker run e778362ca7cf
```

You could also use the CMD instruction in a Dockerfile. This has the advantage that you can overwrite the CMD behavior when you launch a container, by passing a new CMD as an argument to docker run. Let's build a new image by using the CMD instruction, like so:

```
FROM ubuntu:14.04

CMD ["/bin/echo" , "Hi Docker !"]
```

Let's build it and run it:

```
$ docker build .
...
$ docker run eff764828551
Hi Docker !
```

 In the preceding build command, you specified the root directory. The Dockerfile that you just created was automatically used for the build. If you want to do a build of an image based on a Dockerfile that is in a different location, you use the -f option of docker build and specify the path.

It looks the same, but if you pass a new executable as an argument to the docker run command, this command will be executed instead of the /bin/echo defined in the Dockerfile:

```
$ docker run eff764828551 /bin/date
Thu Dec 11 02:49:06 UTC 2014
```

Discussion

A Dockerfile is a text file that represents the way a Docker image is built and what happens when a container is started with this image. Starting with three simple instructions, you can build a fully functioning container: FROM, ENTRYPOINT, CMD. Of course, this is quite limited in this recipe. Read the Dockerfile reference (*https://docs.docker.com/reference/builder/*) to learn about all the other instructions, or go to Recipe 2.4 for a more detailed example.

 The CentOS project maintains a large set of Dockerfile examples. Check out this repository (*https://github.com/CentOS/CentOS-Dockerfiles*) and run a few of their examples to get more familiar with Dockerfile files.

Remember that CMD can be overwritten by an argument to docker run, while ENTRY POINT can be overwritten only by using the --entrypoint option of docker run. Also, you saw that after a command is finished, the container exits. A process that you want to run in a container needs to run in the foreground; otherwise, the container will stop.

Once your first build is done, a new image is created with, in this case, the ID e778362ca7cf. Note that no repository or tag is defined because you did not specify any. You can rebuild the image with the repository cookbook as the name and the tag hello, using the -t option of docker build. As long as you are doing this locally, the choice of repository and tag is up to you, but once you start publishing this image into a registry, you will need to follow a naming convention.

```
$ docker build -t cookbook:hello .
$ docker images
REPOSITORY          TAG         IMAGE ID        CREATED         VIRTUAL SIZE
cookbook            hello       e778362ca7cf    4 days ago      192.7 MB
ubuntu              14.04       9bd07e480c5b    10 days ago     192.7 MB
```

 The docker build command has a couple of options to deal with intermediate containers:

```
$ docker build -h

Usage: docker build [OPTIONS] PATH | URL | -

Build a new image from the source code at PATH

    --force-rm=false      Always remove intermediate containers...
    --no-cache=false      Do not use cache when building the ...
    -q, --quiet=false     Suppress the verbose output generated...
    --rm=true             Remove intermediate containers after ...
    -t, --tag=""          Repository name (and optionally a tag)...
```

See Also

- Dockerfile reference (*https://docs.docker.com/reference/builder/*)
- Best practices for writing a Dockerfile (*https://docs.docker.com/articles/dockerfile_best-practices/*)
- The CentOS project's large set of Dockerfiles (*https://github.com/CentOS/CentOS-Dockerfiles*)

2.4 Packaging a Flask Application Inside a Container

Problem

You have a web application built with the Python framework Flask (*http:// flask.pocoo.org*), running in Ubuntu 14.04. You want to run this application in a container.

Solution

As an example, you are going to use the simple Hello World (*http://flask.pocoo.org*) application defined by the following Python script:

```
#!/usr/bin/env python

from flask import Flask
app = Flask(__name__)

@app.route('/hi')
def hello_world():
    return 'Hello World!'

if __name__ == '__main__':
    app.run(host='0.0.0.0', port=5000)
```

To get this application running inside a Docker container, you need to write a Dockerfile that installs the prerequisites for running the application by using the RUN key and exposes the port that the application runs on by using the EXPOSE key. You also need to move the application inside the container filesystem by using the ADD key.

This Dockerfile will be as follows:

```
FROM ubuntu:14.04

RUN apt-get update
RUN apt-get install -y python
RUN apt-get install -y python-pip
RUN apt-get clean all

RUN pip install flask

ADD hello.py /tmp/hello.py

EXPOSE 5000

CMD ["python","/tmp/hello.py"]
```

This Dockerfile is not optimized intentionally; when you understand the basic principles, see Recipe 2.5 to build images following best practices to write Dockerfiles. The RUN command allows you to execute specific shell commands during the container image build time. Here you update the repository cache, install Python as well as Pip, and install the Flask micro-framework.

To copy the application inside the container image, you use the `ADD` command. It copies the file *hello.py* in the */tmp/* directory.

The application uses port 5000, and you expose this port on the Docker host.

Finally, the `CMD` command specifies that the container will run `python /tmp/ hello.py` at runtime.

What is left to do is to build the image:

```
$ docker build -t flask .
```

This creates a *flask* Docker image:

```
$ docker images
REPOSITORY       TAG       IMAGE ID        CREATED        VIRTUAL SIZE
flask            latest    d381310506ed    4 days ago     354.6 MB
cookbook         echo      e778362ca7cf    4 days ago     192.7 MB
ubuntu           14.04     9bd07e480c5b    10 days ago    192.7 MB
```

To run the application, you use the `-d` option of `docker run`, which daemonizes the container, and you also use the `-P` option of `docker run` to let Docker choose a port on the Docker host that will be mapped to the exposed port specified in the Docker-file (e.g., 5000):

```
$ docker run -d -P flask
5ac72ed12a72f0e2bec0001b3e78f11660905d20f40e670d42aee292263cb890
$ docker ps
CONTAINER ID    IMAGE           COMMAND            ... PORTS
5ac72ed12a72    flask:latest    "python /tmp/hello.p ... 0.0.0.0:49153->5000/tcp
```

The container returns, it is daemonized, and you are not logged in to an interactive shell. `PORTS` shows a mapping between port 5000 of the container and port 49153 of the Docker host. A simple `curl` to *http://localhost:49153/hi* returns `Hello World`, or you can open your browser to the same URL.

 If you are using Boot2Docker, you will have to use the IP address of the bridge network, instead of `localhost`. If you do want to use `localhost`, add port forwarding rules in VirtualBox.

Discussion

Since your Dockerfile specified a command to run via `CMD`, you do not need to specify a command after the name of the image to use. However, you can override this command and start the container in interactive mode by starting a bash shell like so:

```
$ docker run -t -i -P flask /bin/bash
root@fc1514ced93e:/# ls -l /tmp
total 4
-rw-r--r-- 1 root root 194 Dec  8 13:41 hello.py
root@fc1514ced93e:/#
```

2.5 Optimizing Your Dockerfile by Following Best Practices

Problem

You want to follow best practices to write your Dockerfiles and optimize your Docker images.

Solution

The Docker documentation has published best practices (*https://docs.docker.com/arti cles/dockerfile_best-practices/*) to write Dockerfiles. This recipe highlights a few of them to put you on your way to building good images:

1. Run a single process per container. Although you can run multiple processes per container (e.g., Recipe 1.15), building images that will run only one process or at least one functional service per container will help you build decoupled applications that can scale. Take advantage of container linking (see Recipe 3.3) or other container-networking techniques (see Chapter 3) to have the containers communicate with each other.

2. Do not assume that your containers will live on; they are ephemeral and will be stopped and restarted. You should treat them as immutable entities, which means that you should not modify them but instead restart them from your base image. Therefore, manage runtime configuration and data outside the containers and hence the image. Use Docker volumes (see Recipe 1.18 and Recipe 1.19) for this.

3. Use a *.dockerignore* file. When building images, Docker will copy the content of the working directory where the Dockerfile exists (i.e., the *build context*) inside the image. Using *.dockerignore*, you can exclude files and directories from being copied during the build process. If you do not use a *.dockerignore* file, make sure to build your image in a directory that has only the minimum required. Check the syntax (*https://docs.docker.com/reference/builder/#dockerignore-file*) for the *.dockerignore* file.

4. Use official (*https://registry.hub.docker.com/search?q=library*) images from Docker Hub instead of writing your own from scratch. These images are maintained and blessed by the projects authoring the software. You can also use ONBUILD images (see Recipe 2.10) to simplify even further your images.

5. Finally, minimize the number of layers of your images and take advantage of the image cache. Docker uses union filesystems to store images. This means that each image is made of a base image plus a collection of *diffs* that adds the required changes. Each *diff* represents an additional layer of an image. This has a direct impact on how your write your Dockerfile and use the various directives. The following section illustrates this point further.

Discussion

In Recipe 2.4, you saw your first Dockerfile, which starts with the following directives:

```
FROM ubuntu:14.04

RUN apt-get update
RUN apt-get install -y python
RUN apt-get install -y python-pip
RUN apt-get clean

RUN pip install flask

ADD hello.py /tmp/hello.py
...
```

It contains several faux-pas that illustrate a couple of best practices to follow instead.

The fact that it uses the *ubuntu:14.04* official image is good. However, you then proceeded to install a few packages using multiple RUN commands. This is bad practice, as it will add unnecessary layers to the image. You also used the ADD command to copy a simple file. Instead in this example, you should use the COPY command (ADD allows more-complex file copy scenarios).

Therefore, the Dockerfile should instead be written like so:

```
FROM ubuntu:14.04

RUN apt-get update && apt-get install -y \
    python
    python-pip
RUN pip install flask

COPY hello.py /tmp/hello.py
...
```

It could even be made better with the use of a Python official image:

```
FROM python:2.7.10

RUN pip install flask
```

```
COPY hello.py /tmp/hello.py
...
```

This is not meant to be exhaustive, but gives you a taste of how to optimize your Dockerfile. For more detailed information, see the recommended best practices (*https://docs.docker.com/articles/dockerfile_best-practices/*).

2.6 Versioning an Image with Tags

Problem

You are creating multiple images and multiple versions of the same image. You would like to keep track of each image and its versions easily, instead of using an image ID.

Solution

Tag the image with the `docker tag` command. This allows you to rename an existing image, or create a new tag for the same name.

When you committed an image (see Recipe 2.1) you already used tags. The naming convention for images is that everything after a colon is a tag.

> A tag is optional. If you do not specify a tag, Docker will implicitly try to use a tag called `latest`. If such a tag for the image being referenced does not exist in the repository, Docker will fail to download the image.

For example, let's rename the *ubuntu:14.04* image to *foobar*. You will not specify a tag, just change the name; hence Docker will use the `latest` tag automatically:

```
$ docker images
REPOSITORY          TAG          IMAGE ID          CREATED          VIRTUAL SIZE
ubuntu              14.04        9bd07e480c5b      12 days ago      192.7 MB

$ docker tag ubuntu foobar
2014/12/17 09:57:48 Error response from daemon: No such id: ubuntu

$ docker tag ubuntu:14.04 foobar

$ docker images
REPOSITORY          TAG          IMAGE ID          CREATED          VIRTUAL SIZE
foobar              latest       9bd07e480c5b      12 days ago      192.7 MB
ubuntu              14.04        9bd07e480c5b      12 days ago      192.7 MB
```

The first thing that you see in the preceding example is that when you try to tag the *ubuntu* image, Docker throws an error. That is because the *ubuntu* image has only a *14.04* tag and no *latest* tag. In your second attempt you specify the existing tag by using a colon, and the tagging is successful. Docker creates a new *foobar* image and automatically adds the *latest* tag. If you specify a tag by using a colon after the new name for the image, you get this:

```
$ docker tag ubuntu:14.04 foobar:cookbook

$ docker images
REPOSITORY        TAG          IMAGE ID       CREATED        VIRTUAL SIZE
foobar            cookbook     9bd07e480c5b   12 days ago    192.7 MB
foobar            latest       9bd07e480c5b   12 days ago    192.7 MB
ubuntu            14.04        9bd07e480c5b   12 days ago    192.7 MB
```

All the images you used so far are local to your Docker host. But when you want to share these images through registries, you need to name them appropriately. Specifically, you need to follow the *USERNAME/NAME* convention when preparing an image for Docker Hub (*https://hub.docker.com*). When using a private registry, you need to specify the registry host, an optional username and the name of the image (i.e., *REGISTRYHOST/USERNAME/NAME*). And, of course, you can still use a tag (i.e., *:TAG*).

Discussion

Properly tagging an image is an important part of sharing it on Docker Hub (see Recipe 2.9) or using a private registry (see Recipe 2.11). The `docker tag` help information is pretty succint but shows the proper naming convention, which references the proper namespace, be it local, on Docker Hub, or on a private registry:

```
$ docker tag -h

Usage: docker tag [OPTIONS] IMAGE[:TAG] [REGISTRYHOST/][USERNAME/]NAME[:TAG]

Tag an image into a repository

  -f, --force=false    Force
```

2.7 Migrating from Vagrant to Docker with the Docker Provider

Problem

You have been using Vagrant (*http://vagrantup.com*) for your testing and development work and would like to reuse some of your Vagrantfiles to work with Docker.

Solution

Use the Vagrant Docker provider (*https://docs.vagrantup.com/v2/docker/index.html*). You can keep writing Vagrant files to bring up new containers and develop your Dockerfiles.

Here is an example Vagrantfile that uses the Docker provider:

```ruby
# -*- mode: ruby -*-
# vi: set ft=ruby :

VAGRANTFILE_API_VERSION = "2"

Vagrant.configure(VAGRANTFILE_API_VERSION) do |config|

  config.vm.provider "docker" do |d|
     d.build_dir = "."
  end

  config.vm.network "forwarded_port", guest: 5000, host: 5000

end
```

The `build_dir` option looks for a Dockerfile in the same directory as the Vagrantfile. Vagrant then issues a `docker build` in turn, and starts the container:

```
$ vagrant up --provider=docker
Bringing machine 'default' up with 'docker' provider...
==> default: Building the container from a Dockerfile...
    default: Sending build context to Docker daemon 8.704 kB
    default: Step 0 : FROM ubuntu:14.04
...
==> default: Creating the container...
    default:    Name: provider_default_1421147689
    default:   Image: 324f2babf057
    default: Volume: /vagrant/provider:/vagrant
    default:    Port: 5000:5000
    default:
    default: Container created: efe111afb8b9d3ff
==> default: Starting container...
==> default: Provisioners will not be run since container doesn't support SSH.
```

Once the `vagrant up` is over, the container will be running and an image will have been created. You can use the regular Docker commands to interact with the container or use the new `vagrant docker-logs` and `vagrant docker-run` commands. Standard commands like `vagrant status` and `vagrant destroy` will also work with your containers.

It is likely that you will not install SSH in your container. Therefore, the Vagrant provisioners will not be able to run. Any software installation within your container will need to happen through the Dockerfile.

Discussion

I created a simple environment to help you test this recipe. Similarly to other recipes, you can clone the Git repository that accompanies this book and head over to the recipe examples. An Ubuntu 14.04 virtual machine will be started, and Docker will be installed as well as Vagrant. In the */vagrant/provider* directory, you will find yet another Vagrantfile (shown previously), and a Dockerfile. This Dockerfile builds a simple Flask application in the container:

```
$ git clone
$ cd ch02/vagrantprovider/
$ vagrant up
$ vagrant ssh
$ cd /vagrant/provider
$ vagrant up --provider=docker
```

The possible configurations of the Vagrantfile are almost a one-to-one match with directives in a Dockerfile. You can define what software to install in a container, what environment variables to pass, which ports to expose, which containers to link to, and which volumes to mount. The interesting thing is that Vagrant will attempt to translate the regular Vagrant configuration into Docker run options. For instance, forwarding ports from a Docker container to the host can be done with the regular Vagrant command:

```
config.vm.network "forwarded_port", guest: 5000, host: 5000
```

Overall, it is my opinion that the Docker support in Vagrant should be seen as a transitioning step for developers who might have invested a lot of work with Vagrant and would like to slowly adopt Docker.

 Vagrant also features a Docker provisioner (*https://docs.vagrantup.com/v2/provisioning/docker.html*). It can be used when you are starting virtual machines, provisioning them with configuration management solutions (e.g., Puppet or Chef) but would also like to start containers within those virtual machines.

See Also

- Vagrant Docker provider configuration (*https://docs.vagrantup.com/v2/docker/configuration.html*)

- Vagrant Docker provider documentation (*https://docs.vagrantup.com/v2/docker/index.html*)

2.8 Using Packer to Create a Docker Image

Problem

You have developed several configuration management recipes using Chef (*http://www.getchef.com*), Puppet (*http://www.getchef.com*), Ansible (*http://www.ansible.com/home*), or SaltStack (*http://www.saltstack.com*). You would like to reuse those recipes to build Docker images.

Solution

Use Packer (*https://www.packer.io*) from HashiCorp. Packer is a tool to create identical machine images for multiple platforms from a single template definition. For example, from a template it can automatically create images for Amazon EC2 (an Amazon Machine Image, or AMI), VMware, VirtualBox, and DigitalOcean. One of those target platforms is Docker.

This means that if you define a Packer template, you can automatically generate a Docker image. You can also post-process it to tag the image and push it to Docker Hub (see Recipe 2.9).

The following template shows three main steps. First it specifies a *builder*; here you use Docker and specify to use the base image *ubuntu:14.04*. Second, it defines the provisioning step. Here we use a simple shell provisioning. Finally, it lists post-processing steps. Here we tag only the resulting image:

```
{
"builders": [
  {
    "type": "docker",
    "image": "ubuntu:14.04",
    "commit": "true"
  }
],
"provisioners": [
  {
    "type": "shell",
    "script": "bootstrap.sh"
  }
],
"post-processors": [
    {
      "type": "docker-tag",
      "repository": "how2dock/packer",
```

```
        "tag": "latest"
      }
    ]
  }
```

You can validate the template and launch a build of the image with two commands:

```
$ packer validate template.json
$ packer build template.json
```

 Set up several builders in your template and output different images for your application (e.g., Docker and AMI).

To help you test Packer, I created a Vagrantfile that starts an Ubuntu 14.04 virtual machine, installs Docker on it, and downloads Packer. Test it like this:

```
$ git clone https://github.com/how2dock/docbook.git
$ cd ch02/packer
$ vagrant up
$ vagrant ssh
$ cd /vagrant
$ /home/vagrant/packer validate template.json
Template validated successfully.
$ /home/vagrant/packer build template.json
...
==> docker: Creating a temporary directory for sharing data...
==> docker: Pulling Docker image: ubuntu:14.04
...
==> Builds finished. The artifacts of successful builds are:
--> docker: Imported Docker image: 3ebae8e2f2a8af8f2c5f366c603091c5e9c8e234bff8
--> docker: Imported Docker image: how2dock/packer:latest
$ docker images
REPOSITORY        TAG       IMAGE ID        CREATED          VIRTUAL SIZE
how2dock/packer   latest    3ebae8e2f2a8    20 seconds ago   210.8 MB
ubuntu            14.04     8eaa4ff06b53    11 days ago      192.7 MB
```

In this example, you can now run Nginx (which has been installed via the *boostrap.sh* script):

```
$ docker run -d -p 80:80 how2dock/packer /usr/sbin/nginx -g "daemon off;"
```

But because a Dockerfile was not used to create this image, no CMD or ENTRYPOINT was defined. Nginx will not be started when the container is launched; hence a container started from the image generated without specifying how to run Nginx will exit right away.

Discussion

Packer is a great tool that can help you migrate some of your work from previous DevOps workflows into a Docker-based workflow. However, Docker containers run applications in the foreground and encourage running single-application processes per container. Hence, creating a Docker image with Packer that would have, for example, MySQL, Nginx, and WordPress in the same image would be contrary to the Docker philosophy and might prove difficult to run without some additional manual post-processing with something like Supervisor (see Recipe 1.15).

The preceding solution features a basic shell provisioning. If you have existing configuration management recipes, you can also use them to create a Docker image. Packer features shell, Ansible, Chef, Puppet, and Salt provisioners (*https:// www.packer.io/docs/provisioners/shell.html*). As an example, the *template-ansible.json* file in the repository used previously makes use of the Ansible local provisioner. The Packer template gets modified like so:

```
{
"builders": [
  {
    "type": "docker",
    "image": "ansible/ubuntu14.04-ansible:stable",
    "commit": "true"
  }
],
"provisioners": [
  {
    "type": "ansible-local",
    "playbook_file": "local.yml"
  }
],
"post-processors": [
  {
    "type": "docker-tag",
    "repository": "how2dock/packer",
    "tag": "ansible"
  }
]
}
```

It uses a special Docker image, pulled from Docker Hub, that has Ansible installed in it. Packer will use the local Ansible CLI to run the Ansible playbook *local.yml*. The playbook defined in the template file installs Nginx locally:

```
---
- hosts: localhost
  connection: local
  tasks:
  - name: install nginx
    apt: pkg=nginx state=installed update_cache=true
```

The result of building with Packer will be a working Docker image *how2dock/packer:ansible*

```
$ /home/vagrant/packer build template-ansible.json
...
==> docker: Creating a temporary directory for sharing data...
==> docker: Pulling Docker image: ansible/ubuntu14.04-ansible:stable
    docker: Pulling repository ansible/ubuntu14.04-ansible
...
==> docker: Provisioning with Ansible...
    docker: Creating Ansible staging directory...
    docker: Creating directory: /tmp/packer-provisioner-ansible-local
    docker: Uploading main Playbook file...
...
    docker:
    docker: PLAY [localhost] *************************************
    docker:
    docker: GATHERING FACTS *************************************
    docker: ok: [localhost]
    docker:
    docker: TASK: [install nginx] *******************************
    docker: changed: [localhost]
    docker:
    docker: PLAY RECAP *****************************************
    docker: localhost  : ok=2    changed=1    unreachable=0    failed=0
    docker:
==> docker: Committing the container
..
    docker (docker-tag): Repository: how2dock/packer:ansible
Build 'docker' finished.
```

A new image is now available, *how2dock/packer:ansible*, that was built using an Ansible playbook. You can start a container based on this image and launch the application as you did before. This interesting workflow allows you to keep the benefit of your configuration management recipes/playbooks while starting to use containers instead of virtual machines.

2.9 Publishing Your Image to Docker Hub

Problem

You write a Dockerfile and build an image for a useful container. You want to share this image with everyone.

Solution

Share this image on the Docker Hub (*http://hub.docker.com*). Docker Hub is to Docker what GitHub (*https://github.com*) is to source code. It allows anyone to host its image online and share it publicly or keep it private. To share an image on Docker Hub, you need to do the following:

- Create an account on Docker Hub.
- Log in to the hub on your Docker host.
- Push your image.

Let's get started. Registering requires only a valid email address. Head over to the signup page (*https://hub.docker.com/*) and create an account. After verifying the email address that you used to create the account, your registration will be complete. This free account will allow you to publish public images as well as have one private repository. If you want to have more than one private repository, you will need to pay a subscription.

Now that you have an account created, you can head back to your Docker host, select one of your images, and use the Docker CLI to publish this image on your public repository. This will be a three-step process:

1. Log in with `docker login`. This will ask for your Docker Hub credentials.
2. Tag an existing image with your username from Docker Hub.
3. Push the newly tagged image.

The login step will store your Docker Hub credentials in a *~/.dockercfg* file:

```
$ docker login
Username: how2dock
Password:
Email: how2dock@gmail.com
Login Succeeded
$ cat ~/.dockercfg
{"https://index.docker.io/v1/":{"auth":"..........",
                                "email":"how2dock@gmail.com"}}
```

If you check the list of images that you currently have, you see that your Flask image from Recipe 2.4 is using a local repository and has a tag called `latest`:

```
$ docker images
REPOSITORY      TAG         IMAGE ID        CREATED       VIRTUAL SIZE
flask           latest      88d6464d1f42    5 days ago    354.6 MB
...
```

To push this image to your Docker Hub account, you need to tag this image with your own Docker Hub repository with the `docker tag` command (see Recipe 2.6):

```
$ docker tag flask how2dock/flask
sebimac:flask sebgoa$ docker images
REPOSITORY          TAG         IMAGE ID        CREATED       VIRTUAL SIZE
```

```
flask              latest        88d6464d1f42     5 days ago    354.6 MB
how2dock/flask     latest        88d6464d1f42     5 days ago    354.6 MB
```

You now have your Flask image with the repository of *how2dock/flask*, which follows the proper naming convention for repositories. You are ready to push the image. Docker will attempt to push the various layers that make the image; if the layer is pre-existing on the Docker Hub, it will skip it. Once the push is finished, the *how2dock/flask* image will be visible in your Docker Hub page, and anyone will be able to docker pull how2dock/flask (see Figure 2-1):

```
$ docker push how2dock/flask
The push refers to a repository [how2dock/flask] (len: 1)
Sending image list
Pushing repository how2dock/flask (1 tags)
511136ea3c5a: Image already pushed, skipping
01bf15a18638: Image already pushed, skipping
...
dc4a9a43bb7f: Image successfully pushed
e394b9fbe3fa: Image successfully pushed
3f7abcdc10d4: Image successfully pushed
88d6464d1f42: Image successfully pushed
Pushing tag for rev [88d6464d1f42] on
{https://cdn-registry-1.docker.io/v1/repositories/how2dock/flask/tags/latest}
```

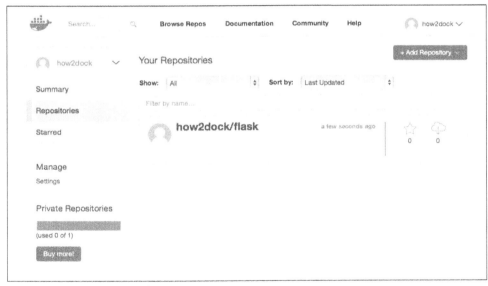

Figure 2-1. Docker Hub Flask image

Discussion

The docker tag command allows you to change the repository and tag of an image. In this example, you did not specify a tag, so Docker assigned it the latest tag. You could choose to specify tags and push these to Docker Hub, maintaining several versions of an image in the same repository.

This recipe introduced two new docker CLI commands: docker tag and docker push. One more is worth noting, in terms of image management: docker search. It allows you to search for images in Docker Hub. For example, if you are looking for an image that would give you postgres:

```
$ docker search postgres
NAME                      DESCRIPTION            STARS   OFFICIAL   AUTOMATED
postgres                  The PostgreSQL   ...    402     [OK]
paintedfox/postgresql     A docker image   ...    50                 [OK]
helmi03/docker-postgis    PostGIS 2.1 in   ...    20                 [OK]
atlassianfan/jira         Atlassian Jira   ...    17                 [OK]
orchardup/postgresql      https://github   ...    16                 [OK]
abevoelker/ruby           Ruby 2.1.2, Post ...    13                 [OK]
slafs/sentry              my approach for  ...    12                 [OK]
...
```

The command returns over 600 images. The first one is the official Postgres image maintained by the Postgres team. The other ones are images created by users of Docker Hub. Some of the images are built and pushed automatically, and you will learn about automated builds in Recipe 2.12.

See Also

- Docker Hub reference (*http://bit.ly/dockerhub-ref*)

2.10 Using ONBUILD Images

Problem

You have seen Dockerfiles in software repositories that have a single line like FROM golang:1.3-onbuild and you are wondering how this image can work.

Solution

The magic happens thanks to the ONBUILD directive that you can use in a Dockerfile. This directive defines a trigger that gets executed at a later time. The trigger is a regular Dockerfile directive like RUN or ADD. An image containing ONBUILD directives is called a *parent image*. When a parent image is used as a base image (i.e., using the FROM directive), the image being built—also called the child—triggers the directives defined by ONBUILD in the parent.

In other words, the parent image tells the child image what to do at build time.

You can still add directives in the Dockerfile of the child, but the ONBUILD directives of the parent will be executed first.

This is handy for building minimalistic Dockerfiles and providing consistency across all your images.

Check the following references for examples of parent images that use the ONBUILD image:

- Node.js (*http://bit.ly/node-dockerfile*)
- Golang (*http://bit.ly/golang-dockerfile*)
- Python (*http://bit.ly/python-dockerfile*)
- Ruby (*http://bit.ly/ruby-dockerfile*)

For Node.js applications, for instance, you can use a parent image defined by this Dockerfile:

```
FROM node:0.12.6

RUN mkdir -p /usr/src/app
WORKDIR /usr/src/app

ONBUILD COPY package.json /usr/src/app/
ONBUILD RUN npm install
ONBUILD COPY . /usr/src/app

CMD [ "npm", "start" ]
```

Your child image would be defined like this (at a minimum):

```
FROM node:0.12.6-onbuild
```

When building your child image, Docker would automatically copy the *package.json* file from your local context to */usr/src/app*, it would execute npm install and copy the entire context to *usr/src/app*.

See Also

- Understanding the ONBUILD directive (*http://www.eikonomega.com/dockerfile-understand-onbuild/*)
- ONBUILD reference (*http://docs.docker.com/reference/builder/#onbuild*)

2.11 Running a Private Registry

Problem

Using the public Docker Hub is easy. However, you might have data governance concerns with your images being hosted outside your own infrastructure. Therefore, you would like to run your own Docker registry, hosting it on your own infrastructure.

Solution

Use the Docker registry image (*https://hub.docker.com/_/registry/*) and start a container from it. You will have your private registry.

Pull the official *registry* image and run it as a detached container. You should then be able to curl *http://localhost:5000/v2* for a quick test that the registry is running:

```
$ docker pull registry:2
$ docker run -d -p 5000:5000 registry:2
$ curl -i http://localhost:5000/v2/
HTTP/1.1 200 OK
Content-Length: 2
Content-Type: application/json; charset=utf-8
Docker-Distribution-Api-Version: registry/2.0
Date: Wed, 19 Aug 2015 23:07:47 GMT
```

The preceding reponse shows that you are running the Docker registry with API version v2. You can now prepare a local image that you have created previously (e.g., a *flask* image, Recipe 2.4) and tag it with the proper naming convention for use with a private registry. In our case, the registry is running at *http://localhost:5000*, so we will prefix our tag with localhost:5000 and then push this image to the private registry. You can also use the IP address of your Docker host:

```
$ docker tag busybox localhost:5000/busy
$ docker push localhost:5000/busy
The push refers to a repository [localhost:5000/busy] (len: 1)
8c2e06607696: Image successfully pushed
6ce2e90b0bc7: Image successfully pushed
cf2616975b4a: Image already exists
latest: digest: sha256:3b5b980...a4d59f24f9c7253fce29 size: 5049
```

If you try to access this private registry from another machine, you will get an error message telling you that your Docker client does not allow you to use an insecure registry. For testing purposes only, edit your Docker configuration file to use the insecure-registry option. For instance, on Ubuntu 14.04, edit */etc/default/docker* and add this line:

```
DOCKER_OPTS="--insecure-registry <IP_OF_REGISTRY>:5000"
```

Then restart Docker on your machine (sudo service docker restart) and try to access the remote private registry again. (Remember that this is done on a different machine than where you are running the registry.)

Discussion

This short example uses the default setup of the registry. It assumes no authentication, an insecure registry, local storage, and a SQLAlchemy search backend. All of these can be set via environmental variables or by editing a configuration file. This is well documented (*https://github.com/docker/distribution*).

The registry that is running via the *registry* Docker image is a Golang application that exposes an HTTP REST API (*https://docs.docker.com/registry/spec/api/*), and that you can access with your own registry client or even curl.

For example, to list all images stored in the private registry, you can use the */v2/_catalog* URI:

```
$ curl http://localhost:5000/v2/_catalog
{"repositories":["busy"]}
```

If you push another *busybox* image to the private registry but tagged differently, you will see it being added to the catalog:

```
$ docker tag busybox localhost:5000/busy1
$ docker push localhost:5000/busy1
...
$ curl http://localhost:5000/v2/_catalog
{"repositories":["busy","busy1"]}
```

Each image in the registry is described by a manifest. You can get this manifest via the API as well at the */v2/<name>/manifests/<reference>* URI, where <name> is the name of the image and <reference> is a tag of the image:

```
$ curl http://localhost:5000/v2/busy1/manifests/latest
{
   "schemaVersion": 1,
   "name": "busy1",
   "tag": "latest",
   "architecture": "amd64",
   "fsLayers": [
      {
         "blobSum": "sha256:a3ed95caeb02ffe68cdd9fd84406680ae93d633cb16422d..."
      },
      {
         "blobSum": "sha256:1db09adb5ddd7f1a07b6d585a7db747a51c7bd17418d47e..."
      },
      {
         "blobSum": "sha256:a3ed95caeb02ffe68cdd9fd84406680ae93d633cb16422d..."
      }
```

```
        ],
...
```

Each *blob* seen in the preceding code corresponds to a layer of the image. You can upload, retrieve, and delete blobs through the registry API. Details are available in the API specification documentation page (*https://docs.docker.com/registry/spec/api/#deleting-an-image*).

To list all tags for a specific image, use the *v2/<name>/tags/list* URI like so:

```
$ curl http://localhost:5000/v2/busy1/tags/list
{"name":"busy1","tags":["latest"]}
$ docker tag busybox localhost:5000/busy1:foobar
$ docker push localhost:5000/busy1:foobar
$ curl http://localhost:5000/v2/busy1/tags/list
{"name":"busy1","tags":["foobar","latest"]}
```

These examples using `curl` are meant to give you a sense of the registry API. Complete API documentation is available on the Docker website (*https://docs.docker.com/reference/api/registry_api/#set-a-tag-for-a-specified-image-id*).

See Also

- The Docker registry page on Docker Hub (*https://hub.docker.com/*)
- The more extensive documentation on GitHub (*https://github.com/docker/distribution*)
- Deployment instructions (*https://docs.docker.com/registry/deploying/*)

2.12 Setting Up an Automated Build on Docker Hub for Continuous Integration/Deployment

Problem

You have access to Docker Hub (*https://hub.docker.com*) (see Recipe 2.9) and already pushed an image to it. However, this is a manual process. You want to automate the build of this image every time you commit a change to it.

Solution

Instead of setting up a standard repository, create an *Automated Build* repository and point to your application on GitHub (*https://github.com*) or Bitbucket (*https://bitbucket.org*).

On your Docker Hub page, click the Add Repository button and select Automated Build (Figure 2-2). You will then have the choice between GitHub and Bitbucket (Figure 2-3).

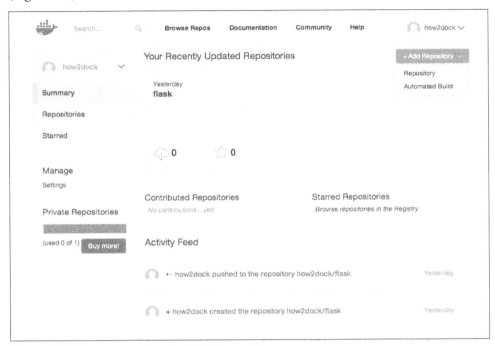

Figure 2-2. Create an automated build repository

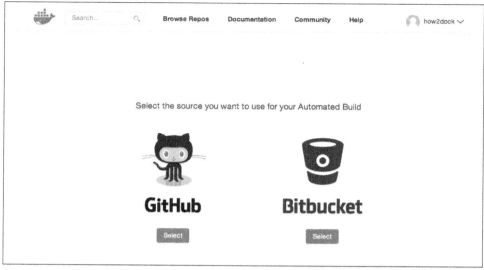

Figure 2-3. Choosing between GitHub and Bitbucket

 Docker Hub allows you to set up an automated build as a public or private repository pointing to a public or private code repository. If you are setting up a private automated build, Docker Hub will need read and write access to your GitHub account.

After selecting the type of online version control system you want to use, you can select the project you want to build from (Figure 2-4). This should be a project on GitHub or Bitbucket that contains the Dockerfile you want to build. Next, you can give a name to the Docker Hub repository you are creating, select the branch, and specify the location of the Dockerfile. This is handy, as it allows you to maintain several Dockerfiles inside a single GitHub/Bitbucket repository. Docker Hub creates a GitHub hook in your GitHub repository.

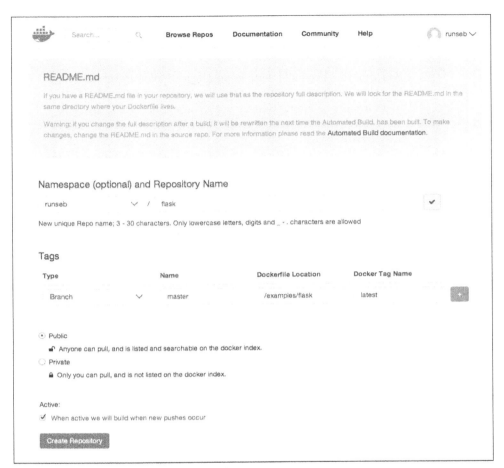

Figure 2-4. *Entering details of the build*

The name of the Docker Hub repository you are creating does not have to be the same as the GitHub/Bitbucket repository you select.

Once you have set up the build, you have access to the build details. The status changes from *pending* to *building* to *pushing* and finally to *finished*. When the build is finished, you can pull the new image:

```
$ docker pull runseb/flask
```

The Dockerfile tab automatically populates with the content of your Dockerfile in your GitHub repository. The Information tab automatically populates with the content of the *README.md* file if it exists.

As soon as you push a new commit to the GitHub repo used for the build, a new build is triggered. When the build finishes, the new image will be available.

 You can edit the build settings to trigger builds from different branches and specify a different tag. For instance, you can decide to build from your master branch and associate the latest tag to it, and use a release branch to build a different tag (i.e., 1.0 tag from a 1.0 release branch).

Discussion

In addition to builds being automatically triggered when you push to your GitHub or Bitbucket repository, you can trigger builds by sending an HTTP POST request to a specific URL generated on the Build Trigger page (see Figure 2-5). To prevent abusing the system, builds may be ignored.

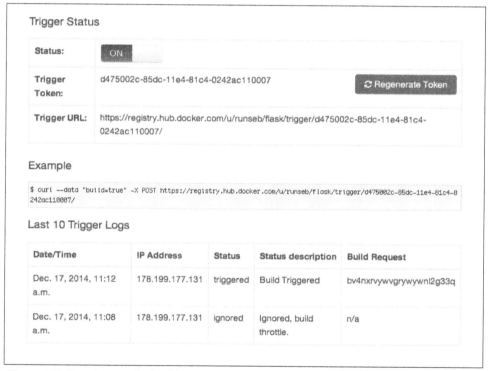

Figure 2-5. Turning on the build trigger

Finally, whether you build automatically or use a trigger on your own, you can also use webhooks. Webhook URLs are useful for integrating with other tools, like Jenkins (*https://jenkins-ci.org*). Various tools can trigger image builds and chain several steps of a continuous delivery pipeline. In the Build Details page of your automated build, you will be able to access the Web Hooks page. In it you can add URLs that will receive an HTTP POST when a successful build happens. The body of this POST request will contain a callback URL. In response, you will need to send another HTTP POST with a JSON payload containing the `state` key and the value of either `success`, `failure`, or `error`. On receiving a successfull state, the automated build can call another webhook, henceforth allowing you to chain several actions together.

See Also

- The automated build reference (*https://docs.docker.com/docker-hub/builds/*) documentation

2.13 Setting Up a Local Automated Build by Using a Git Hook and a Private Registry

Problem

Automated builds using Docker Hub and GitHub or Bitbucket are great (see Recipe 2.12), but you might be using a private registry (i.e., local hub) and may want to trigger Docker builds when you commit to your local Git projects.

Solution

Create a `post-commit` Git hook that triggers a build and pushes the new image to your private registry.

In the root tree of your Git project, create a bash script, *./git/hooks/post-commit*, that contains something as simple as this:

```
#!/bin/bash

tag=`git log -1 HEAD --format="%h"`
docker build -t flask:$tag /home/sebgoa/docbook/examples/flask
```

Make it executable with `chmod +x .git/hooks/post-commit`.

Now every time you make a commit to this Git project, this *post-commit* bash script will run. It will create a `tag` using the short version of the SHA of the latest commit and then trigger the build based on the Dockerfile referenced. It will then create a new image with the name *flask* and the computer tag:

```
$ git commit -m "fixing hook"
9c38962
Sending build context to Docker daemon 3.584 kB
```

```
Sending build context to Docker daemon
Step 0 : FROM ubuntu:14.04
 ---> 9bd07e480c5b
Step 1 : RUN apt-get update
 ---> Using cache
 ---> e659c9e9ba21
<snip>
Removing intermediate container 05c13744c7bf
Step 8 : CMD python /tmp/hello.py
 ---> Running in 124cd2ada52d
 ---> 9a50c7b2bee9
Removing intermediate container 124cd2ada52d
Successfully built 9a50c7b2bee9
[master 9c38962] fixing hook
 1 file changed, 1 insertion(+), 1 deletion(-)
$ docker images
REPOSITORY          TAG            IMAGE ID        CREATED        VIRTUAL SIZE
flask               9c38962        9a50c7b2bee9    5 days ago     354.6 MB
```

Although this works nicely and is achieved with two lines of bash, if the build were to take a long time, it would not be practical to build the image as a post-commit task. It would be better to use the post-commit hook to trigger a remote build and then register this image in a private repo.

Discussion

For example, you could use a Git hook to trigger an image build on one of your Jenkins servers and then let Jenkins push the new image to your private repository.

2.14 Using Conduit for Continuous Deployment

Problem

You know how to set up an automated build (see Recipe 2.12) on Docker Hub but would like to set up a hook so that when the build completes, the new image is deployed automatically on a Docker host.

Solution

Docker Hub features webhooks (*https://docs.docker.com/docker-hub/builds/#web hooks*) that are called when a successful push to a Docker Hub repository has been made.

The webhook is an HTTP POST request that will be sent to a defined endpoint. Processing this HTTP request and parsing the payload allows the endpoint to pull the image and potentially start a new container. Webhooks in Docker Hub can also be chained to trigger multiple events.

Chaining webhooks can be used to build continuous integration and continuous deployment pipelines. A development team will make changes to the source code of their applications (e.g., on GitHub); if the source code contains a Dockerfile and an automated build is set up, every commit will result in a new image. To validate the image, a team usually runs integration tests. While a lot of web services allow you to do that (including Travis CI (*https://travis-ci.org*), CircleCI (*https://circleci.com*), and Codeship (*https://codeship.com*)), you can do it on your own by using Jenkins or another testing framework. Once an image is validated, it can be used in production and deployed automatically by calling a second webhook.

To test this capability, you will use a single hook in Docker Hub that will reach an application that can process the payload and deploy the image. This application is available on the Docker Hub itself and is called Conduit.

 Conduit is an experimental system and should not be used in production.

See Also

- Official Docker documentation of Docker Hub webhooks (*https://docs.docker.com/docker-hub/builds/#webhooks*)
- Conduit Docker Hub page (*https://registry.hub.docker.com/u/ehazlett/conduit/*)
- Conduit GitHub page (*https://github.com/ehazlett/conduit*)

## CHAPTER 3

Docker Networking

3.0 Introduction

As you build your distributed application, services that compose it will need to be able to communicate with each other. These services, running in containers, might be on a single host or on multiple hosts and even across data centers. Therefore container networking is a critical enabler of any Docker-based distributed application.

The techniques used for networking containers are very similar to the techniques used to network virtual machines. Containers on a host can be attached to a software switch, and iptables are used to control network traffic between containers and expose processes running in the container on ports of the host.

At installation time, the Docker engine sets up multiple default networking behaviors on your hosts, which gives you a fully working setup from the start. In Recipe 3.1 we start by introducing some Docker commands that let you find the IP addresses of your containers, then we show you how to expose a container port on a host port in Recipe 3.2. In Recipe 3.3 we take a deeper a look at container linking, a mechanism to help with service discovery of multiple containers.

Networking is such an important topic for distributed applications that we felt it necessary to dive deeper into the nuts and bolts of it. Recipe 3.4 explains the default Docker bridge setup while Recipe 3.6 shows you how to change the defaults by modifying the Docker engine options. Recipe 3.8 and Recipe 3.9 go even deeper and show you how to create your own network switch and use it for networking your containers. While not necessary, understanding how container networking works and being able to modify it will help you with operating your applications in production.

While container networking is very similar to virtual machine networking, there exists a major difference. With containers you can choose the networking stack being used (Recipe 3.5). For example, you can share the networking stack of your host with a container, so this allows you to give a container the same IP address than your host. It also allows you to share the same network stack between containers. A lot is possible with container networking, and to explore all the possibilities Recipe 3.7 introduces a nice utility: pipework. Spending a little bit of time with pipework and trying to understand what it does will greatly enhance your understanding of containers and networking.

So far all the recipes presented have been for a single host; however, in a real distributed application, dozens, hundreds, or even thousands of hosts might be involved. In Recipe 3.10 we give a basic example of creating a tunnel between two hosts to provide a common IP subnet for containers running on two different hosts. This recipe is only shown for training purposes and should not be considered a production solution. Instead, Recipe 3.11, Recipe 3.12, and Recipe 3.13 are recipes that introduce Weave Net and Flannel. They have been contributed by Fintan Ryan and Eugene Yakubovich and introduce production-ready solutions for multihost container networking.

The chapter ends with a peek at Docker network (Recipe 3.14) and a deep dive into the VXLAN configuration being used (Recipe 3.15). Docker network is currently under development but should soon be part of the standard Docker release. Solutions like Weave Net, Flannel, and Calico should be usable in Docker network through the plug-in mechanism being developed.

To summarize what you will learn in this chapter, the first few recipes will cover some basic concepts that use the default Docker networking configuration. These should be enough for developers. System administrators looking at supporting Docker-based applications in production should consider diving deeper into the network configuration of the Docker engine and getting a good understanding of the defaults being set as well as how the networking namespaces are being used. Finally, for production use across multiple hosts, you should check the recipes about Weave and Flannel as well as start learning Docker network.

3.1 Finding the IP Address of a Container

Problem

You have started a container and would like to find its IP address.

Solution

There are many ways to find the IP address of a container started with the default Docker networking. This recipe presents a few of them.

The first method is to use the docker inspect command (see Recipe 9.1 for details) and the Go template format:

```
$ docker run -d --name nginx nginx
$ docker inspect --format '{{ .NetworkSettings.IPAddress }}' nginx
172.17.0.2
```

You can also use the docker exec command and check the IP address by using a command that executes within the container:

```
$ docker exec -ti nginx ip add | grep global
    inet 172.17.0.2/16 scope global eth0
```

You could also check the /etc/hosts file in the container, assuming the image does set it properly:

```
$ docker run -d --name foobar -h foobar busybox sleep 300
$ docker exec -ti foobar cat /etc/hosts | grep foobar
172.17.0.4      foobar
```

Finally, you can enter a shell in the container and issue standard Linux commands at the prompt:

```
$ docker exec -ti nginx bash
root@a3c1f7edb00a:/# cat /etc/hosts
```

See Also

- To understand how Docker networking works and go beyond finding a container IP address, see Recipe 3.4
- 10 examples (*http://networkstatic.net/10-examples-of-how-to-get-docker-container-ip-address/*) of how to get a Docker container IP address

3.2 Exposing a Container Port on the Host

Problem

You want to access a service running in a container over the network.

Solution

Docker can dynamically map a network port in a container to a port on the host by using the -P option of docker run. You can also manually specify a mapping by using the -p option.

Let's say that you have built an image that runs a Python Flask application using the Dockerfile shown here:

```
FROM python:2.7.10

RUN pip install flask
COPY hello.py /tmp/hello.py

CMD ["python","/tmp/hello.py"]
```

This is similar to what you saw in Recipe 2.4. Let's build this image and run a container without any port mapping flags:

```
$ docker build -t flask
$ docker run -d --name foobar flask
```

You can find the IP address and reach the Flask application on port 5000 from within the host like so:

```
$ docker inspect -f '{{.NetworkSettings.IPAddress}}' foobar
172.17.0.2
$ curl http://172.17.0.2:5000/
Hello World!
```

However, you cannot reach this application from *outside* the host. To make this work, you are going to run the container again but this time using port mapping:

```
$ docker kill foobar
$ docker rm foobar
$ docker run -d -p 5000 --name foobar flask
$ docker ps
CONTAINER ID  IMAGE   COMMAND            ... PORTS                   NAMES
2cc258827b34  flask   "python /tmp/hello.p ... 0.0.0.0:32768->5000/tcp  foobar
```

You see that the PORTS column of docker ps now returns a mapping between port 32768 and port 5000 of the container. The host listens on interface 0.0.0.0, TCP port 32768 and forwards the requests to port 5000 of the container. Try to curl the Docker host on port 32768, and you will see that you reach the Flask application.

> While docker ps returns the port-mapping information and you can use docker inspect, Docker also has the useful command docker port to list only the port mappings of a container. Try this:
>
> ```
> $ docker port foobar 5000
> 0.0.0.0:32768
> ```

You might have noticed that your Dockerfile does not contain an EXPOSE statement as it did in Recipe 2.4. If you add this statement, you can use the -P flag to expose the port and you do not have to specify the application port. Docker will automatically set the proper mapping. Add the EXPOSE 5000 statement to the Dockerfile, build a new image, and run the container like so:

```
$ docker run -d -P flask
```

You will see that the mapping was done automatically.

Discussion

You can expose multiple container ports and choose TCP or UDP protocols; for example, if you wanted to expose port 5000 over TCP and port 53 over UDP (assuming your application uses port 53 as well), you would do this:

```
$ docker run -d -p 5000/tcp -p 53/udp flask
```

This port mapping is made possible via two mechanisms.

First, by default Docker can manipulate the IP table of the host. If you check your IP tables rules when running the preceding Flask application, you will find a new rule in the Docker chain:

```
$ sudo iptables -L
...

Chain DOCKER (1 references)
target      prot opt source           destination
ACCEPT      tcp  --  anywhere         172.17.0.2            tcp dpt:5000
```

Second, Docker starts a small proxy on your host that listens on the host interface using the port that was chosen dynamically. If you list the processes, you will find this:

```
$ ps -ef | grep docker
root     29969     1 ... /usr/bin/docker -d
root     30851 29969 ... docker-proxy -proto tcp -host-ip 0.0.0.0 \
                                              -host-port 32769 \
                                              -container-ip 172.17.0.5 \
                                              -container-port 5000
```

You could change this default behavior by not allowing Docker to change your `ipta bles` but you will have to handle networking on your own (see Recipe 3.6).

3.3 Linking Containers in Docker

Problem

When building a distributed application that is made of several services, you need a way to discover where those services are so that various components of the system can reach the other ones. You could manually extract IP addresses of each service (running in a container), but in order to scale, you need a self-discovery system.

Solution

A first-order solution in Docker is to *link* containers. This is achieved by using the `--link` option of the `docker run` command.

 Container linking works well on a single host, but large-scale systems need other discovery mechanisms. Solutions like Recipe 7.13 coupled with a key-value store and DNS might be chosen. Docker network (see Recipe 3.14) has a built-in mechanism that exposes container services without defining *links*.

To illustrate linking, let's build a three-tier system made of a database, a web application, and a load-balancer. You will start the database, link it to the web application container, and then start the load-balancer with a link to the web application. To ease linking, you will name each container. Because this is a toy example, where the application does not need to do anything, you will use the image *runseb/hostname*, a Flask application that returns the hostname of the container.

Let's start those three containers:

```
$ docker run -d --name database -e MYSQL_ROOT_PASSWORD=root mysql
$ docker run -d --link database:db --name web runseb/hostname
$ docker run -d --link web:application --name lb nginx
$ docker ps
CONTAINER ID  IMAGE            COMMAND                 ... PORTS              NAMES
507edee2bbcf  nginx            "nginx -g 'daemon of ... 80/tcp, 443/tcp    lb
62c321acb102  runseb/hostname  "python /tmp/hello   ... 5000/tcp           web
cf17b64e7017  mysql            "/entrypoint.sh mysq ... 3306/tcp           database
```

The result of linking is that the application container now contains environment variables that point to the database. Similarly, the load-balancer contains environment variables that point to the application container:

```
$ docker exec -ti web env | grep DB
DB_PORT=tcp://172.17.0.13:3306
DB_PORT_3306_TCP=tcp://172.17.0.13:3306
DB_PORT_3306_TCP_ADDR=172.17.0.13
DB_PORT_3306_TCP_PORT=3306
DB_PORT_3306_TCP_PROTO=tcp
DB_NAME=/web/db
DB_ENV_MYSQL_ROOT_PASSWORD=root
DB_ENV_MYSQL_MAJOR=5.6
DB_ENV_MYSQL_VERSION=5.6.25

$ docker exec -ti lb env | grep APPLICATION
APPLICATION_PORT=tcp://172.17.0.14:5000
APPLICATION_PORT_8080_TCP=tcp://172.17.0.14:5000
APPLICATION_PORT_8080_TCP_ADDR=172.17.0.14
APPLICATION_PORT_8080_TCP_PORT=5000
```

```
APPLICATION_PORT_8080_TCP_PROTO=tcp
APPLICATION_NAME=/lb/application
```

You can use these environment variables to dynamically configure your application and load-balancer.

The */etc/hosts* file is also automatically updated to contain information for name resolution:

```
$ docker exec -ti web cat /etc/hosts
172.17.0.14     62c321acb102
172.17.0.13     db cf17b64e7017 database

$ docker exec -ti lb cat /etc/hosts
172.17.0.15     507edee2bbcf
172.17.0.14     application 62c321acb102 web
```

 If you restart a container, the */etc/hosts* file of containers that were linked to it will be updated, but the environment variables will be unchanged. Therefore, using the content of */etc/hosts* is the recommended way of extracting the IP address of a linked container.

Discussion

When you started the containers, you saw that we named all of them. The container name was used to define the link. It took this form:

```
--link <container_name>:<alias>
```

The alias specified was found in the */etc/host* entry and was used as a prefix in the environment variables defined.

When you have containers running, you can use the inspect method to know what links are present. It will return a mapping between the linked container name and its alias in the container:

```
$ docker inspect -f "{{.HostConfig.Links}}" application
[/database:/application/db]
$ docker inspect -f "{{.HostConfig.Links}}" lb
[/application:/lb/app]
```

Although container linking is useful for development on a single machine, in large-scale deployments it will show its limitations, including when containers get restarted often. A system based on either DNS or a dynamic container registration system will scale and be updated automatically.

See Also

- Official documentation on linking containers (*https://docs.docker.com/userguide/dockerlinks/*)

3.4 Understanding Docker Container Networking

Problem

You would like to understand the basics of networking Docker containers.

Solution

To use Docker and get network connectivity working between your containers, you don't have to use the solution presented here. It is presented in detail to provide enough information so that you can customize the networking behavior to your liking.

In the default installation of Docker, Linux bridge docker0 is created on the Docker host. This bridge gets a private address and a subnet associated to it. The subnet assigned to the docker0 bridge is chosen as the first nonconflicting subnet among the following list: `172.[17-31].42.1/16, 10.[0-255].42.1/16, 192.168.[42-44].1/24`. Hence, most of the time your docker0 bridge will get the address 172.17.42.1. All containers that will attach to this bridge will get an address in the 172.17.42.0/24 network. Containers' networking interfaces get attached to this bridge and will use the docker0 interface as a networking gateway. When a container is created, Docker creates a pair of "peer" network interfaces that are placed in two separate networking namespaces: one interface in the networking namespace of the container (i.e., eth0) and one interface in the networking namespace of the host, attached to the docker0 bridge.

To illustrate this setup, let's look at a Docker host and start a container. You can use an existing Docker host or use the Vagrant box prepared for this book:

```
$ git clone https://github.com/how2dock/docbook
$ cd ch03/simple
$ vagrant up
$ vagrant ssh
```

Figure 3-1 shows the network configuration of this Vagrant box. It contains a single NAT interface to get to the outside network. Inside the host is Linux bridge docker0, and two containers are depicted.

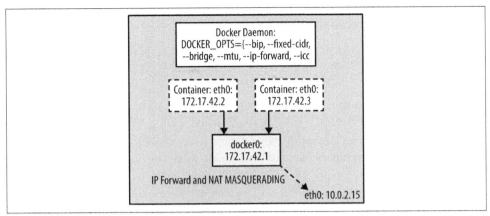

Figure 3-1. Network diagram of single Docker host

After connecting to the host, if you list the network links, you will see the loopback device, an `eth0` interface, and the `docker0` bridge, as depicted in the diagram. Docker starts when the machine is booted and automatically creates a bridge and assigns a subnet to it:

```
$ ip -d link show
1: lo: <LOOPBACK,UP,LOWER_UP> mtu 65536 qdisc noqueue state UNKNOWN ...
    link/loopback 00:00:00:00:00:00 brd 00:00:00:00:00:00 promiscuity 0
2: eth0: <BROADCAST,MULTICAST,UP,LOWER_UP> mtu 1500 qdisc pfifo_fast ...
    link/ether 08:00:27:98:a7:ad brd ff:ff:ff:ff:ff:ff promiscuity 0
3: docker0: <NO-CARRIER,BROADCAST,MULTICAST,UP> mtu 1500 qdisc noqueue ...
    link/ether 00:00:00:00:00:00 brd ff:ff:ff:ff:ff:ff promiscuity 0
    bridge
```

Now let's start a container and check its network interface:

```
$ docker run -ti --rm ubuntu:14.04 bash
root@4e3ffb9bc381:/# ip addr show eth0
6: eth0: <BROADCAST,UP,LOWER_UP> mtu 1500 qdisc noqueue state UP group default
    link/ether 02:42:ac:11:2a:03 brd ff:ff:ff:ff:ff:ff
    inet 172.17.42.3/24 scope global eth0
...
```

Indeed the container has an IP (i.e., 172.17.42.3) in the 172.17.42.1/16 network. On the host itself, a virtual interface (i.e., `veth450b81a` in the following code) is created and attached to the bridge. You can see this by listing the links on the Docker host with the `ip` tool (or `ifconfig`) and the `brctl` tool if you installed the *bridge-utils* package. The `ip` command represents a collection of utilities for controlling TCP/IP traffic in Linux. You can find the project documentation at the Linux Foundation website (*http://bit.ly/iproute2*).

```
$ ip -d link show
...
```

```
3: docker0: <BROADCAST,MULTICAST,UP,LOWER_UP> mtu 1500 qdisc noqueue state UP ...
    link/ether aa:85:e0:61:69:2d brd ff:ff:ff:ff:ff:ff promiscuity 0
    bridge
7: veth450b81a: <BROADCAST,UP,LOWER_UP> mtu 1500 qdisc pfifo_fast master docker0
    link/ether aa:85:e0:61:69:2d brd ff:ff:ff:ff:ff:ff promiscuity 1
    veth
$ brctl show
bridge name     bridge id            STP enabled     interfaces
docker0         8000.aa85e061692d    no              veth450b81a
```

From the container, you can ping the network gateway 172.17.42.1 (i.e., docker0), other containers on the same host, and the outside world.

 Start another container on a separate terminal and try to ping each container. Verify that the second container interface is also attached to the bridge. Since there are no IP table rules dropping traffic, both containers can communicate with each other on any port.

Discussion

Outbound networking traffic is forwarded to the other interfaces of your Docker host via IP forwarding and will go through NAT translation using an IP table masquerading rule. On your Docker host you can check that IP forwarding has been enabled:

```
$ cat /proc/sys/net/ipv4/ip_forward
1
```

 Try turning off IP forwarding, and you will see that your container will lose outbound network connectivity:

```
# echo 0 > /proc/sys/net/ipv4/ip_forward
```

You can also check the NAT rule that does the IP masquerading for outbound traffic:

```
$ sudo iptables -t nat -L
...
Chain POSTROUTING (policy ACCEPT)
target      prot opt source              destination
MASQUERADE  all  --  172.17.42.0/24      anywhere
...
```

In Recipe 3.7, you will see how to create this configuration from scratch.

See Also

- Docker official networking documentation (*https://docs.docker.com/articles/networking/*)

3.5 Choosing a Container Networking Namespace

Problem

When starting a container, you want to be able to choose a specific network namespace. For certain applications that you run in containers, you may be required to use a different network setup than default bridge networking or you may not need any networking at all.

Solution

In Recipe 3.4, you started a container using the defaults of the docker run command. This attached the container to a Linux bridge and created the appropriate network interfaces. It takes advantage of IP forwarding and IP tables managed by the Docker engine to provide outbound network connectivity and NAT.

However, you can start a container with a different type of networking. You can choose between the host networking namespace, no networking namespace at all, or the networking namespace of another container by using the --net option of docker run.

Let's start a container on a Docker host without any networking namespace by using --net=none:

```
$ docker run -it --rm --net=none ubuntu:14.04 bash
root@3a22f5076f9a:/# ip -d link show
1: lo: <LOOPBACK,UP,LOWER_UP> mtu 65536 qdisc noqueue state UNKNOWN mode DEFAULT
    link/loopback 00:00:00:00:00:00 brd 00:00:00:00:00:00 promiscuity 0
root@3a22f5076f9a:/# route
        Kernel IP routing table
        Destination     Gateway         Genmask         Flags Metric Ref    Use Iface
```

When listing the networking links, you see only a link local address. There are no other network interfaces and no networking routes. You will have to bring up the network manually if you need it (see Recipe 3.7).

Now let's start a container with the networking namespace of the host by using --net=host:

```
$ docker run -it --rm --net=host ubuntu:14.04 bash
root@foobar-server:/# ip -d link show
1: lo: <LOOPBACK,UP,LOWER_UP> mtu 65536 qdisc noqueue state UNKNOWN mode DEFAULT
```

```
        link/loopback 00:00:00:00:00:00 brd 00:00:00:00:00:00 promiscuity 0
  2: eth0: <BROADCAST,MULTICAST,UP,LOWER_UP> mtu 1500 qdisc pfifo_fast state ...
        link/ether 08:00:27:98:a7:ad brd ff:ff:ff:ff:ff:ff promiscuity 0
  3: docker0: <BROADCAST,MULTICAST,UP,LOWER_UP> mtu 1500 qdisc noqueue state ...
        link/ether c6:4b:6b:b7:4b:98 brd ff:ff:ff:ff:ff:ff promiscuity 0
        bridge
```

When listing the networking links within this container, you see exactly the same interfaces as in the host, including the docker0 bridge. This means that while the container processes are isolated in their own namespace and resources are limited through cgroups, the network namespace of the container is the same as the one of the host. You see in the preceding example that the hostname of the container is the Docker host hostname (you cannot use the -h option to set a hostname when using the host networking stack). Note, however, that you will not be able to reconfigure the host network from such a container. For example, you cannot bring down interfaces:

```
root@foobar-server:/# ifconfig eth0 down
SIOCSIFFLAGS: Operation not permitted
```

Although host networking can be handy, it needs to be handled with lots of care.

 Starting a container with --net=host can be dangerous, especially if you start a privileged container with --privileged=true. Host networking will allow you to change your host network configuration from within the container. If you were to run an application as root in a privileged container started with --net=host, a vulnerability of your application would let an intruder control your Docker host networking entirely. However, it can also be useful for processes that need a lot of network I/O.

The final option is to use the network stack of another already running container. Let's start a container with the hostname *cookbook*:

```
$ docker run -it --rm -h cookbook ubuntu:14.04 bash
root@cookbook:/# ifconfig
eth0      Link encap:Ethernet  HWaddr 02:42:ac:11:00:02
          inet addr:172.17.0.2  Bcast:0.0.0.0  Mask:255.255.0.0
          ...
```

You see at the prompt that the hostname has been set to *cookbook* and that the IP is 172.17.02. It is attached to the docker0 bridge. Now let's start another container and use the same network namespace. First you list the running containers to get the name of the container just started. The convention is to use --net=container:CONTAINER_NAME_OR_ID:

```
$ docker ps
CONTAINER ID    IMAGE         COMMAND  ...    NAMES
```

```
cc7f72826c36    ubuntu:14.04   "bash"   ...    cocky_galileo
$ docker run -ti --rm --net=container:cocky_galileo ubuntu:14.04 bash
root@cookbook:/# ifconfig
eth0      Link encap:Ethernet  HWaddr 02:42:ac:11:00:02
          inet addr:172.17.0.2  Bcast:0.0.0.0  Mask:255.255.0.0
              ...
```

As you see, the new container has the same hostname as the first container started and of course has the same IP. The processes in each container will be isolated and exist in their own process namespace, but they share the same networking namespace and can communicate on the loopback device.

Discussion

Which networking namespace to use is up to the application you are running and what you want the network to look like. Docker networking is extremely flexible and will allow you to build any topology and secure network scenarios between your container processes.

See Also

- How Docker networks containers (*https://docs.docker.com/articles/networking/#container-networking*)

3.6 Configuring the Docker Daemon IP Tables and IP Forwarding Settings

Problem

You may not like that by default the Docker daemon turned on IP forwarding as well as modified your IP tables. You would like more control on how traffic flows on your host, between your containers and with the outside world.

Solution

The default Docker behavior will most likely be fine for most readers. However, this behavior is customizable when you start the Docker daemon with the `--ip-forward=false`, `--iptables=false` options. This recipe shows you to make those customizations.

To try this, stop the Docker daemon on the host that you are using. On Ubuntu/Debian-based systems, edit */etc/default/docker* and set these options to `false` (on CentOS/RHEL systems edit */etc/sysconfig/docker*):

```
$ sudo service docker stop
$ sudo su
# echo DOCKER_OPTS=\"--iptables=false --ip-forward=false\" >> /etc/default/docker
# service docker restart
```

 You may have to remove the postrouting rule manually first as well as set the IP forwarding rule to zero, before restarting the Docker daemon. To do this, try the following on your Docker host:

```
# iptables -t nat -D POSTROUTING 1
# echo 0 > /proc/sys/net/ipv4/ip_forward
# service docker restart
```

With this configuration, traffic on the Docker bridge docker0 will not be forwarded to the other networking interfaces and the postrouting masquerading rule will not be present. This means that all outbound connectivity from your containers to the outside world will be dropped.

Verify this behavior by starting a container and trying to reach the outside world. For example:

```
$ docker run -it --rm ubuntu:14.04 bash
WARNING: IPv4 forwarding is disabled.

root@ba12d578e6c8:/# ping -c 2 -W 5 8.8.8.8
PING 8.8.8.8 (8.8.8.8) 56(84) bytes of data.

--- 8.8.8.8 ping statistics ---
2 packets transmitted, 0 received, 100% packet loss, time 1009ms
```

To re-enable communication to the outside manually, enable IP forwarding and set the postrouting rule on the Docker host like so:

```
# echo 1 > /proc/sys/net/ipv4/ip_forward
# iptables -t nat -A POSTROUTING -s 172.17.0.0/16 -j MASQUERADE
```

Go back to the terminal of your container and try pinging 8.8.8.8 again. Traffic should now be routed outside your host.

 With --iptables=false set for the Docker daemon, you will not be able to restrict traffic between containers (i.e., use --icc=false) since Docker will not be able to manage the IP table rules. This means that all containers started on the same bridge will be able to communicate on all ports. See the following Discussion for more on this topic.

Discussion

By default the Docker daemon is allowed to manage the IP table rules on the Docker host. This means that it can add rules that restrict traffic between containers and provide network isolation between them.

If you disallow Docker to manipulate the IP table rules, it will not be able to add rules that restrict traffic between containers.

If you do allow Docker to manipulate the IP table rules, you can set the `--icc=false` option for the Docker daemon. This will add a default drop rule for all packets on the bridge, and containers will not be able to reach each other.

You can try this by editing the Docker config file (i.e., */etc/default/docker* on Ubuntu/Debian and */etc/sysconfig/docker* on CentOS/RHEL) and adding the `--icc=false` option. Restart Docker and start two containers on your host, and you will see that you cannot ping one container from another.

Since this drastically restricts traffic between containers, how can you have them communicating? This is solved with container linking, which creates specific IP table rules (see Recipe 3.3).

Allow ping from the Docker host to all the containers:

```
$ sudo iptables -A DOCKER -p icmp --icmp-type echo-request -j ACCEPT
$ sudo iptables -A DOCKER -p icmp --icmp-type echo-reply -j ACCEPT
```

3.7 Using pipework to Understand Container Networking

Problem

Docker built-in networking capabilities work great, but you would like a hands-on approach that enables you to use traditional networking tools to create network interfaces for your containers.

Solution

This is an advanced recipe aimed at providing more in-depth knowledge of how Docker networking happens. You do not need this recipe and the tooling presented here to use Docker. However, to better understand Docker networking, you might want to use pipework (*https://github.com/jpetazzo/pipework*). Pipework, created by Jerome Petazzoni from Docker back in 2013, manipulates cgroups and network namespaces to build networking scenarios for your containers. At first it supported pure LXC containers and now it also supports Docker containers. If you start a container with the `--net=none` option, pipework is handy for adding networking to that container. This is a really nice exercise if you want to gain more detailed knowledge about Docker networking, although it's not needed for day-to-day use and production deployment.

 Using pipework is not needed to use Docker and manage the connectivity of your containers. This recipe is included for those who want to gain advanced knowledge in creating network stacks in the container network namespaces by hand. pipework allows you to do this, and having a look at the bash script gives you even more knowledge, as you will learn all the detailed step-by-step commands that are needed to build the network of a container.

While almost everything you can do with pipework is built in within Docker, it is a great tool to reverse-engineer Docker networking and get a deeper understanding of how the containers communicate with each other and the outside world. This recipe shows you a few examples so you can deconstruct Docker networking capabilities and become a little more comfortable dealing with different networking namespaces.

pipework is a single bash script that you can download for free (*https://raw.githubusercontent.com/jpetazzo/pipework/master/pipework*). For convenience, I created a Vagrant box that contains pipework. You can get it by cloning the repository and starting the Vagrant VM:

```
$ git clone https://github.com/how2dock/docbook
$ cd ch03/simple
$ vagrant up
$ vagrant ssh
vagrant@foobar-server:~$ cd /vagrant
vagrant@foobar-server:/vagrant$ ls
pipework  Vagrantfile
```

Let's start a container without any network by using --net=none as shown in Recipe 3.5:

```
$ docker run -it --rm --net none --name cookbook ubuntu:14.04 bash
root@556d04d8637e:/# ip -d link show
1: lo: <LOOPBACK,UP,LOWER_UP> mtu 65536 qdisc noqueue state UNKNOWN mode ...
    link/loopback 00:00:00:00:00:00 brd 00:00:00:00:00:00 promiscuity 0
```

In another terminal on the Docker host, let's use pipework to create a bridge br0, assign an IP address to the container, and set the correct routing from the container to the bridge:

```
$ cd /vagrant
$ sudo ./pipework br0 cookbook 192.168.1.10/24@192.168.1.254
Warning: arping not found; interface may not be immediately reachable
```

In the container, verify that the interface eth1 is up and that the routing is in place:

```
root@556d04d8637e:/# ip -d link show eth1
7: eth1: <BROADCAST,MULTICAST,UP,LOWER_UP> mtu 1500 qdisc pfifo_fast state UP ...
```

```
    link/ether a6:95:12:b9:8f:55 brd ff:ff:ff:ff:ff:ff promiscuity 0
    veth
root@556d04d8637e:/# route
Kernel IP routing table
Destination     Gateway         Genmask         Flags Metric Ref    Use Iface
default         192.168.1.254   0.0.0.0         UG    0      0        0 eth1
192.168.1.0     *               255.255.255.0   U     0      0        0 eth1
```

Now if you list the network links on the host, you will see a bridge br0 in addition to the default docker0 bridge, and if you list the bridges (using brctl from the *bridge-utils* package), you will see the virtual Ethernet interface attached to br0 by pipework:

```
$ ip -d link show
...
3: docker0: <NO-CARRIER,BROADCAST,MULTICAST,UP> mtu 1500 qdisc noqueue state \
DOWN mode DEFAULT group default
    link/ether 00:00:00:00:00:00 brd ff:ff:ff:ff:ff:ff promiscuity 0
    bridge
8: br0: <NO-CARRIER,BROADCAST,MULTICAST,UP> mtu 1500 qdisc noqueue state \
DOWN mode DEFAULT group default
    link/ether 22:43:24:f5:91:7e brd ff:ff:ff:ff:ff:ff promiscuity 0
    bridge
10: veth1pl31668: <NO-CARRIER,BROADCAST,MULTICAST,UP> mtu 1500 qdisc \
pfifo_fast master br0 state DOWN mode DEFAULT group default qlen 1000
    link/ether 22:43:24:f5:91:7e brd ff:ff:ff:ff:ff:ff promiscuity 1
    veth
$ brctl show
bridge name     bridge id               STP enabled     interfaces
br0             8000.224324f5917e       no              veth1pl31668
docker0         8000.000000000000       no
```

At this stage, you can reach the container from the host or reach any other containers from the container cookbook. However, if you try to reach outside the Docker host, you will notice that it will not work. There is no NAT masquerading rule in place that is added automatically by Docker when you use the defaults. Add the rule manually on the Docker host and try to ping 8.8.8.8 (for example) from the container interactive terminal:

```
# iptables -t nat -A POSTROUTING -s 192.168.0.0/16 -j MASQUERADE
```

On the container, verify that you can reach outside your Docker host:

```
root@556d04d8637e:/# ping 8.8.8.8
PING 8.8.8.8 (8.8.8.8) 56(84) bytes of data.
64 bytes from 8.8.8.8: icmp_seq=1 ttl=61 time=22.6 ms
64 bytes from 8.8.8.8: icmp_seq=2 ttl=61 time=23.8 ms
64 bytes from 8.8.8.8: icmp_seq=3 ttl=61 time=23.9 ms
```

pipework can do a lot more, so make sure to check the *README* file (*https://github.com/jpetazzo/pipework*) and to pick inside the bash script to gain an even greater understanding of the networking namespace.

Discussion

Although pipework is extremely powerful and allowed you to build a proper networking stack for a container started with --net=none, it also hid some of the details of manipulating the container network namespace. If you read the code of pipework, you will see what it does. A good explanation is also available in the Docker documentation (*https://docs.docker.com/articles/networking/#container-networking*) and is a good exercise, both in networking and containers. I highly recommend reading it.

 This discussion is not about pipework specifically; it aims to show you all the steps necessary to build a networking stack for a container. It is extremely useful to obtain a better understanding of container networking and reverse-engineer how Docker works.

Let's look back at this single pipework command:

```
$ sudo ./pipework br0 cookbook 192.168.1.10/24@192.168.1.254
```

This command did several almost magical things at once:

- It created a bridge br0 on the host.
- It assigned IP address 192.168.1.254.
- It created a network interface inside the container and assigned it IP address 192.168.1.10.
- Finally it added a route inside the container, setting up the bridge as the default gateway.

Let's do it step by step but without pipework this time. To get started, let's add a bridge br0 and give it the IP 192.168.1.254. If you have worked on virtual machine virtualization before, this should be familiar. If not, follow along: you create the bridge with the brctl utility, use ip to add the IP address to the bridge, and finish by bringing the bridge up.

If you have followed along, you might want to delete the existing br0 bridge:

```
$ sudo ip link set br0 down
$ sudo brctl delbr br0
```

You are now ready to do it all over again, but by hand this time:

```
$ sudo brctl addbr br0
$ sudo ip addr add 192.168.1.254/24 dev br0
$ sudo ip link set dev br0 up
```

The tricky part compared to full network virtualization comes from the fact that you are dealing with containers and that the networking stack is in fact a different network namespace on the host. To assign network interfaces to the container, you need to assign an interface to the network namespace that the container will use. The interfaces that you can assign to a specific network namespace are virtual Ethernet interface pairs. These pairs act as a pipe, with one end of the pipe in the container namespace and the other end on the bridge that you just created on the host.

Therefore, let's create a veth pair *foo, bar* and attach *foo* to the bridge br0:

```
$ sudo ip link add foo type veth peer name bar
$ sudo brctl addif br0 foo
$ sudo ip link set foo up
```

The result can be seen with ip -d link show; a new bridge br0 and foo interface of type veth attached to it:

```
$ ip -d link
1: lo: <LOOPBACK,UP,LOWER_UP> mtu 65536 qdisc noqueue state UNKNOWN mode DEFAULT \
group default
    link/loopback 00:00:00:00:00:00 brd 00:00:00:00:00:00 promiscuity 0
2: eth0: <BROADCAST,MULTICAST,UP,LOWER_UP> mtu 1500 qdisc pfifo_fast state \
UNKNOWN mode DEFAULT group default qlen 1000
    link/ether 08:00:27:98:a7:ad brd ff:ff:ff:ff:ff:ff promiscuity 0
3: docker0: <NO-CARRIER,BROADCAST,MULTICAST,UP> mtu 1500 qdisc noqueue state \
DOWN mode DEFAULT group default
    link/ether 00:00:00:00:00:00 brd ff:ff:ff:ff:ff:ff promiscuity 0
    bridge
6: br0: <BROADCAST,MULTICAST,UP,LOWER_UP> mtu 1500 qdisc noqueue state UP mode \
DEFAULT group default
    link/ether ee:7d:7e:f7:6f:18 brd ff:ff:ff:ff:ff:ff promiscuity 0
    bridge
8: foo: <BROADCAST,MULTICAST,UP,LOWER_UP> mtu 1500 qdisc pfifo_fast master br0 \
state UP mode DEFAULT group default qlen 1000
    link/ether ee:7d:7e:f7:6f:18 brd ff:ff:ff:ff:ff:ff promiscuity 1
    veth
$ brctl show
bridge name     bridge id           STP enabled    interfaces
br0             8000.ee7d7ef76f18   no             foo
docker0         8000.000000000000   not
```

 Do not call each end of your veth pair the traditional eth0 or eth1 as it could conflict with existing physical interfaces on the host.

To complicate things a bit, when you started your container with --net=none, it did create a network namespace but there was nothing in it except the loopback device. Now that you want to configure it (e.g., adding an interface, setting up a route), you need to find the network namespace ID. Docker keeps its network namespaces in */var/run/docker/netns*, which is a nondefault location. To be able to use the ip tool properly, you are going to do a little nonconventional hack and symlink */var/run/docker/netns* to */var/run/netns*, which is the default location where the `ip` tool looks for network namespaces. Doing so, you can list the existing network namespaces. Next, you see that the namespace ID of your container is the container ID:

```
$ cd /var/run
$ sudo ln -s /var/run/docker/netns netns
$ sudo ip netns
c785553b22a1
$ NID=$(sudo ip netns)
```

Now, let's put the *bar* veth in the container namespace by using `ip link set netns` and use `ip netns exec` to give it a name and a MAC address inside this namespace:

```
$ sudo ip link set bar netns $NID
$ sudo ip netns exec $NID ip link set dev bar name eth1
$ sudo ip netns exec $NID ip link set eth1 address 12:34:56:78:9a:bc
$ sudo ip netns exec $NID ip link set eth1 up
```

The final thing to do is to assign an IP address to *eth1* of the container and define a default route so that the container can reach the Docker host and beyond:

```
$ sudo ip netns exec $NID ip addr add 192.168.1.1/24 dev eth1
$ sudo ip netns exec $NID ip route add default via 192.168.1.254
```

That's it. At this stage, your container should have the exact same networking stack as the one built with pipework earlier with a single command.

 Remember that if you want to reach outside your container, you need to add the IP NAT masquerading rule:

```
$ sudo iptables -t nat -A POSTROUTING -s 192.168.0.0/24
-j MASQUERADE
```

See Also

- pipework's (*https://github.com/jpetazzo/pipework*) extensive *README* covers multiple scenarios
- How Docker networks (*https://docs.docker.com/articles/networking/#container-networking*) containers
- `ip netns` man page (*http://man7.org/linux/man-pages/man8/ip-netns.8.html*)
- Introduction to Linux nework namespace (*http://blog.scottlowe.org/2013/09/04/introducing-linux-network-namespaces/*)

3.8 Setting Up a Custom Bridge for Docker

Problem

You would like to set up your own bridge for Docker to use instead of using the default.

Solution

Create a bridge and change the start-up options of the Docker daemon to use it.

In the Recipe 3.7 solution section, you saw how to create a full networking stack for a container started with the --net=none option. That section showed how to create a bridge. Let's reuse what we discussed there.

First let's turn off the Docker daemon, delete the docker0 bridge created by default, and create a new bridge called cookbook:

```
$ sudo service docker stop
$ sudo ip link set docker0 down
$ sudo brctl delbr docker0
$ sudo brctl addbr cookbook
$ sudo ip link set cookbook up
$ sudo ip addr add 10.0.0.1/24 dev cookbook
```

Now that the bridge is up, you can edit the Docker daemon configuration file and restart the daemon (e.g., on Ubuntu):

```
$ sudo su
# echo 'DOCKER_OPTS="-b=cookbook"' >> /etc/default/docker
# service docker restart
```

You can start a container and list the IP address assigned to it and check network connectivity:

```
root@c557cdb072ba:/# ip addr show eth0
10: eth0: <BROADCAST,UP,LOWER_UP> mtu 1500 qdisc noqueue state UP group default
    link/ether 02:42:0a:00:00:02 brd ff:ff:ff:ff:ff:ff
    inet 10.0.0.2/24 scope global eth0
      ...
```

Automatically as expected, Docker also creates the NAT rule for this bridge:

```
$ sudo iptables -t nat -L
...
Chain POSTROUTING (policy ACCEPT)
target     prot opt source             destination
MASQUERADE  all  --  10.0.0.0/24        anywhere
```

Discussion

Although you can do this manually, there is nothing different between the bridge cookbook that you just created and the default docker0 bridge.

If you wanted to change the IP range that Docker uses for the containers started with the default networking (i.e., bridge), you could use the --bip option. You could also restrict this IP range with the --fixed-cidr option as well as set the MTU size with --mtu.

To bring down the bridge, execute the following two commands:

```
$ sudo ip link set cookbook down
$ sudo brctl delbr cookbook
```

3.9 Using OVS with Docker

Problem

You know how to use your own bridge to network your Docker containers (see Recipe 3.8), but you would like to use the Open vSwitch (OVS) virtual switch instead of the standard Linux bridge. Maybe you want to build your own GRE, or VXLAN-based overlay, or you want to build a software-defined network solution with a network controller. OVS provides programmatic extensions and control using the Open-Flow protocol (*https://www.opennetworking.org/openflow*) and the OVSDB management protocol (*https://tools.ietf.org/html/rfc7047*).

Solution

As of Docker 1.7, Open vSwitch is not yet supported natively. You can use it, but you will need to use a tool like pipework (see Recipe 3.7) or a utility called ovs-docker (*https://github.com/openvswitch/ovs/blob/master/utilities/ovs-docker*), a manual process to build the network stack of the containers. It should be supported in a future version of Docker Network (see Recipe 3.14).

Use Open vSwitch (*http://openvswitch.org*) (OVS) as your bridge and specify its name in the Docker daemon configuration file.

On your Docker host, start by installing the packages for OVS; for example, on Ubuntu 14.04:

```
$ sudo apt-get -y install openvswitch-switch
```

If you want a more recent version of Open vSwitch, you can build it from source (*https://github.com/openvswitch/ovs*) relatively easily.

Now create a bridge and bring it up:

```
$ sudo ovs-vsctl add-br ovs-cookbook
$ sudo ip link set ovs-cookbook up
```

You are now ready to use pipework (see Recipe 3.7) to build the network stack of containers attached to this Open vSwitch bridge. You will need to start containers without a network stack (i.e., --net=none)—for example:

```
$ docker run -it --rm --name foobar --net=none ubuntu:14.04 bash
root@8fda6e33eb88:/#
```

In a different shell on your Docker host, use pipework to create a network interface (you will need to install pipework) in your *foobar* container:

```
$ sudo su
# ./pipework ovs-cookbook foobar 10.0.0.10/24@10.0.0.1
# ovs-vsctl list-ports ovs-cookbook
veth1pl31350
```

Your bridge will also have been assigned the IP address 10.0.0.1 by pipework:

```
$ ifconfig
ovs-cookbook  Link encap:Ethernet  HWaddr 36:b1:d3:e5:fc:44
              inet addr:10.0.0.1  Bcast:0.0.0.0  Mask:255.255.255.0
                   . . .
```

Your container will now have a network interface:

```
root@8fda6e33eb88:/# ifconfig
eth1      Link encap:Ethernet  HWaddr 52:fe:9f:78:b7:fc
          inet addr:10.0.0.10  Bcast:0.0.0.0  Mask:255.255.255.04
. . . .
```

You could also create the interface by hand by using ip netns, as you did in the discussion section of Recipe 3.7.

See Also

- The Open vSwitch website (*http://openvswitch.org*)

3.10 Building a GRE Tunnel Between Docker Hosts

Problem

You need to have network connectivity between containers on multiple hosts using their own IP addresses.

Solution

Several recipes (see Recipe 3.11 and Recipe 3.13) show solutions that can be used in production deployment. This recipe presents a step-by-step example of how to set up multihost networking, to help you build a solid foundation for understanding Docker networking.

To build a toy setup that provides network connectivity between containers on multiple hosts, build a Generic Routing Encapsulation (GRE) tunnel to encapsulate IPv4 traffic and provide a route between containers using their private addresses. To showcase this technique, you are going to bring up two Docker hosts and set up the network configuration that you can see in Figure 3-2.

Host 1 has IP address `192.168.33.11`. We will give the `docker0` bridge IP address `172.17.0.1` and create a GRE tunnel endpoint with IP address `172.17.0.2`. Docker will give containers addresses in the `172.17.0.0/17` network.

Host 2 has IP address `192.168.33.12`. We will give the `docker0` bridge IP address `172.17.128.1` and create a GRE tunnel endpoint with IP address `171.17.128.2`. Docker will give containers addresses in the `172.17.128.0/17` network.

Splitting a `/16` network in two `/17` networks and assigning each subnet to the two different hosts ensures that containers will not get conflicting IP addresses.

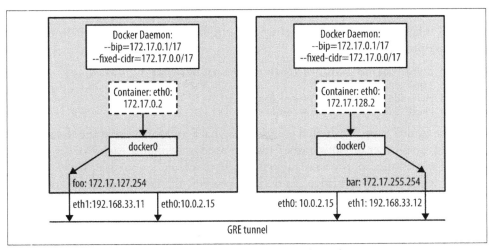

Figure 3-2. Network diagram of a two-hosts GRE tunnel overlay

You can start this configuration with a Vagrantfile (*http://bit.ly/gresimple-vagrant*). Each host has the latest stable version of Docker and two network interfaces: one NAT interface that gives outbound connectivity and one interface on a private network.

The first thing to do to avoid any issues is to stop the Docker engine and remove that docker0 bridge that was started during the Docker provisioning step. You will need to do this on all your hosts:

```
$ sudo su
# service docker stop
# ip link set docker0 down
# ip link del docker0
```

Now you can create a GRE tunnel between the two hosts. You do not need Open vSwitch for this; you can just use the ip tool. If you used the Vagrantfile mentioned earlier, on your first host with IP 192.168.33.11 do the following:

```
# ip tunnel add foo mode gre local 192.168.33.11 remote 192.168.33.12
# ip link set foo up
# ip addr add 172.17.127.254 dev foo
# ip route add 172.17.128.0/17 dev foo
```

If you did not use the Vagrantfile mentioned, replace the IP addresses for the local and remote endpoints in the preceding ip tunnel command with the IP addresses of your two Docker hosts. In the previous four commands, you created a GRE tunnel named foo. You brought the interface up and assigned an IP address to it. Then you set up a route that sends all 172.17.128.0/17 traffic in the tunnel.

On your second host, repeat the previous step to create the other end of the tunnel. You call this other end bar and set up a route that sends all `172.17.0.0/17` traffic over this tunnel:

```
# ip tunnel add bar mode gre local 192.168.33.12 remote 192.168.33.11
# ip link set bar up
# ip addr add 172.17.255.254 dev bar
# ip route add 172.17.0.0/17 dev bar
```

Once the tunnel is up, verify that you can ping back and forth using the tunnel. Now let's bring up Docker on both hosts. First you need to configure each Docker daemon so that it uses the appropriate subnets for its containers and uses the correct IP address for the `docker0` bridge. To do this, you edit the Docker daemon configuration file and use the `--bip` and `--fixed-cidr` options.

On host 1 that would be as follows:

```
# echo DOCKER_OPTS=\"--bip=172.17.0.1/17 --fixed-cidr=172.17.0.0/17\" \
>> /etc/default/docker
```

And on host 2:

```
# echo DOCKER_OPTS=\"--bip=172.17.128.1/17 --fixed-cidr=172.17.128.0/17\" \
>> /etc/default/docker
```

If you have chosen a different partitioning schema or have more than two hosts, repeat this with your values.

 Since Docker will turn on IP forwarding, all traffic on `docker0` will get forwarded to `foo` and `bar`, so there is no need to attach the tunnel endpoints to any bridges.

All that is left now is to restart Docker. Then you can start one container on each host and you will see that they have direct network connectivity using the private IP address given to them by Docker.

Discussion

There are multiple ways to build a networking overlay for your Docker host. Docker Network (see Recipe 3.14), which should be released in Docker 1.8, allows you to build VXLAN overlays using Docker built-in features. Other third-party solutions exist, such as Weave (see Recipe 3.11) or Flannel (see Recipe 3.13). As the Docker plug-in framework matures, this type of functionality will change significantly. For instance, Weave and Flannel will be available as Docker plug-ins, instead of a separate network setup.

See Also

- The blog post from Vincent Viallet on Wiredcraft (*http://wiredcraft.com/blog/multi-host-docker-network/*) that inspired this recipe

3.11 Running Containers on a Weave Network

Contributed by Fintan Ryan

Problem

You wish to create a network for your containers that scales from a single host to thousands of hosts across multiple data centers, with automatic IP address allocation and integrated service discovery via DNS.

Solution

Use Weave Net (*http://github.com/weaveworks/weave*) from Weaveworks (*http://weave.works*).

To help you experiment with Weave Net, I have created a Vagrantfile that starts two hosts running Ubuntu 14.04, and installs Docker, Weave Net, and two example containers. You can test it as follows:

```
$ git clone https://github.com/how2dock/docbook.git
$ cd ch03/weavesimple
$ vagrant up
```

Here are our Vagrant hosts in this example:

- `172.17.8.101 weave-gs-01`
- `172.17.8.102 weave-gs-02`

Next you will launch Weave Net on both hosts. Notice that you provide the IP address of the first host when launching Weave Net on the second host:

```
$ vagrant ssh weave-gs-01
$ weave launch
$ vagrant ssh weave-gs-02
$ weave launch 172.17.8.101
```

At this point, you have have created a network that will automatically allocate IP addresses to any container launched with Weave Net, and integrated service discovery with DNS.

Containers that you launch that are aware of Weave Net will be automatically allocated unique IP addresses, and, where an -h option is provided to Docker, registered with DNS.

Next you will launch containers on each host. To allow you to easily launch containers on your network, you set your DOCKER_HOST environment variable using weave env:

```
$ vagrant ssh weave-gs-01
$ eval $(weave env)
$ docker run -d -h lb.weave.local fintanr/myip-scratch
$ docker run -d -h lb.weave.local fintanr/myip-scratch
$ docker run -d -h hello.weave.local fintanr/weave-gs-simple-hw

$ vagrant ssh weave-gs-02
$ eval $(weave env)
$ docker run -d -h lb.weave.local fintanr/myip-scratch
$ docker run -d -h hello-host2.weave.local fintanr/weave-gs-simple-hw
```

You have done two things here. First, you have launched a container with a simple Hello World application on your hosts. Second, you have used DNS to create a load-balanced service across the containers named *lb*.

Let's launch a container on your Weave network and make some requests to the various containers you have launched:

```
$ vagrant ssh weave-gs-01
$ eval $(weave env)
$ C=$(docker run -d -ti fintanr/weave-gs-ubuntu-curl)
$ docker attach $C
root@ad6b7c0b1c6e:/#
root@ad6b7c0b1c6e:/# curl lb
Welcome to Weave, you probably want /myip
root@ad6b7c0b1c6e:/# curl lb/myip
10.128.0.2
root@ad6b7c0b1c6e:/# curl lb/myip
10.160.0.1
root@ad6b7c0b1c6e:/# curl hello
{
    "message" : "Hello World",
    "date" : "2015-07-09 15:59:50"
}
```

You also provide a script for the preceding commands, launching your container to make requests:

```
$ ./launch-simple-demo.sh
```

Discussion

Weave Net allows you to quickly and easily launch containers on a scalable network with automatic IP address allocation and service discovery.

In this example, you launched a Weave router container on your first host, `weave-gs-01`. On your second host, `weave-gs-02`, you launched another Weave router container with the IP address of your first host. This command tells Weave on `weave-gs-02` to peer with the Weave router on `weave-gs-01`.

Any containers you launch after this using Weave are visible within the Weave network to all other containers, no matter what host they are on. The containers will be automatically allocated an IP address that is unique on the network, and automatically registered with the Weave DNS service if Docker is called with an `-h` option.

To examine the containers launched, you can also use Weave `Scope` (see Recipe 9.12). On each host, run:

```
$ scope launch
```

See Also

- Weave Getting Started Guides (*http://weave.works/guides*)

3.12 Running a Weave Network on AWS

Contributed by Fintan Ryan

Problem

You would like to use Weave Net and WeaveDNS on instances deployed in AWS.

Solution

As prerequisites, you will need the following:

- An account on AWS
- A set of access and secret API keys
- Ansible installed, with the boto package

To help you experiment with Weave on AWS, I have created an Ansible playbook that starts two hosts running Ubuntu 14.04 on EC2, installs Docker, and installs Weave. I have provided a second playbook specifically for launching a simple demo application using HAProxy as a load-balancer in front of containers across your two hosts:

```
$ git clone https://github.com/how2dock/docbook.git
$ cd ch03/weaveaws
$ ansible-playbook setup-weave-ubunu-aws.yml
```

 You can change your AWS region and AMI in the file *ansi-ble_aws_variables.ym*.

To launch your containers, call the following:

```
$ ansible-playbook launch-weave-haproxy-aws-demo.yml
```

I have provided a script to quickly connect to your HAProxy container and cycle through a number of requests. Each container will return its hostname as part of its JSON output:

```
$ ./access-aws-hosts.sh

Connecting to HAProxy with Weave on AWS demo

{
    "message" : "Hello Weave - HAProxy Example",
    "hostname" : ws1.weave.local",
    "date" : "2015-03-13 11:23:12"
}

{
    "message" : "Hello Weave - HAProxy Example",
    "hostname" : ws4.weave.local",
    "date" : "2015-03-13 11:23:12"
}

{
    "message" : "Hello Weave - HAProxy Example",
    "hostname" : ws5.weave.local",
    "date" : "2015-03-13 11:23:12"
}
....
```

Discussion

Using Weave Net, you have placed HAProxy as a load-balancing solution in front of a number of containers running a simple application distributed across a number of hosts.

See Also

- Weave Getting Started Guides (*http://weave.works/guides*)

3.13 Deploying flannel Overlay Between Docker Hosts

Contributed by Eugene Yakubovich

Problem

You want containers on different hosts to communicate with each other without port mapping.

Solution

Use `flannel` to create an overlay network for containers. Each container will be assigned an IP that can be reachable from other hosts. Start by bringing up two virtual machines from a Vagrantfile:

```
$ git clone https://github.com/how2dock/docbook.git
$ cd ch03/flannel
$ vagrant up
```

This defines two virtual machines installed with Docker: `etcd` and `flannel`. The "master" will run a key-value store (`etcd`) that `flannel` uses for coordination.

Next, `vagrant ssh master` and start `etcd` in the background:

```
$ cd /opt/coreos/etcd-v2.0.13-linux-amd64
$ nohup ./etcd --listen-client-urls=http://0.0.0.0:2379 \
            --advertise-client-urls=http://192.168.33.10:2379 &
```

Before starting the `flannel` daemon, write the overlay network configuration into etcd. Be sure to pick a subnet range that does not conflict with other IP addresses:

```
$ ./etcdctl set /coreos.com/network/config '{ "Network": "10.100.0.0/16" }'
```

Now start the `flannel` daemon. Notice that the `--iface` option specifies the IP of the private network given in the Vagrantfile. `flannel` will forward encapsulated packets over this interface:

```
$ cd /opt/coreos/flannel-0.5.1
$ sudo ./flanneld --iface=192.168.33.10 --ip-masq &
$ sudo ./mk-docker-opts.sh -c -d /etc/default/docker
```

`flannel` will acquire a lease for a /24 subnet to be assigned to the docker0 bridge. The acquired subnet will be written out to the */run/flannel/subnet.env* file. The `mk-docker-opts.sh` utility converts this file into a set of command-line options for the Docker daemon.

Finally, start the Docker daemon. Verify that everything is running as expected by checking the IP of the `docker0` bridge. It should be within the 10.100.0.0/16 range:

```
$ sudo service docker start
$ ifconfig docker0
docker0   Link encap:Ethernet  HWaddr 56:84:7a:fe:97:99
          inet addr:10.100.63.1  Bcast:0.0.0.0  Mask:255.255.255.0
...
```

Over on the "worker" node, repeat the procedure of bringing up `flannel`. Since `etcd` is running on the "master," do not launch it on this node. Instead, point `flannel` to use the instance running on "master":

```
$ cd /opt/coreos/flannel-0.5.1
$ sudo ./flanneld --etcd-endpoints=http://192.168.33.10:2379 \
                  --iface=192.168.33.11 --ip-masq &
$ sudo ./mk-docker-opts.sh -c -d /etc/default/docker
$ sudo service docker start
```

With both nodes bootstrapped into the `flannel` network, bring up a simple busybox container on each of the nodes. The containers will have an IP pingable from the remote container.

Discussion

All `flannel` members use `etcd` for coordination. Upon start-up, the `flannel` daemon reads the overlay network configuration from `etcd` as well as all other subnets in use by other nodes. It then picks a used subnet (/24 by default) and attempts to claim it by creating a key for it in `etcd`. If the creation succeeds, the node has acquired a 24-hour lease on the subnet. The associated value contains the host's IP.

Next, `flannel` uses the TUN device to create a `flannel0` interface. IP fragments routed to `flannel0` from the `docker0` bridge will be delivered to the `flannel` daemon. It encapsulates each IP fragment in a UDP packet and uses the subnet information from `etcd` to forward it to the correct host. The receiving end unwraps the IP fragment from its encapsulation and sends it to `docker0` via the TUN device.

`flannel` continues to watch `etcd` for changes in the memberships to keep its knowledge current. Additionally, the daemon will renew its lease an hour before its expiration.

3.14 Networking Containers on Multiple Hosts with Docker Network

Problem

Although you could build tunnels between your Docker hosts manually (see Recipe 3.10), you want to take advantage of the new Docker Network feature and use a VXLAN overlay.

Solution

Docker Network is a new feature, currently available on the Docker experimental channel. This recipe is a preview that will give you a taste of what you will be able to find in future Docker releases.

As of this writing, Docker Network relies on Consul for key-value stores, uses Serf for discovery of the nodes, and builds a VXLAN overlay by using the standard Linux bridge. Since Docker Network is under heavy development, these requirements and methods may change in the near future.

As is common in this book, I prepared a Vagrantfile that will start three virtual machines. One will act as a Consul server, and the other two will act as Docker hosts. The experimental version of Docker is installed on the two Docker hosts, while the latest stable version of Docker is installed on the machine running the Consul server.

The setup is as follows:

- `consul-server`, the Consul server node based on Ubuntu 14.04, has IP 192.168.33.10.
- `net-1`, the first Docker host based on Ubuntu 14.10, has IP 192.168.33.11.
- `net-2`, the second Docker host based on Ubuntu 14.10, has IP 192.168.33.12.

Figure 3-3 illustrates this setup.

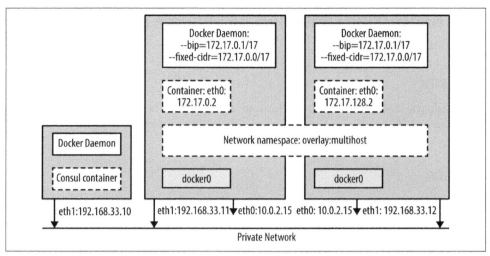

Figure 3-3. Network diagram of a two-hosts Docker network VXLAN overlay with an additional Consul node

Clone the repository, change to the *docbook/ch03/networks* directory, and let Vagrant do the work:

```
$ git clone https://github.com/how2dock/docbook/
$ cd docbook/ch03/network
$ vagrant up
$ vagrant status
Current machine states:

consul-server            running (virtualbox)
net-1                    running (virtualbox)
net-2                    running (virtualbox)
```

You are now ready to `ssh` to the Docker hosts and start containers. You will see that you are running the Docker experimental version `-dev`. The version number that you see may be different, depending on where you are in the release cycle:

```
$ vagrant ssh net-1
vagrant@net-1:~$ docker version
Client version: 1.9.0-dev
...<snip>...
```

Check that Docker Network is functional by listing the default networks:

```
vagrant@net-1:~$ docker network ls
NETWORK ID          NAME                TYPE
4275f8b3a821        none                null
80eba28ed4a7        host                host
64322973b4aa        bridge              bridge
```

No service has been published so far, so `docker service ls` will return an empty list:

```
$ docker service ls
SERVICE ID          NAME                NETWORK             CONTAINER
```

Start a container and check the content of *etc/hosts*:

```
$ docker run -it --rm ubuntu:14.04 bash
root@df479e660658:/# cat /etc/hosts
172.21.0.3      df479e660658
127.0.0.1       localhost
::1     localhost ip6-localhost ip6-loopback
fe00::0 ip6-localnet
ff00::0 ip6-mcastprefix
ff02::1 ip6-allnodes
ff02::2 ip6-allrouters
172.21.0.3      distracted_bohr
172.21.0.3      distracted_bohr.multihost
```

In a separate terminal on net-1, list the networks again. You will see that the multi host overlay now appears. The overlay network multihost is your default network. This was set up by the Docker daemon during the Vagrant provisioning. Check */etc/default/docker* to see the options that were set:

```
vagrant@net-1:~$ docker network ls
NETWORK ID          NAME                TYPE
4275f8b3a821        none                null
80eba28ed4a7        host                host
64322973b4aa        bridge              bridge
b5c9f05f1f8f        multihost           overlay
```

Now in a separate terminal, ssh to net-2, and check the network and services. The networks will be the same, and the default network will also be multihost of type overlay. But the service will show the container started on net-1:

```
$ vagrant ssh net-2
vagrant@net-2:~$ docker service ls
SERVICE ID          NAME                NETWORK             CONTAINER
b00f2bfd81ac        distracted_bohr     multihost           df479e660658
```

Start a container on net-2 and check */etc/hosts*:

```
vagrant@net-2:~$ docker run -ti --rm ubuntu:14.04 bash
root@2ac726b4ce60:/# cat /etc/hosts
172.21.0.4      2ac726b4ce60
127.0.0.1       localhost
::1     localhost ip6-localhost ip6-loopback
fe00::0 ip6-localnet
ff00::0 ip6-mcastprefix
ff02::1 ip6-allnodes
ff02::2 ip6-allrouters
172.21.0.3      distracted_bohr
172.21.0.3      distracted_bohr.multihost
172.21.0.4      modest_curie
172.21.0.4      modest_curie.multihost
```

You will see not only the container that you just started on net-2, but also the container that you started earlier on net-1. And, of course, you will be able to ping each container.

Discussion

The solution uses the default network overlay that was configured at start-up time by specifying it in the */etc/default/docker* configuration file. You can, however, use a non-default overlay network. This means that you can create as many overlays as you want, and the container started in each overlay will be isolated.

In the previous test, you started containers with regular options -ti --rm. These containers were placed automatically in the default network, which was set to be the multihost network of type overlay.

But you could create your own overlay network and start containers in it. Let's try this. First, create a new overlay network with the docker network create command.

On one of your Docker hosts, net-1 or net-2, run the following:

```
$ docker network create -d overlay foobar
8805e22ad6e29cd7abb95597c91420fdcac54f33fcdd6fbca6dd4ec9710dd6a4
$ docker network ls
NETWORK ID          NAME                TYPE
a77e16a1e394        host                host
684a4bb4c471        bridge              bridge
8805e22ad6e2        foobar              overlay
b5c9f05f1f8f        multihost           overlay
67d5a33a2e54        none                null
```

Automatically, the second host will also see this network. To start a container on this new network, use the --publish-service option of docker run:

```
$ docker run -it --rm --publish-service=bar.foobar.overlay ubuntu:14.04 bash
```

 You could directly start a container with a new overlay by using the --publish-service option, and it will create the network automatically.

Check the docker services now:

```
$ docker service ls
SERVICE ID          NAME                NETWORK             CONTAINER
b1ffdbfb1ac6        bar                 foobar              6635a3822135
```

Repeat the getting started steps by starting another container in this new overlay on the other host, check the */etc/hosts* file, and try to ping each container.

3.15 Diving Deeper into the Docker Network Namespaces Configuration

Problem

You would like to better understand what Docker Network (see Recipe 3.14) does, especially where the VXLAN interfaces exist.

Solution

The new Docker overlay networking in Docker Network is made possible via VXLAN tunnels and the use of network namespaces. In Recipe 3.7, you already saw how to explore and manipulate network namespaces. The same can be done for Docker Network.

 This is an advanced recipe included so you can gain a deep understanding of how the network namespaces of a Docker host are used to build a VXLAN network overlay. This recipe is not needed to use default single-host Docker networking or multihost Docker Network or other multihost networking solutions like the ones presented in Recipe 3.11 and Recipe 3.13.

Check the design documentation (*https://github.com/docker/libnetwork/blob/master/docs/design.md*) for all the details. But to explore these concepts a bit, nothing beats an example.

Discussion

With a running container in one overlay, check the network namespace:

```
$ docker inspect -f '{{ .NetworkSettings.SandboxKey}}' 6635a3822135
/var/run/docker/netns/6635a3822135
```

This is not a default location for network namespaces, which might confuse things a bit. So let's become `root`, head over to this directory that contains the network namespaces of the containers, and check the interfaces:

```
$ sudo su
root@net-2:/home/vagrant# cd /var/run/docker/
root@net-2:/var/run/docker# ls netns
6635a3822135
8805e22ad6e2
```

To be able to check the interfaces in those network namespaces by using the `ip` command, create a symlink for `netns` that points to */var/run/docker/netns*:

```
root@net-2:/var/run# ln -s /var/run/docker/netns netns
root@net-2:/var/run# ip netns show
6635a3822135
8805e22ad6e2
```

The two namespace IDs returned are the ones of the running container on that host and the overlay network the container is in:

```
root@net-2:/var/run/docker# ip netns exec 6635a3822135 ip addr show eth0
15: eth0: <BROADCAST,UP,LOWER_UP> mtu 1500 qdisc noqueue state UP group default
    link/ether 02:42:b3:91:22:c3 brd ff:ff:ff:ff:ff:ff
    inet 172.21.0.5/16 scope global eth0
       valid_lft forever preferred_lft forever
    inet6 fe80::42:b3ff:fe91:22c3/64 scope link
       valid_lft forever preferred_lft forever
```

You get back the network interface of your running container, with the same MAC address, and the same IP. If you check the links of the overlay namespace, you see your VXLAN interface and the VLAN ID being used:

```
root@net-2:/var/run/docker# ip netns exec 8805e22ad6e2 ip -d link show
...<snip>...
14: vxlan1: <BROADCAST,UP,LOWER_UP> mtu 1500 qdisc noqueue master br0 state \
UNKNOWN mode DEFAULT group default
    link/ether 7a:af:20:ee:e3:81 brd ff:ff:ff:ff:ff:ff promiscuity 1
    vxlan id 256 srcport 32768 61000 dstport 8472 proxy l2miss l3miss ageing 300
    bridge_slave
16: veth2: <BROADCAST,UP,LOWER_UP> mtu 1500 qdisc pfifo_fast master br0 state \
UP mode DEFAULT group default qlen 1000
    link/ether 46:b1:e2:5c:48:a8 brd ff:ff:ff:ff:ff:ff promiscuity 1
    veth
    bridge_slave
```

If you sniff packets on these interfaces, you will see the traffic between your containers.

## CHAPTER 4

Docker Configuration and Development

4.0 Introduction

If you have read all the chapters so far, you have learned all the basics of using Docker. You can install the Docker engine, start and manage containers, create and share images, and you have a good understanding of container networking including networking across multiple hosts. This chapter will now look at more advanced Docker topics, first for developers and then for configuration.

Recipe 4.1 looks at how to configure the Docker engine, then Recipe 4.2 shows how to compile Docker from source. Recipe 4.3 presents how to run all the tests to verify your build and Recipe 4.4 shows how to use this newly built binary instead of the official released Docker engine.

Developers might also want to look at the nsenter utility in Recipe 4.5. While not needed for using Docker, it is of use to better understand how Docker leverages Linux namespaces to create containers. Recipe 4.6 is a sneak peek at the underlying library used to managed containers. Originally called libcontainer, runc has been donated to the Open Container Initiative to be the seed source code to help drive a standard for container runtime and image format.

To dive deeper into configuration and how to access the Docker engine, Recipe 4.7 presents how to access Docker remotely and Recipe 4.8 introduces the application programming interface (API) exposed by Docker. The Docker client uses this API to manage containers. Accessing this API remotely and securely is described in Recipe 4.9, it shows how to set up TLS-based access to the Docker engine. To finish the configuration topics, Recipe 4.12 shows how to change the underlying storage driver that provides a union filesystem to support Docker images.

If you are a user of Docker, you will benefit from looking at Recipe 4.10 and Recipe 4.11. These two recipes present `docker-py`, a Python module to communicate with the Docker API. This is not the only client library available for Docker, but it provides an easy entrypoint to learn the API.

4.1 Managing and Configuring the Docker Daemon

Problem

You would like to start, stop, and restart the Docker daemon. Additionally, you would like to configure it in specific ways, potentially changing things such as the path to the Docker binary or using a different network bridge.

Solution

Use the `docker` init script to manage the Docker daemon. On most Ubuntu/Debian-based systems, it will be located in the */etc/init.d/docker* file. Like most other init services, it can be managed via the `service` command. The Docker daemon runs as `root`:

```
# service docker status
docker start/running, process 2851
# service docker stop
docker stop/waiting
# service docker start
docker start/running, process 3119
```

The configuration file is located in */etc/default/docker*. On Ubuntu systems, all configuration variables are commented out. The */etc/default/docker* file looks like this:

```
# Docker Upstart and SysVinit configuration file

# Customize location of Docker binary (especially for development testing).
#DOCKER="/usr/local/bin/docker"

# Use DOCKER_OPTS to modify the daemon startup options.
#DOCKER_OPTS="--dns 8.8.8.8 --dns 8.8.4.4"

# If you need Docker to use an HTTP proxy, it can also be specified here.
#export http_proxy="http://127.0.0.1:3128/"

# This is also a handy place to tweak where Docker's temporary files go.
#export TMPDIR="/mnt/bigdrive/docker-tmp"
```

For example, if you wanted to configure the daemon to listen on a TCP socket to enable remote API access, you would edit this file as explained in Recipe 4.7.

Discussion

On `systemd`-based systems like Ubuntu 15.05 or CentOS 7, you need to modify the `systemd` unit file for Docker. It can be located in the */etc/systemd/system/docker.service.d* directory or it can be the */etc/systemd/system/docker.service* file. For more details on Docker daemon configuration using `systemd`, see this article (*https://docs.docker.com/articles/systemd/*) from the Docker documentation.

Finally, although you can start Docker as a Linux daemon, you can also start it interactively by using the `docker -d` command or, starting with Docker 1.8, the `docker daemon` command. You would then pass the options directly to the command. Check the help to see what options can be set:

```
$ docker daemon --help

Usage:  docker daemon [OPTIONS]

Enable daemon mode

  --api-cors-header=         Set CORS headers in the remote API
  -b, --bridge=              Attach containers to a network bridge
  --bip=                     Specify network bridge IP
  -D, --debug=false          Enable debug mode
  --default-gateway=         Container default gateway IPv4 address
  ...
```

4.2 Compiling Your Own Docker Binary from Source

Problem

You would like to develop the Docker software and build your own Docker binary.

Solution

Use Git to clone the Docker repository from GitHub (*https://github.com/docker/docker*) and use a Makefile to create your own binary.

Docker is built within a Docker container. In a Docker host, you can clone the Docker repository and use the Makefile rules to build a new binary. This binary is obtained by running a privileged Docker container. The Makefile contains several targets, including a `binary` target:

```
$ cat Makefile
...
default: binary

all: build
    $(DOCKER_RUN_DOCKER) hack/make.sh
```

```
binary: build
    $(DOCKER_RUN_DOCKER) hack/make.sh binary
...
```

Therefore, it is as easy as `sudo make binary`:

 The *hack* directory in the root of the Docker repository has been moved to the *project* directory. Therefore, the *make.sh* script is in fact at *project/make.sh*. It uses scripts for each bundle that are stored in the *project/make/* directory.

```
$ sudo make binary
...
docker run --rm -it --privileged \
            -e BUILDFLAGS -e DOCKER_CLIENTONLY -e DOCKER_EXECDRIVER \
            -e DOCKER_GRAPHDRIVER -e TESTDIRS -e TESTFLAGS \
            -e TIMEOUT \
            -v "/tmp/docker/bundles:/go/src/github.com/docker/docker/\
                              bundles" \
            "docker:master" hack/make.sh binary
---> Making bundle: binary (in bundles/1.9.0.-dev/binary)
Created binary: \
/go/src/github.com/docker/docker/bundles/1.9.0-dev/binary/docker-1.9.0-dev
```

You see that the `binary` target of the Makefile will launch a privileged Docker container from the *docker:master* image, with a set of environment variables, a volume mount, and a call to the `hack/make.sh binary` command.

With the current state of Docker development, the new binary will be located in the *bundles/1.9.0-dev/binary/* directory. The version number might differ, depending on the state of Docker releases.

Discussion

To ease this process, you can clone the repository that accompanies this cookbook. A Vagrantfile is provided that starts an Ubuntu 14.04 virtual machine, installs the latest stable Docker release, and clones the Docker repository:

```
$ git clone https://github.com/how2dock/docbook
$ cd docbook/ch04/compile/
$ vagrant up
```

Once the machine is up, `ssh` to it and go to the */tmp/docker* directory, which should have been created during the Vagrant provisioning process. Then run `make`. The first time you run the Makefile, the stable Docker version installed on the machine will pull the base image being used by the Docker build process *ubuntu:14.04*, and then build the *docker:master* image defined in */tmp/docker/Dockerfile*. This can take a bit of time the first time you do it:

```
$ vagrant ssh
$ cd /tmp/docker
$ sudo make binary
docker build -t "docker:master" .
Sending build context to Docker daemon 55.95 MB
Sending build context to Docker daemon
Step 0 : FROM ubuntu:14.04
...
```

Once this completes, you will have a new Docker binary:

```
$ cd bundles/1.9.0-dev/binary/docker
$ ls
docker  docker-1.9.0-dev  docker-1.9.0-dev.md5  docker-1.9.0-dev.sha256
```

See Also

- How to contribute to Docker on GitHub (*https://github.com/docker/docker/blob/master/CONTRIBUTING.md*)

4.3 Running the Docker Test Suite for Docker Development

Problem

You have made some changes to the Docker source and have successfully built a new binary. You also need to make sure that you pass all the tests.

Solution

Use the Makefile `test` target to run the four sets of tests present in the Docker source. Alternatively, pick only the set of tests that matters to you:

```
$ cat Makefile
...
test: build
  $(DOCKER_RUN_DOCKER) hack/make.sh binary cross \
                                  test-unit test-integration \
                                  test-integration-cli test-docker-py

test-unit: build
  $(DOCKER_RUN_DOCKER) hack/make.sh test-unit

test-integration: build
  $(DOCKER_RUN_DOCKER) hack/make.sh test-integration
```

```
test-integration-cli: build
  $(DOCKER_RUN_DOCKER) hack/make.sh binary test-integration-cli

test-docker-py: build
  $(DOCKER_RUN_DOCKER) hack/make.sh binary test-docker-py
...
```

You can see in the Makefile that you can choose which set of tests you want to run. If you run all of them with `make test`, it will also build the binary:

```
$ sudo make test
....
---> Making bundle: test-docker-py (in bundles/1.9.0-dev/test-docker-py)
+++ exec docker --daemon --debug --storage-driver vfs \
              -exec-driver native \
              --pidfile \
              /go/src/github.com/docker/docker/bundles/1.9.0-dev/ \
              test-docker-py/docker.pid
.........................................................
-------------------------------------------------------------------
Ran 56 tests in 75.366s

OK
```

Depending on test coverage, if all the tests pass, you have some confidence that your new binary works.

See Also

- Official Docker development environment documentation (*https://docs.docker.com/project/software-required/*)

4.4 Replacing Your Current Docker Binary with a New One

Problem

You have built a new Docker binary and run the unit and integration tests described in Recipe 4.2 and Recipe 4.3. Now you would like to use this new binary on your host.

Solution

Start from within the virtual machine setup in Recipe 4.2.

Stop the current Docker daemon. On Ubuntu 14.04, edit the */etc/default/docker* file to uncomment the `DOCKER` variable that defines where to find the binary and set it to

`DOCKER="/usr/local/bin/docker"`. Copy the new binary to *usr/local/bin/docker*, and finally, restart the Docker daemon:

```
$ pwd
/tmp/docker
$ sudo service docker stop
docker stop/waiting
$ sudo vi /etc/default/docker
$ sudo cp bundles/1.8.0-dev/binary/docker-8.0-dev /usr/local/bin/docker
$ sudo cp bundles/1.8.0-dev/binary/docker-1.8.0-dev /usr/bin/docker
$ sudo service docker restart
stop: Unknown instance:
$ docker version
Client:
 Version:      1.8.0-dev
 API version:  1.21
 Go version:   go1.4.2
 Git commit:   3e596da
 Built:        Tue Aug 11 16:51:56 UTC 2015
 OS/Arch:      linux/amd64

Server:
 Version:      1.8.0-dev
 API version:  1.21
 Go version:   go1.4.2
 Git commit:   3e596da
 Built:        Tue Aug 11 16:51:56 UTC 2015
 OS/Arch:      linux/amd64
```

You are now using the latest Docker version from the master development branch (i.e., master branch at Git commit 3e596da at the time of this writing).

Discussion

The Docker bootstrap script used in the Vagrant virtual machine provisioning installs the latest stable version of Docker with the following:

```
sudo curl -sSL https://get.docker.com/ubuntu/ | sudo sh
```

This puts the Docker binary in *usr/bin/docker*. This may conflict with your new binary installation. Either remove it or replace it with the new one if you see any conflicts when running `docker version`.

4.5 Using nsenter

Problem

You would like to enter a container for debugging purposes, you are using a Docker version older than 1.3.1, or you do not want to use the `docker exec` command.

Solution

Use `nsenter` (*https://github.com/jpetazzo/nsenter*). Starting with Docker 1.3, `docker exec` allows you to easily enter a running container, so there is no need to do things like running an SSH server and exposing port 22 or using the now deprecated `attach` command.

`nsenter` was created to solve the problem of entering the namespace (hence, *nsenter*) of a container prior to the availability of `docker exec`. Nonetheless, it is a useful tool that merits a short recipe in this book.

Let's start a container that sleeps for the duration of this recipe, and for completeness, let's enter the running container with `docker exec`:

```
$ docker pull ubuntu:14.04
$ docker run -d --name sleep ubuntu:14.04 sleep 300
$ docker exec -ti sleep bash
root@db9675525fab:/#
```

`nsenter` gives the same result. Conveniently, it comes as an image in Docker Hub. Pull the image, run the container, and use `nsenter`.

```
$ docker pull jpetazzo/nsenter
$ sudo docker run docker run --rm -v /usr/local/bin:/target jpetazzo/nsenter
```

At this time, it is useful to have a look at the Dockerfile (*https://github.com/jpetazzo/nsenter/blob/master/Dockerfile*) for `nsenter` and check the `CMD` option. You will see that it runs a script called *installer*. This small bash script does nothing but detect whether a mount point exists at */target*. If it does, it copies a script called *docker-enter* and a binary called *nsenter* to that mount point. In the `docker run` command, since you specified a volume (i.e., `-v /usr/local/bin:/target`), running the container will have the effect of copying *nsenter* on your local machine. Quite a nice trick with a powerful effect:

```
$ which docker-enter nsenter
/usr/local/bin/docker-enter
/usr/local/bin/nsenter
```

> To copy the files in */usr/local/bin*, I run the container with `sudo`. If you do not want to use this mount-point convenience, you can copy the files locally with a command like this:
>
> ```
> $ docker run --rm jpetazzo/nsenter cat /nsenter \
>         > /tmp/nsenter && chmod +x /tmp/nsenter
> ```

You are now ready to enter the container. You can pass a command, if you do not want to get an interactive shell in the container:

```
$ docker-enter sleep
root@db9675525fab:/#
$ docker-enter sleep hostname
db9675525fab
```

`docker-enter` is nothing more than a wrapper around `nsenter`. You could use `nsen`ter directly after finding the process ID of the container with `docker inspect`, like so:

```
$ docker inspect --format {{.State.Pid}} sleep
9302
$ sudo nsenter --target 9302 --mount --uts --ipc --net --pid
root@db9675525fab:/#
```

Discussion

Starting with Docker 1.3, you do not need to use `nsenter`; use `docker exec` instead:

```
$ docker exec -h

Usage: docker exec [OPTIONS] CONTAINER COMMAND [ARG...]

Run a command in a running container

  -d, --detach=false          Detached mode: run command in the background
  --help=false                Print usage
  -i, --interactive=false     Keep STDIN open even if not attached
  -t, --tty=false             Allocate a pseudo-TTY
```

See Also

- GitHub page from Jerome Petazzoni (*https://github.com/jpetazzo/nsenter*) `nsen`ter repository

4.6 Introducing runc

Problem

You want to become familiar with the upcoming standard around the container format and runtime `runc`.

Solution

The Open Container Project (OCP) was established in June 2015, and the specifications coming from that project are still not done. However, Docker Inc. donated its libcontainer (*https://github.com/docker/libcontainer*) codebase as an early implementation of a standard runtime for containers. This runtime is called `runc`.

The OCP was just launched, so the specifications are not out yet. Expect many changes until the specifications and reference implementations are considered stable and official.

This recipe will give you a quick feel for `runc`, including instructions to compile the Go codebase. As always, I prepared a Vagrant box that gives you a Docker host, a Go 1.4.2 installation, and a clone of the `runc` code. To get started with this box, use the following:

```
$ git clone https://github.com/how2dock/docbook.git
$ cd dockbook/ch04/runc
$ vagrant up
$ vagrant ssh
```

Once you are on a terminal inside this VM, you need to grab all the dependencies of `runc` by using the `go get` command. Once this completes, you can build `runc` and install. Verify that you have a running `runc` in your path:

Expect a change in the build process sometime soon. Most likely the build will use Docker itself.

```
$ cd go/src
$ go get github.com/opencontainers/runc
$ cd github.com/opencontainers/runc/
$ make
$ sudo make install
$ runc -v
runc version 0.2
```

To run a container with `runc`, you need a root filesystem describing your container image. The easiest way to get one is to use Docker itself and the `docker export` command. So let's pull a Docker image, start a container, and export it to a tarball:

```
$ cd ~
$ mkdir foobar
$ cd foobar
$ docker run --name foobar -d ubuntu:14.04 sleep 30
$ docker export -o foobar.tar foobar
$ sudo -xf foobar.tar
$ rm foobar.tar
```

To run this container, you need to generate a configuration file. This is most easily done with the `runc spec` command. To get a container started quickly, you will need to get only one change, which is the location of the root filesystem. In that JSON file, edit the path to it; you see an excerpt here:

```
$ runc spec > config.json
$ vi config.json
...
  "root": {
    "path": "./",
    "readonly": true
...
```

You are now ready to start your container with `runc` as root, and you will get a shell inside your container:

```
$ sudo runc
#
```

This is the low-level plumbing of Docker and what should evolve to become the Open Container standard runtime. You can now explore the configuration file and see how you can define a start-up command for your container, as well as a network namespace and various volume mounts.

Discussion

The Open Container Project is good news. In late 2014, CoreOS had started developing an open standard for container images, including a new trust mechanism, `appc` (*https://github.com/appc/spec*). CoreOS also developed a container runtime implementation for running `appc`-based containers. As part of the OCP, `appc` developers will help develop the new `runc` specification. This will avoid fragmentation in the container image format and runtime implementation.

If you look at an application container image (i.e., ACI (*https://github.com/coreos/rkt/blob/master/Documentation/app-container.md#ACI*)) manifest, you will see high similarities with the configuration file obtained from `runc spec` in the preceding solution section. You might see some of the `rkt` implementation features being ported back into `runc`.

If you care about standards, watch the specifications coming out of the Open Container Project.

See Also

- The blog post on cloudgear.net that inspired this recipe (*https://www.cloudgear.net/blog/2015/getting-started-with-runc/*)

- The Open Container Project (*https://www.opencontainers.org*)
- The App container spec (*https://github.com/appc/spec*)
- The rkt runtime (*https://github.com/coreos/rkt*)

4.7 Accessing the Docker Daemon Remotely

Problem

The default Docker daemon listens on a local Unix socket, /var/run/docker.sock, which is accessible only locally. However, you would like to access your Docker host remotely, calling the Docker API from a different machine.

Solution

Switch the listening protocol that the Docker daemon is using by editing the configuration file in *etc/default/docker* and issue a remote API call.

In *etc/default/docker*, add a line that sets DOCKER_HOST to use tcp on port 2375. Then restart the Docker daemon with sudo service docker restart:

```
$ cat /etc/default/docker
...
# Use DOCKER_OPTS to modify the daemon startup options.
#DOCKER_OPTS="--dns 8.8.8.8 --dns 8.8.4.4"
DOCKER_OPTS="-H tcp://127.0.0.1:2375"
...
```

You will then be able to use the Docker client by specifying a host accessed using TCP:

```
$ docker -H tcp://127.0.0.1:2375 images
REPOSITORY       TAG            IMAGE ID         CREATED        VIRTUAL SIZE
ubuntu           14.04          04c5d3b7b065     6 days ago     192.7 MB
```

This method is unencrypted and unauthenticated. You should not use this on a publicly routable host. This would expose your Docker daemon to anyone. You will need to properly secure your Docker daemon if you want to do this in production. (See Recipe 4.9.)

Discussion

With the Docker daemon listening over TCP you can now use curl to make API calls and explore the response. This is a good way to learn the Docker remote API:

```
$ curl -s http://127.0.0.1:2375/images/json | python -m json.tool
[
    {
        "Created": 1418673175,
        "Id": "04c5d3b7b0656168630d3ba35d8889bdaafcaeb32bfbc47e7c5d35d2",
        "ParentId": "d735006ad9c1b1563e021d7a4fecfd384e2a1c42e78d8261b83d6271",
        "RepoTags": [
            "ubuntu:14.04"
        ],
        "Size": 0,
        "VirtualSize": 192676726
    }
]
```

We pipe the output of the `curl` command through `python -m json.tool` to make the JSON object that is returned readable. And the `-s` option removes the information of the data transfer.

4.8 Exploring the Docker Remote API to Automate Docker Tasks

Problem

After being able to access the Docker daemon remotely (see Recipe 4.7), you want to explore the Docker remote API in order to write programs. This will allow you to automate Docker tasks.

Solution

The Docker remote API is fully documented (*https://docs.docker.com/reference/api/docker_remote_api_v1.20/*). It is currently on version 1.21. It is a REST API, in the sense that it manipulates resources (e.g., images and containers) through HTTP calls using various HTTP methods (e.g., GET, POST, DELETE). The *attach* and *pull* APIs are not purely REST, as noted in the documentation (*https://docs.docker.com/reference/api/docker_remote_api_v1.20/*).

You already saw how to make the Docker daemon listen on a TCP socket (Recipe 4.7) and use `curl` to make API calls. Tables 4-1 and 4-2 show a summary of the remote API calls that are available.

Table 4-1. A sample of the API for container actions

Action on containers	HTTP method	URI
List containers	GET	/containers/json
Create container	POST	/containers/create

Action on containers	HTTP method	URI
Inspect a container	GET	/containers/(id)/json
Start a container	POST	/containers/(id)/start
Stop a container	POST	/containers/(id)/stop
Restart a container	POST	/containers/(id)/restart
Kill a container	POST	/containers/(id)/kill
Pause a container	POST	/containers/(id)/pause
Remove a container	DELETE	/containers/(id)

Table 4-2. A sample of the API for image actions

Action on images	HTTP method	URI
List images	GET	/images/json
Create an image	POST	/images/create
Tag an image into a repository	POST	/images/(name)/tag
Remove an image	DELETE	/images/(name)
Search images	GET	/images/search

For example, let's download the Ubuntu 14.04 image from the public registry (a.k.a. Docker Hub), create a container from that image, and start it. Remove it and then remove the image. Note that in this toy example, running the container will cause it to exit immediately because you are not passing any commands:

```
$ curl -X POST -d "fromImage=ubuntu" -d "tag=14.04"
                              http://127.0.0.1:2375/images/create
$ curl -X POST -H 'Content-Type: application/json'
            -d '{"Image":"ubuntu:14.04"}'
        http://127.0.0.1:2375/containers/create
{"Id":"6b6bd46f483a5704d4bced62ff58a0ac5758fb0875ec881fa68f0e...",\
"Warnings":null}
$ docker ps
CONTAINER ID    IMAGE           COMMAND         CREATED         STATUS    ...
$ docker ps -a
CONTAINER ID    IMAGE           COMMAND         CREATED         STATUS    ...
6b6bd46f483a    ubuntu:14.04    "/bin/bash"     16 seconds ago            ...
$ curl -X POST http://127.0.0.1:2375/containers/6b6bd46f483a/start
$ docker ps -a
```

```
CONTAINER ID      IMAGE          COMMAND        CREATED             ...
6b6bd46f483a      ubuntu:14.04   "/bin/bash"    About a minute ago  ...
```

Now let's clean things up:

```
$ curl -X DELETE http://127.0.0.1:2375/containers/6b6bd46f483a
$ curl -X DELETE http://127.0.0.1:2375/images/04c5d3b7b065
[{"Untagged":"ubuntu:14.04"}
,{"Deleted":"04c5d3b7b0656168630d3ba35d8889bd0e9caafcaeb3004d2bfbc47e7c5d35d2"}
,{"Deleted":"d735006ad9c1b1563e021d7a4fecfd75ed36d4384e2a1c42e78d8261b83d6271"}
,{"Deleted":"70c8faa62a44b9f6a70ec3a018ec14ec95717ebed2016430e57fec1abc90a879"}
,{"Deleted":"c7b7c64195686444123ef370322b5270b098c77dc2d62208e8a9ce28a11a63f9"}
,{"Deleted":"511136ea3c5a64f264b78b5433614aec563103b4d4702f3ba7d4d2698e22c158"}
$ docker ps -a
CONTAINER ID      IMAGE          COMMAND        CREATED      STATUS   ...
$ docker images
REPOSITORY        TAG            IMAGE ID       CREATED      VIRTUAL SIZE
```

After enabling remote API access, you can set the `DOCKER_HOST` variable to its HTTP endpoint. This relieves you from passing it to the docker command as an `-H` option. For example, instead of `docker -H http://127.0.0.1:2375 ps`, you can use `export DOCKER_HOST=tcp://127.0.0.1:2375` and you will be able to simply use `docker ps`.

Discussion

Although you can use `curl` or write your own client, existing Docker clients like *docker-py* (see Recipe 4.10) can ease calling the API.

The list of APIs presented in Table 4-1 and Table 4-2 is not exhaustive, and you should check the complete API documentation (*https://docs.docker.com/reference/api/docker_remote_api_v1.16/*) for all API calls, query parameters, and response examples.

4.9 Securing the Docker Daemon for Remote Access

Problem

You need to access your Docker daemon remotely and securely.

Solution

Set up TLS-based (*http://tools.ietf.org/html/rfc5246*) access to your Docker daemon. This will use public-key cryptography to encrypt and authenticate communication between a Docker client and the Docker daemon that you have set up with TLS.

The basic steps to test this security feature are described on the Docker website (*https://docs.docker.com/articles/https/#daemon-modes*). However, it shows how to create your own certificate authority (CA) and sign server and client certificates using the CA. In a properly set up infrastructure, you need to contact the CA that you use routinely and ask for server certificates.

To conveniently test this TLS setup, I created an image (*https://regis try.hub.docker.com/u/runseb/dockertls/*) containing a script that creates the CA and the server and client certificates and keys. You can use this image to create a container and generate all the needed files.

You start with an Ubuntu 14.04 machine, running the latest Docker version (see Recipe 1.1). Download the image and start a container. You will need to mount a volume from your host and bind mount it to the */tmp/ca* inside the Docker container. You will also need to pass the hostname as an argument to running the container (in the following example, *<hostname>*). Once you are done running the container, all CA, server, and client keys and certificates will be available in your working directory:

```
$ docker pull runseb/dockertls
$ docker run -ti -v $(pwd):/tmp/ca runseb/dockertls <hostname>
$ ls
cakey.pem  ca.pem  ca.srl  clientcert.pem  client.csr  clientkey.pem
extfile.cnf  makeca.sh  servercert.pem  server.csr  serverkey.pem
```

Stop the running Docker daemon. Create an */etc/docker* directory and a *~/.docker* directory. Copy the CA, server key, and server certificates to */etc/docker*. Copy the CA, client key, and certificate to *~/.docker*:

```
$ sudo service docker stop
$ sudo mkdir /etc/docker
$ mkdir ~/.docker
$ sudo cp {ca,servercert,serverkey}.pem /etc/docker
$ cp ca.pem ~/.docker/
$ cp clientkey.pem ~/.docker/key.pem
$ cp clientcert.pem ~/.docker/cert.pem
```

Edit the */etc/default/docker* (you need to be root) configuration file to specify DOCKER_OPTS (replace *test* with your own hostname):

```
DOCKER_OPTS="-H tcp://<test>:2376 --tlsverify \
                        --tlscacert=/etc/docker/ca.pem \
                        --tlscert=/etc/docker/servercert.pem \
                        --tlskey=/etc/docker/serverkey.pem"
```

Then restart the Docker service with sudo service docker restart and try to connect to the Docker daemon:

```
$ docker -H tcp://test:2376 --tlsverify images
REPOSITORY          TAG         IMAGE ID        CREATED         VIRTUAL SIZE
runseb/dockertls    latest      5ed60e0f6a7c    17 minutes ago  214.7 MB
```

Discussion

 The *runseb/dockertls* convenience image is automatically built from the `https://github.com/how2dock/docbook/ch04/tls` Dockerfile. Check it out.

By setting up a few environment variables (`DOCKER_HOST` and `DOCKER_TLS_VERIFY`), you can easily configure the TLS connection from the CLI:

```
$ export DOCKER_HOST=tcp://test:2376
$ export DOCKER_TLS_VERIFY=1
$ docker images
REPOSITORY          TAG         IMAGE ID        CREATED          VIRTUAL SIZE
runseb/dockertls    latest      5ed60e0f6a7c    19 minutes ago   214.7 MB
```

You can still use `curl` as discussed in Recipe 4.7, but you need to specify the client key and certificate:

```
$ curl --insecure --cert ~/.docker/cert.pem --key ~/.docker/key.pem \
      -s https://test:2376/images/json | python -m json.tool
[
    {
        "Created": 1419280147,
        "Id": "5ed60e0f6a7ce3df3614d20dcadf2e4d43f4054da64d52709c1559ac",
        "ParentId": "138f848eb669500df577ca5b7354cef5e65b3c728b0c241221c611b1",
        "RepoTags": [
            "runseb/dockertls:latest"
        ],
        "Size": 0,
        "VirtualSize": 214723529
    }
]
```

Note that you used the `--insecure curl` option, because you created your own certificate authority. By default, `curl` will check the certificates against the CAs contained in the default CA bundle installed on your server. If you were to get server and client keys and certificates from a trusted CA listed in the default CA bundle, you would not have to make an `--insecure` connection. However, this does not mean that the connection is not properly using TLS.

4.10 Using docker-py to Access the Docker Daemon Remotely

Problem

Although the Docker client is powerful, you would like to access the Docker daemon through a Python client. Specifically, you would like to write a Python program that calls the Docker remote API.

Solution

Import the *docker-py* Python module from Pip. In a Python script or interactive shell, create a connection to a remote Docker daemon and start making API calls.

 Although this recipe is about *docker-py*, it serves as an example that you can use your own client to communicate with the Docker daemon and you are not restricted to the default Docker client. Docker clients exist in several programming languages (*https://docs.docker.com/reference/api/remote_api_client_libraries/*) (e.g., Java, Groovy, Perl, PHP, Scala, Erlang, etc.), and you can write your own by studying the API reference (*https://docs.docker.com/reference/api/docker_remote_api_v1.16/*).

docker-py is a Python client for Docker. It can be installed from source (*https://github.com/docker/docker-py*) or simply fetched from the Python Package Index (*https://pypi.python.org/pypi*) by using the `pip` command. First install `python-pip`, and then get the *docker-py* package. On Ubuntu 14.04:

```
$ sudo apt-get install python-pip
$ sudo pip install docker-py
```

The documentation (*http://docker-py.readthedocs.org/en/latest/*) tells you how to create a connection to the Docker daemon. Create an instance of the `Client()` class by passing it a `base_url` argument that specifies how the Docker daemon is listening. If it is listening locally on a Unix socket:

```
$ python
Python 2.7.6 (default, Mar 22 2014, 22:59:56)
[GCC 4.8.2] on linux2
Type "help", "copyright", "credits" or "license" for more information.
>>> from docker import Client
>>> c=Client(base_url="unix://var/run/docker.sock")
>>> c.containers()
[]
```

If it is listening over TCP, as you set it up in Recipe 4.7:

```
$ python
Python 2.7.6 (default, Mar 22 2014, 22:59:56)
[GCC 4.8.2] on linux2
Type "help", "copyright", "credits" or "license" for more information.
>>> from docker import Client
>>> c=Client(base_url="tcp://127.0.0.1:2375")
>>> c.containers()
[]
```

You can explore the methods available via *docker-py* by using help(c) at the Python prompt in the interactive sessions.

Discussion

The *docker-py* module has a few basics documented (*http://docker-py.readthedocs.org/en/latest/*). Of note is the integration with Boot2Docker (Recipe 1.7), which has a helper function to set up the connection (*http://docker-py.readthedocs.org/en/latest/boot2docker/*). Since the latest Boot2Docker uses TLS for added security in accessing the Docker daemon, the setup is slightly different than what we presented. In addition, there is currently a bug that is worth mentioning for those who will be interested in testing *docker-py*.

Start Boot2Docker:

```
$ boot2docker start
Waiting for VM and Docker daemon to start...
...............oooo
Started.
Writing /Users/sebgoa/.boot2docker/certs/boot2docker-vm/ca.pem
Writing /Users/sebgoa/.boot2docker/certs/boot2docker-vm/cert.pem
Writing /Users/sebgoa/.boot2docker/certs/boot2docker-vm/key.pem

To connect the Docker client to the Docker daemon, please set:
    export DOCKER_HOST=tcp://192.168.59.103:2376
    export DOCKER_CERT_PATH=/Users/sebgoa/.boot2docker/certs/boot2docker-vm
    export DOCKER_TLS_VERIFY=1
```

This returns a set of environment variables that need to be set. Boot2Docker provides a nice convenience utility, $(boot2docker shellinit), to set everything up. However, for *docker-py* to work, you need to edit your */etc/hosts* file and set a different DOCKER_HOST. In */etc/hosts* add a line with the IP of boot2docker and its local DNS name (i.e., boot2docker) and then export DOCKER_HOST=tcp://boot2docker:2376. Then in a Python interactive shell:

```
>>> from docker.client import Client
>>> from docker.utils import kwargs_from_env
>>> client = Client(**kwargs_from_env())
>>> client.containers()
[]
```

4.11 Using docker-py Securely

Problem

You want to use the *docker-py* Python client to access a remote Docker daemon set up with TLS secure access.

Solution

After setting up a Docker host as explained in Recipe 4.9, verify that you can connect to the Docker daemon with TLS. For example, assuming a host with the hostname dockerpytls and client certificate, key, and CA located in the default location at *~/.docker/*, try this:

```
$ docker -H tcp://dockerpytls:2376 --tlsverify ps
CONTAINER ID    IMAGE        COMMAND      CREATED      STATUS      PORTS      NAMES
```

 Make sure you have installed *docker_py*:

```
sudo apt-get -y install python-pip
sudo pip install docker-py
```

Once this is successful, open a Python interactive shell and create a *docker-py* client instance by using the following configuration:

```
tls_config = docker.tls.TLSConfig(
  client_cert=('/home/vagrant/.docker./cert.pem', \
               '/home/vagrant/.docker/key.pem'), \
  ca_cert='/home/vagrant/.docker/ca.pem')
client = docker.Client(base_url='https://host:2376', tls=tls_config)
```

This is equivalent to calling the Docker daemon on the command line as follows:

```
$ docker -H tcp://host:2376 --tlsverify --tlscert /path/to/client-cert.pem \
                            --tlskey /path/to/client-key.pem \
                            --tlscacert /path/to/ca.pem ...
```

See Also

- Documentation of docker=py (*http://docker-py.readthedocs.org/en/latest/tls/*)
- Docker article on HTTPS support (*https://docs.docker.com/articles/https/*)

4.12 Changing the Storage Driver

Problem

You would like to use a different storage driver than the default used on your system during Docker installation.

Solution

This recipe illustrates how to change the storage backend used by Docker. You will start from a Ubuntu 14.04 installation with a 3.13 kernel and a Docker 1.7 setup with Another Union File System (AUFS), and you will switch to the overlay filesystem. As before, you can grab a Vagrantfile from the repository that comes with this book. Let's do it:

```
$ git clone https://github.com/how2dock/docbook.git
$ cd docbook/ch04/overlay
$ vagrant up
$ vagrant ssh
$ uname -r
3.13.0-39-generic
$ docker info | grep Storage
Storage Driver: aufs
$ docker version | grep Server
Server version: 1.7.0
```

The overlay filesystem is available in the Linux kernel starting with 3.18. Therefore to switch storage backends, you first need to upgrade (*http://bit.ly/linux-318*) the kernel of your machine to 3.8 and restart:

```
$ cd /tmp
$ wget http://kernel.ubuntu.com/~kernel-ppa/mainline/v3.18-vivid/\
  linux-headers-3.18.0-031800-generic_3.18.0-031800.201412071935_amd64.deb
$ wget http://kernel.ubuntu.com/~kernel-ppa/mainline/v3.18-vivid/\
  linux-headers-3.18.0-031800_3.18.0-031800.201412071935_all.deb
$ wget http://kernel.ubuntu.com/~kernel-ppa/mainline/v3.18-vivid/\
  linux-image-3.18.0-031800-generic_3.18.0-031800.201412071935_amd64.deb
$ sudo dpkg -i linux-headers-3.18.0-*.deb linux-image-3.18.0-*.deb
$ sudo update-grub
$ sudo shutdown -r now
```

Once the machine has restarted, connect to it again. You can now edit the Docker configuration file and specify Overlay as a storage driver by using the -s option in starting the Docker daemon:

```
$ uname -r
3.18.0-031800-generic
$ sudo su
# service docker stop
```

```
# echo DOCKER_OPTS=\"-s overlay\" >> /etc/default/docker
# service docker start
```

You now switch the storage backend for Docker:

```
$ docker info | grep Storage
Storage Driver: overlay
```

 AUFS has been the default storage backend for 3.13–3.16 kernels, especially on Ubuntu systems. Overlay is now in the upstream kernel starting with 3.18, and AUFS is not available. Consider switching to Overlay.

Discussion

Docker can use multiple storage backends to store images and container filesystems. The storage abstraction in Docker tries to minimize the space used by images and container filesystems by keeping them in layers and tracking only the modifications from layer to layer. It relies on union-based filesystems to accomplish this.

You can choose between the following storage backends:

- vfs
- devicemapper
- btrfs
- aufs
- overlay

Analyzing the differences in stability and performance of each of these solutions as Docker storage backends is beyond the scope of this recipe.

See Also

- Upgrade to 3.18 Linux kernel on Ubuntu 14.04 (*http://bit.ly/linux-318*)
- Docker deep dive into storage drivers (*http://bit.ly/petazzoni*)
- Docker-supported filesystems (*http://www.projectatomic.io/docs/filesystems/*)

## CHAPTER 5

Kubernetes

5.0 Introduction

Contributed by Joe Beda

As applications grow beyond what can be safely handled on a single host, a need has arisen for what has come to be called an *orchestration system*. An orchestration systems helps users view a set of hosts (also referred to as *nodes*) as a unified programmable reliable cluster. That cluster can be viewed and used as a giant computer.

Kubernetes (*http://kubernetes.io*) (often abbreviated as *k8s*) is an open source system started by Google to fill this need. Kubernetes is based on ideas validated through internal Google systems over the last 10 years (Borg (*http://bit.ly/google-borg*) and Omega (*http://bit.ly/g-omega*)). These systems are used to run and manage all of the myriad Google services, including Google Search, Google Mail, and more. Many of the engineers who built and operated Borg clusters at scale are helping to design and build Kubernetes.

Traditionally, Borg has been one of the key things that ex-Google engineers miss from their time at the company. But now Kubernetes fills this need for engineers who don't happen to work for Google. Kubernetes features some enhanced capabilities and new concepts.

Enhanced capabilities

A Kubernetes cluster coordinates Docker across multiple nodes and provides a unified programming model with enhanced capabilities:

Reliable container restart
   Kubernetes can monitor the health of a container and restart it when it fails.

Self-healing

If a node fails, the Kubernetes management system can automatically reschedule work onto healthy nodes. Dynamic service membership ensures that those new containers can be found and used.

High-cluster utilization

By scheduling a diverse set of workloads on a common set of machines, users can drive dramatically higher utilization compared to static manual placement. The larger the cluster and the more diverse the workloads, the better the utilization.

Organization and grouping

With large clusters, keeping track of all the containers that are running can be difficult. Kubernetes provides a flexible labeling system that allows both users and other systems to think in sets of containers. In addition, Kubernetes supports the idea of namespaces so different users or teams can have isolated views into the cluster.

Horizontal scaling and replication

Kubernetes is built to enable easy horizontal scaling. Scaling and load balancing are intrinsic concepts.

Microservice friendly

Kubernetes clusters are a perfect companion for teams adopting a microservices architecture. Applications can be broken into smaller parts that are easier to develop, scale, and reason about. Kubernetes provides ways for a service to find (commonly called *discovery*) and communicate with other services.

Streamlined operations

Kubernetes allows for specialized ops teams. Management of the Kubernetes system and the nodes that it runs on can be driven by a dedicated team or outsourced to a cloud service. Operational teams for specific apps (or the development team itself) can then focus on running that application without managing the details of individual nodes.

New concepts

While Docker is great for dealing with containers running on a single node, Kubernetes addresses the additional challenges around cross-node communication and scale. To help, Kubernetes introduces a set of new concepts:

Cluster scheduling

The process of placing a container on a specific node to optimize the reliability and utilization of the cluster.

Pods

A group of containers that *must* be placed on a single node and work together as a team. Allowing a set of containers to work closely together on a single node is a powerful way to make applications even more manageable.

Labels

Data attached to pods in order to organize a group for monitoring and management.

Replication controllers

Agents that work to make sure that a horizontal scaling group or pod is reliably maintained.

Network services

A way to communicate between not just pods, but groups of pods by using dynamically configured naming and network proxies.

With that, let's jump into understanding and using Kubernetes!

5.1 Understanding Kubernetes Architecture

Problem

You need a container management system that provides scale and fault-tolerance, and you would like to understand the architecture of Kubernetes (see Figure 5-1).

Solution

The main architecture of a Kubernetes cluster includes the following:

Kubernetes master services

These centralized services (that can run in Docker containers) provide an API, collect and surface the current state of the cluster, and assign pods to nodes. Most users will always interact directly with the master API. This provides a unified view of the entire cluster.

Master storage

Currently all persistent Kubernetes state is stored in etcd. New storage engines likely will be built out over time.

Kubelet

This agent runs on every node and is responsible for driving Docker, reporting status to the master, and setting up node-level resources (like remote disk storage).

Kubernetes proxy

This proxy runs on every node (and can run elsewhere) and provides local containers a single network endpoint to reach an array of pods.

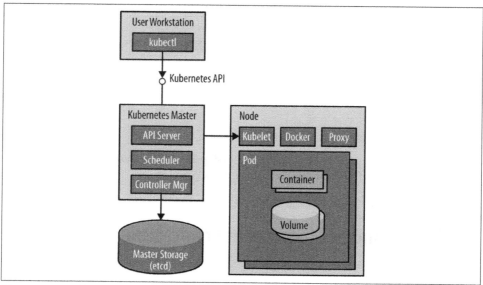

Figure 5-1. Kubernetes architecture

Discussion

A user interacts with a Kubernetes master through tools (such as kubectl) that call the Kubernetes API. API documentation (automatically generated from source) is available on the Kubernetes site (*http://kubernetes.io/third_party/swagger-ui/*). The master is responsible for storing a description of what users want to run (referred to as a spec in the API). It then works to turn that specification into reality. It reports the current state of the cluster as status.

Running on every worker node in the cluster are the kubelet and the proxy. The kubelet is responsible for driving Docker and setting up other node-specific states, like storage volumes. The proxy is responsible for providing a stable local endpoint for talking to services (frequently implemented by a set of containers running in the cluster).

Kubernetes works to manage pods. *Pods* are a grouping of compute resources that provide context for a set of containers. Users can use pods to force a set of containers that work as a team to be scheduled on a single physical node. While simple applications can be built as a single container, pods help to enable advanced scenarios:

- *Multiple Docker containers* can exist in a pod. This allows for some advanced scenarios explored in Recipe 5.7. Each container starts with its filesystem and process as normal.
- Pods define a *shared network interface*. Unlike regular containers, containers in a pod all share the same network interface. This allows for efficient and easy access across containers using `localhost`. It also means that different containers in the same pod cannot use the same network port.
- *Storage volumes* are defined as part of the pod. These volumes can be mapped into multiple containers as needed. Specialized types of volumes also exist, based on the needs of users and the capabilities of the cluster.

Here is the general flow for how work is run with Kubernetes:

1. Via the kubectl tool and the Kubernetes API, the user creates a specification for a replication controller with a pod template and a count for the number of desired replicas.
2. Kubernetes uses the template in the replication controller to create a number of pods.
3. The Kubernetes Scheduler (part of the master) looks at the current state of the cluster (which nodes are available and what resources are available on those nodes) and binds a pod to a specific node.
4. The kubelet on that node watches for a change in the set of pods assigned to the node it is running on. It then starts up or kills pods as necessary. This includes configuring any storage volumes as necessary, downloading the Docker image to that specific node, and calling the Docker API to start/stop individual containers.

Fault-tolerance is implemented at multiple levels. Individual containers within a pod can be health checked and monitored by the local kubelet. If pods stop or fail, they can be restarted automatically. If the entire node fails, the master will notice this and, after a time-out to make sure the node does come back, delete all of the pods on that node. At that point, replication controllers (if used) will create replacements for pods that were on that node. Multiple levels of monitoring and restarting help to keep applications running even when the cluster is experiencing problems (software or hardware).

Pods Get Scheduled Only Once

After a pod is scheduled on a node, it will never be moved. If that node is lost or removed from the cluster, the pod will not be restarted. This is surprising behavior given that a goal of Kubernetes is to reliably keep work running. This is required, as networks are imperfect. In the event that the master cannot talk to a node, any pod on that node is in an indeterminate state as far as the master is concerned—it may or may not be running. If that same pod were restarted on another machine, two pods with the exact same name/identity could be running at the same time. This can cause all sorts of problems. For instance, distributed logs might be written from multiple places, all keyed to the same pod ID. Or the pod ID may be used as part of a master election system, and clients may be confused as to which pod is really the master.

Instead, to reliably run a workload, it is necessary to use a replication controller. This takes a pod template and tries to ensure that a specific number of pods is always running to accomplish that task. In the case of the master not being able to talk to a node, a replication controller is in charge of spinning up a new pod to replace the lost pods. If communication is reestablished, it is up to the replication controller to delete one of the redundant pods.

5.2 Networking Pods for Container Connectivity

Contributed by Joe Beda

Problem

You want to control how network traffic is directed to your containers as they are scheduled across a Kubernetes cluster.

Solution

Use a networking subsystem that gives each container its own IP address so that each can be addressed directly.

Shipping with Kubernetes are a set of scripts that make it easy to launch in various clouds. Many of these cluster deployment systems set up the network appropriately for you automatically. However, if you are digging into the details, an easy system to start with is Flannel (*https://github.com/coreos/flannel*) from CoreOS (see Recipe 6.1).

Other options include the following:

- Build in internal network routing for the cloud you are running on. Support is built in for GCE and Amazon EC2.
- Project Calico (*http://www.projectcalico.org/*) for larger bare-metal deployments.
- Weave (*http://weave.works/*) for a solution that supports encryption across wide areas (see Recipe 3.11).

The solution is to use Kubernetes services. These can be used to communicate between containers within a cluster or to direct external traffic to a set of pods.

Discussion

Kubernetes assumes a network model in which each pod gets an IP. Each pod can then connect to other pods, regardless of which physical node they happen to be running on.

However, just because pods can connect directly doesn't mean that is the best or easiest way to communicate between pods. In the event that a pod fails or is replaced on a new node, the calling code would have to know to reconnect to a new address. This dynamic reconnection is hard to integrate with many existing servers and frameworks. Kubernetes services are the answer to this problem (see Recipe 5.8).

See Also

- Administration guide for Networking in Kubernetes (*http://kubernetes.io/v1.0/docs/admin/networking.html*)

5.3 Creating a Multinode Kubernetes Cluster with Vagrant

Problem

You want to get started with Kubernetes and would like to create a small cluster on your local machine using Vagrant.

Solution

You will need to install Vagrant (*https://vagrantup.com*) and VirtualBox (*http://virtualbox.org*) if you have not done so already. Then set two environment variables: KUBERNETES_PROVIDER to specify that you will use Vagrant, and NUM_MINIONS to set the number of nodes in your cluster (in addition to the master node). Then you will use the installation script (*https://get.k8s.io*) provided by the Kubernetes community. It will read the environment variables, detect your operating system, download the latest stable release of Kubernetes, and untar it in a *kubernetes* directory. The following commands show you these steps on the command line:

```
export KUBERNETES_PROVIDER=vagrant
export NUM_MINIONS=2
curl -sS https://get.k8s.io | bash
```

If you do not specify the NUM_MINIONS environment variables, only one node will be started in addition to the master node.

Each virtual machine started with Vagrant will use 1GB of RAM, so make sure you have enough memory.

Downloading the Vagrant box being used (about 316MB), and provisioning the virtual machines using SaltStack (*http://saltstack.com*) will take a bit of time. Once it is done, the nodes will have gone through a validation step, and you should see a similar output on *stdout*:

```
...
Kubernetes cluster is running.  The master is running at:

  https://10.245.1.2

The user name and password to use is located in ~/.kubernetes_vagrant_auth.

... calling validate-cluster
Found 2 nodes.
        NAME        LABELS                                  STATUS
    1   10.245.1.3  kubernetes.io/hostname=10.245.1.3       Ready
    2   10.245.1.4  kubernetes.io/hostname=10.245.1.4       Ready
Validate output:
NAME                STATUS    MESSAGE               ERROR
etcd-0              Healthy   {"health": "true"}    nil
controller-manager Healthy   ok                    nil
scheduler          Healthy   ok                    nil
Cluster validation succeeded
Done, listing cluster services:

Kubernetes master is running at https://10.245.1.2
KubeDNS is running at https://10.245.1.2/api/v1/proxy/namespaces/kube-system/ \
services/kube-dns
KubeUI is running at https://10.245.1.2/api/v1/proxy/namespaces/kube-system/ \
services/kube-ui
```

The `vagrant status` command lists your running VMs:

```
$ vagrant status
Current machine states:

master              running (virtualbox)
minion-1            running (virtualbox)
minion-2            running (virtualbox)
```

At this point, you have a working Kubernetes cluster running locally within virtual machines.

Discussion

The Vagrant box used to create this cluster is based on Fedora 21 and uses systemd. If you connect to these VMs, you can list the systemd units that are running and make up the Kubernetes system. The networking between the containers uses Open vSwitch to set up a tunnel mesh.

On the master node, you find two services running—the *Addon* object manager along with the *kubelet*. The *kubelet* then runs the rest of the Kubernetes server processes under Docker. This includes an instance of etcd, the *API* server, the *Controller manager*, and the *Scheduler*:

```
workstation$ vagrant ssh master
Last login: Tue Aug  4 23:53:35 2015 from 10.0.2.2
[vagrant@kubernetes-master ~]$ sudo systemctl list-units | grep kube
kube-addons.service     loaded active running   Kubernetes Addon Object Manager
kubelet.service         loaded active running   Kubernetes Kubelet Server
[vagrant@kubernetes-master ~]$ sudo docker ps | grep -e 'k8s_kube\|k8s_etcd' | \
awk '{print $1 " " $2}'
23963ff9ed00 gcr.io/google_containers/etcd:2.0.12
be59784f7885 gcr.io/google_containers/kube-apiserver:f8f32e739d4797f77dc3f85c...
ab3bea447298 gcr.io/google_containers/kube-scheduler:2c6e421dc8d78201f68d4cfa...
f41749ff028d gcr.io/google_containers/kube-controller-manager:4d46d90bb861fdd...
```

On the minions, you find two more Kubernetes-related services: the *Kube-Proxy* server and the *Kubelet* server. Docker is, of course, also running:

```
workstation$ vagrant ssh minion-1
Last login: Tue Aug  4 23:52:47 2015 from 10.0.2.2
[vagrant@kubernetes-minion-1 ~]$ sudo systemctl list-units kube*
UNIT               LOAD   ACTIVE SUB      DESCRIPTION
kube-proxy.service loaded active running Kubernetes Kube-Proxy Server
kubelet.service    loaded active running Kubernetes Kubelet Server
```

To interact with the cluster, you can use the *kubectl.sh* script on your localhost. This script allows you to manage all Kubernetes resources that make up container-scheduling tasks. Here is a snippet of the kubectl help:

```
workstation$ ./cluster/kubectl.sh
kubectl controls the Kubernetes cluster manager.

Find more information at https://github.com/GoogleCloudPlatform/kubernetes.

Usage:
  kubectl [flags]
  kubectl [command]

Available Commands:
  get          Display one or many resources
  describe     Show details of a specific resource or group of resources
  create       Create a resource by filename or stdin
```

```
replace          Replace a resource by filename or stdin.
patch            Update field(s) of a resource by stdin.
delete           Delete a resource by filename, stdin, resource and name,
                 or by resources and label selector.
namespace        SUPERCEDED: Set and view the current Kubernetes namespace
logs             Print the logs for a container in a pod.
rolling-update   Perform a rolling update of the given ReplicationController.
scale            Set a new size for a Replication Controller.
exec             Execute a command in a container.
port-forward     Forward one or more local ports to a pod.
proxy            Run a proxy to the Kubernetes API server
run              Run a particular image on the cluster.
stop             Gracefully shut down a resource by name or filename.
expose           Take a replicated application and expose it as Kubernetes
                 Service
label            Update the labels on a resource
config           config modifies kubeconfig files
cluster-info     Display cluster info
api-versions     Print available API versions.
version          Print the client and server version information.
help             Help about any command
...
```

To test that you can indeed communicate with the Kubernetes API server running on the master node, list the nodes in the cluster:

```
workstation$ ./cluster/kubectl.sh get nodes
NAME           LABELS                                 STATUS
10.245.1.3     kubernetes.io/hostname=10.245.1.3      Ready
10.245.1.4     kubernetes.io/hostname=10.245.1.4      Ready
```

 To destroy all the virtual machines, run the *./cluster/kube-down.sh* script.

You are now ready to head over to Recipe 5.4 and create your first containers using Kubernetes.

See Also

- Documentation on Vagrant provisioning (*http://kubernetes.io/v1.0/docs/getting-started-guides/vagrant.html*)

- Bash script (*https://get.k8s.io*) that automates the creation of a Kubernetes cluster using the latest stable release

5.4 Starting Containers on a Kubernetes Cluster with Pods

Problem

You know how to start containers by using the Docker command-line interface. Now you would like to use Kubernetes to schedule your containers in a cluster.

Solution

You have a Kubernetes cluster available to you, either through Recipe 5.3 or Recipe 5.9 or a public cloud provider like Google Container Engine. In addition, you have downloaded the Kubernetes client `kubectl` and it is set up to use your cluster endpoint with the appropriate authentication (see Recipe 5.15).

As explained in Recipe 5.1, containers are scheduled as a group by defining pods. Therefore, to start your first container, you need to write a pod definition in JSON or YAML and use the `kubectl` client to submit it to the Kubernetes API server.

Let's start with a fun example and run the 2048 game. A Docker image is available on the Docker Hub (*https://registry.hub.docker.com/u/cpk1224/docker-2048/*), and I will leave it to you to check out the Dockerfile. Save the YAML file shown here as *2048.yaml*:

```
apiVersion: v1
kind: Pod
metadata:
  name: "2048"
spec:
  containers:
  - image: cpk1224/docker-2048
    name: "2048"
    ports:
    - containerPort: 80
      hostPort: 80
```

You can now submit it to your cluster:

```
$ kubectl create -f 2048.yaml
pods/2048
```

Once the image is downloaded, the container will start running. You should be able to use your browser and open the 2048 game on the IP of the host that is running it. You will need to open any firewall rules that may prevent you from doing so.

Discussion

The YAML file specifies the API version (i.e., `v1`) and the kind of object it defines (i.e., pod). Then some metadata needs to be set to specify a name for this pod. In this example, a single container is started, but there could be several. All would be defined in the spec section under the container field. The image used and a name for the container are required parameters. In this example, you also define port 80 to be exposed and mapped on port 80 of the host (using the containerPort and hostPort keys).

You can then list the pods that you have running with kubectl get pods. You will see that the pod will enter running state, that there is one container in that pod, what the image is, and its status:

```
$ kubectl get pods
POD        IP          CONTAINER(S)   IMAGE(S)       HOST ...

podname   10.132.1.9                                 k8s-node/1.2.3.4 ...
                       2048           cpk1224/docker-2048 ...
```

To learn the API specification, you can query the pod and return its definition in YAML or JSON:

```
$ ./kubectl get pods -o yaml 2048
apiVersion: v1
kind: Pod
metadata:
  name: "2048"
...<snip>
```

The pod is exposed on port 80 on the host's IP because of the host Port item in the original YAML pod definition file. This is great for debugging but not recommended for production services, as each host port can be forwarded to only a single container. To expose pods in a more scalable way, use services as described in Recipe 5.2.

Once you are done experimenting, you can delete the pod easily:

```
$ kubectl delete pods podname
```

5.5 Taking Advantage of Labels for Querying Kubernetes Objects

Problem

In a large Kubernetes cluster, you may run thousands of pods as well as other cluster objects. You would like to easily query and manipulate sets of objects in multi-dimensional ways by using a tagging system.

Solution

Tag your objects (e.g., pods) by using labels. *Labels* are key/value pairs that can be attached to any Kubernetes object. These labels are defined primarily in the metadata section of an object definition.

Taking the example from Recipe 5.4, you can add a label `foo=bar` by modifying the pod `yaml` metadata description like so:

```
apiVersion: v1
kind: Pod
metadata:
  name: "2048"
  labels:
    foo: bar
    version: "47"
spec:
  containers:
  - image: cpk1224/docker-2048
    name: "2048"
    ports:
    - containerPort: 80
      hostPort: 80
```

Now delete any existing pod named 2048 and start up a new pod with this definition.

The end result is that you can now list pods that have that specific label by using the `--selector` option of the kubectl CLI:

```
$ kubectl get pods --selector="foo=bar"
```

Additionally, you can add labels at runtime by using the kubectl `label` function:

```
$ kubectl label pods 2048 env=production
POD      IP          CONTAINER(S)   IMAGE(S)           HOST ...
2048     10.244.0.6                                    k8s-node/1.2.3.4 ...
                     2048           cpk1224/docker-2048
```

> Labels follow a specific syntax (*https://github.com/GoogleCloudPlat form/kubernetes/blob/master/docs/labels.md*).

In short, labels are a straightforward tagging system that allows users to add metadata to any resource in their cluster. It helps build cross-functional relationships to manage sets of resources in various stages of an application life cycle.

Now delete your pod by identifying it via a label selector:

```
$ kubectl.sh delete pod --selector="foo=bar"
pods/2048
```

See Also

- Introduction, motivation, and syntax of labels (*http://kubernetes.io/v1.0/docs/ user-guide/labels.html*)

5.6 Using a Replication Controller to Manage the Number of Replicas of a Pod

Problem

You need to make sure that several replicas of your pod exist at any time in the cluster.

Solution

Kubernetes is a declarative system: users express what they want the system to do and not how to do it. Using replication controllers, you can specify the number of replicas that you want for a pod. This helps with high load and availability by serving part of an application through a service proxy (see Recipe 5.8).

Replication controllers are one of the three key objects in a Kubernetes cluster (with pods and services). You can list all running replication controllers with `kubectl`:

```
$ kubectl get replicationcontrollers
...
$ kubectl get rc
```

To create a replication controller, you write a JSON or YAML file following the replication controller API specification. It can contain metadata, the number of replicas that you want, a selector to target specific pods, and a template for a pod. Currently, the template is embedded within the replication controller definition, but this may change in future version of Kubernetes.

For example, if you want to create a replication controller for the 2048 game that you ran in a single pod in Recipe 5.4, you can write the following *rc2048.yaml* file:

```
apiVersion: v1
kind: ReplicationController
metadata:
  labels:
    name: rcgame
  name: rcgame
spec:
  replicas: 1
  selector:
    name: game
  template:
```

```
metadata:
  labels:
    name: game
spec:
  containers:
  - image: cpk1224/docker-2048
    name: test
    ports:
    - containerPort: 80
```

The controller itself will have the `rcgame` label, and will target pods with the label `game`. Once started, the controller will ensure that one pod is running at all times. You launch it with `kubectl create`:

```
$ kubectl create -f rc2048.yml
replicationcontrollers/rcgame
$ kubectl get rc
CONTROLLER   CONTAINER(S)   IMAGE(S)              SELECTOR     REPLICAS
rcgame       test           cpk1224/docker-2048   name=game    1
```

Try killing the pod that was created. You will see that a new one automatically starts again.

 You do not need to have an existing pod running before starting a replication controller. It will automatically start a pod that matches the label specified in the definition if it does not exist yet. You can also set the number of replicas to zero.

The magic happens when you want to increase the number of replicas. You can use the `kubectl resize` command, and the number of pods will automatically be adjusted:

```
$ kubectl resize --replicas=4 rc rcgame
resized
```

Discussion

Recipe 5.1 mentioned that every node in a Kubernetes cluster runs a *kubelet*. This process watches over the pods that are scheduled on a node and makes sure they keep running. But what happens if the node dies? Kubernetes needs to have a way to reschedule that pod on another node automatically as well as keep a number of replicas up for availability. This is what replication controllers help you achieve.

Although replication controllers are extremely helpful for guaranteed availability and elasticity, they are also a great way to perform application deployment scenarios such as canary deployment. In fact, Kubernetes has a built-in rolling update mechanism based on replication controllers that is worth investigating:

```
$ ./kubectl rollingupdate -h
Perform a rolling update of the given ReplicationController.

Replaces the specified controller with new controller, updating one pod at a time
to use the new PodTemplate. The new-controller.json must specify the same
namespace as the existing controller and overwrite at least one (common) label
in its replicaSelector.
...<snip>
```

See Also

- Documentation on replication controllers (*http://kubernetes.io/v1.0/docs/user-guide/replication-controller.html*)

5.7 Running Multiple Containers in a Pod

Problem

You know how to run a single container in a pod, but would like to run multiple ones that will be co-located. You might already have some containers in production that use the Docker linking mechanism on a single host and would like to use Kubernetes to do the same.

Solution

A pod definition is not restricted to a single container. You can define as many containers as you want, as well as volumes. Recipe 5.4 created a simple pod definition that started a single container. The following example starts WordPress by using the official images from Docker Hub for WordPress and MySQL. Both run as separate containers and use environment variables to configure the installation. The WordPress container defines the database host through the environment variable WORD PRESS_DB_HOST and sets it to 127.0.0.1. This allows WordPress to reach the MySQL database also started within the pod. This works, because pods get a single IP address in the current Kubernetes networking model (see Recipe 5.2). Create the following *wordpress.yaml* file:

```
apiVersion: v1
kind: Pod
metadata:
  labels:
    name: wp
  name: wp
spec:
  containers:
  - name: wordpress
    env:
```

```
    - name: WORDPRESS_DB_NAME
      value: wordpress
    - name: WORDPRESS_DB_USER
      value: wordpress
    - name: WORDPRESS_DB_PASSWORD
      value: wordpresspwd
    - name: WORDPRESS_DB_HOST
      value: 127.0.0.1
    image: wordpress
    ports:
    - containerPort: 80
      hostPort: 80
  - name: mysql
    env:
    - name: MYSQL_ROOT_PASSWORD
      value: wordpressdocker
    - name: MYSQL_DATABASE
      value: wordpress
    - name: MYSQL_USER
      value: wordpress
    - name: MYSQL_PASSWORD
      value: wordpresspwd
    image: mysql
    ports:
    - containerPort: 3306
```

Create the pod:

```
$ kubectl create -f wordpress.yaml
```

Once the containers start, you will have a working WordPress installation.

 You can view the logs of the containers in your pod with the kubectl client:

```
$ kubectl logs wp wordpress
```

Here, wp is the name of the pod you started and wordpress the name of the container you want to see the logs from.

Discussion

Although starting multiple containers through a pod is straightforward, accessing the application running within a pod requires using Kubernetes services (*http://kuber netes.io/v1.0/docs/user-guide/services.html*). Each pod gets its own IP address in a private network. To access an application from outside the Kubernetes cluster through a public IP address, you need to create a service that will bind the application to a public IP address or make use of an external load-balancer service.

In Google Container Engine, using an external load-balancer in a service definition is done directly in the YAML file describing the service. For instance, to expose the

WordPress application that is running through the pod defined in this recipe, you need to create the service file *sgoogle.yml* like so:

```
apiVersion: v1
kind: Service
metadata:
  labels:
    name: wordpress
  name: wordpress
spec:
  createExternalLoadBalancer: true
  ports:
    - port: 80
  selector:
    name: wp
```

The service has metadata associated with it, but the important part is the selector filed in the spec section. In the preceding example, the selector wp will allow the service to create a proxy that will bind the IP address given by the load-balancer to the pod that matches the wp label. Once you obtain the IP address of the load-balancer, you can access it from the public Internet. The Kubernetes service will proxy the request to the node where the pod is running. If the pod has been started with a replication controller, the service will also load-balance the requests among all the running pods.

On a cloud provider whose load-balancing system is not yet supported by Kubernetes, you can bind the pod to a public IP address manually with a service definition like this (where 1.2.3.4 needs to be replaced with the public IP):

```
apiVersion: v1
kind: Service
metadata:
  labels:
    name: wordpress
  name: wordpress
spec:
  publicIPs: ["1.2.3.4"]
  ports:
    - port: 80
  selector:
    name: wp
```

5.8 Using Cluster IP Services for Dynamic Linking of Containers

Problem

You want to *link* containers across multiple hosts in your cluster instead of running multiple containers per pod. This is the more cloud-native way of designing an appli-

---

cation, where layers that can scale and can operate separately from each other run as separate replication controllers.

Solution

In Recipe 5.7, you started WordPress by running the MySQL and WordPress containers in a single pod. The two containers started on the same host. You took advantage of the fact that a pod has a single IP address to set the WordPress MySQL host to localhost. However, you could imagine running a replicated MySQL service and/or a replicated WordPress frontend. This would mean that the containers would run on different hosts in the cluster.

Kubernetes services are smart proxies that keep track of changes in pod cluster allocation and update their port mapping dynamically when pods get rescheduled.

A better way of running our canonical WordPress example would be to run MySQL as a single pod or replication controller (glancing over the issues with database replication and data persistence) and then exposing this MySQL service through a Kubernetes service definition.

The replication controller would look something like this:

```
apiVersion: v1
kind: ReplicationController
metadata:
  name: wp-mysql
spec:
  replicas: 1
  selector:
    tier: wp-mysql
  template:
    metadata:
      labels:
        tier: wp-mysql
    spec:
      containers:
      - name: mysql
        image: mysql
        ports:
        - containerPort: 3306
        env:
        - name: MYSQL_ROOT_PASSWORD
          value: wordpressdocker
        - name: MYSQL_DATABASE
          value: wordpress
        - name: MYSQL_USER
          value: wordpress
        - name: MYSQL_PASSWORD
          value: wordpresspwd
```

A MySQL service can then be defined as a different type of Kubernetes object. It can be managed through the API. A service definition for MySQL would be as follows:

```
kind: Service
apiVersion: v1
metadata:
  name: mysql
spec:
  selector:
    tier: wp-mysql
  ports:
    - port: 3306
```

Note the `selector` field in the `spec` section. This selector will match all pods that contain the `tier: wp-mysql` label. The service will create a new "cluster IP" that will be accessible to any other pod in the cluster. Any connections to this cluster IP will be proxied and load-balanced to one of the underlying endpoints.

You can inspect the endpoints that are backing this service:

```
$ kubectl describe services/mysql
Name:               mysql
Namespace:          default
Labels:             <none>
Selector:           tier=wp-mysql
Type:               ClusterIP
IP:                 10.0.175.152
Port:               <unnamed>    3306/TCP
Endpoints:          10.244.1.4:3306
Session Affinity:   None
No events.
```

Furthermore, if you are running the (highly recommended) DNS add-on, the cluster IP will be given a logical name that can be used by any clients. You use this in your WordPress pod configuration so that it can find the database no matter where it is. You can see this with the `WORDPRESS_DB_HOST` environment variable:

```
apiVersion: v1
kind: Pod
metadata:
  labels:
    tier: fe
  name: wp
spec:
  containers:
  - env:
    - name: WORDPRESS_DB_NAME
      value: wordpress
    - name: WORDPRESS_DB_USER
      value: wordpress
    - name: WORDPRESS_DB_PASSWORD
      value: wordpresspwd
```

```
    - name: WORDPRESS_DB_HOST
      value: mysql
    image: wordpress
    name: wordpress
    ports:
    - containerPort: 80
      hostPort: 80
      protocol: TCP
```

WordPress is exposed to the public Internet the same way as in Recipe 5.7, through another service of type LoadBalancer:

```
apiVersion: v1
kind: Service
metadata:
  name: wordpress
spec:
  type: LoadBalancer
  ports:
    - port: 80
  selector:
    tier: fe
```

Discussion

Along with pods and replication controllers, services are key entities of Kubernetes. Services bring a locality abstraction on top of pods, which is key to self-discovery and a dynamic behavior in a large-scale cluster when failures happens. With services, a set of pods can be given a stable name that can be reliably accessed no matter where those pods are scheduled.

Creating a Kubernetes service will allocate a new cluster IP address for the service that is independent of any specific pod or node. This creates a stable way to talk to the service no matter where the implementation is running. When a calling pod then establishes a connection to that service, it will be handled by the local Kubernetes proxy that is running on its node. This proxy then forwards the connection to a pod identified by the service definition (usually by a label selector). If multiple pods are backing a service, the proxy will load-balance across those pods. See Figure 5-2.

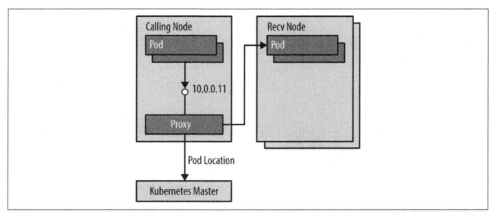

Figure 5-2. Using a Kubernetes cluster

The calling code can find the IP for a service in two ways: environment variables and DNS. The environment variables created for services are similar to Docker link variables. For example, suppose you have a service called redis that exposes port 6379:

```
REDIS_MASTER_SERVICE_HOST=10.0.0.11
REDIS_MASTER_SERVICE_PORT=6379
REDIS_MASTER_PORT=tcp://10.0.0.11:6379
REDIS_MASTER_PORT_6379_TCP=tcp://10.0.0.11:6379
REDIS_MASTER_PORT_6379_TCP_PROTO=tcp
REDIS_MASTER_PORT_6379_TCP_PORT=6379
REDIS_MASTER_PORT_6379_TCP_ADDR=10.0.0.11
```

Much preferred, however, is to use DNS to find your services. When DNS support is configured on a Kubernetes cluster, each service will also be given a resolvable name. In this example, assuming the default namespace of default and a DNS domain root of cluster.local, the service will be exposed as redis.default.cluster.local. However, when working within a single namespace, users can simply use the name of the service: redis.

See Also

- WordPress example in the Kubernetes documentation (*http://bit.ly/mysql-kub*)
- Documentation on Kubernetes Services (*http://kubernetes.io/v1.0/docs/user-guide/services.html*)

5.9 Creating a Single-Node Kubernetes Cluster Using Docker Compose

Problem

You know how to create a Kubernetes cluster by running the various cluster components (e.g., API server, scheduler, kubelet) as `systemd` units. But why not take advantage of Docker itself to run these components? It would simplify deployment of the cluster. To test this deployment scenario, you want to run a one-node Kubernetes cluster locally using only Docker containers.

Solution

The Kubernetes documentation has a good resource (*http://kubernetes.io/v1.0/docs/getting-started-guides/docker.html*) about this scenario. This recipe goes one step further and takes advantage of Docker Compose (see Recipe 7.1). To get started, you will need a Docker host and Docker Compose installed. You can clone the repository that comes with this book and use the Vagrantfile provided:

```
$ git clone https://github.com/how2dock/docbook.git
$ cd docbook/ch05/docker
$ tree
.
├── Vagrantfile
├── k8s.yml
└── kubectl
```

The Vagrantfile contains a small bootstrap script that will install Docker in the virtual machine as well as Docker Compose. The *k8s.yml* is the `docker-compose` definition to start all the components of Kubernetes as containers. Bring up the machine and run `docker-compose`; all the required images will be downloaded and the containers will start:

```
$ vagrant up
$ vagrant ssh
$ cd /vagrant
$ docker-compose -f k8s.yml up -d
$ docker ps
CONTAINER ID   IMAGE                         COMMAND
64e0073615c5   gcr.io/google_containers/...  "/hyperkube controll  ...
9603f3b5b186   gcr.io/google_containers/...  "/hyperkube schedule  ...
3ce44e77989f   gcr.io/google_containers/...  "/hyperkube apiserve  ...
1b0bcbb56d59   kubernetes/pause:go           "/pause"              ...
0b0c3e2735a9   kubernetes/etcd:2.0.5.1       "/usr/local/bin/etcd  ...
459c45ef9389   gcr.io/google_containers/...  "/hyperkube proxy --  ...
005c5ac1de0e   gcr.io/google_containers/...  "/hyperkube kubelet   ...
```

That is it. You now have a one-node Kubernetes *cluster* with all components running as containers; get nodes returns your localhost, and you can create pods, replication controllers, and services:

```
$ ./kubectl get nodes
NAME         LABELS    STATUS
127.0.0.1    <none>    Ready
```

To test that you can create a new pod, you are going to run a single Nginx container:

```
$ ./kubectl run-container nginx --image=nginx --port=80
CONTROLLER    CONTAINER(S)    IMAGE(S)    SELECTOR                REPLICAS
nginx         nginx           nginx       run-container=nginx     1
```

 The run-container command automatically creates a replication controller for this container. List it with ./kubectl get rc.

To access this *nginx* frontend from outside the cluster, you need to expose it as a service. However, when creating the service, you pass the host-only network IP of the virtual machine to the kubectl command. Otherwise, the service will be created, and all future pods will be able to access it, but we will not be able to reach it from outside the cluster:

```
$ ./kubectl expose rc nginx --port=80 --public-ip=192.168.33.10
NAME     LABELS    SELECTOR              IP           PORT
nginx    <none>    run-container=nginx   10.0.0.98    80
```

Once the *nginx* image is downloaded, the pod will enter running state and you will be able to access the Nginx welcome page at http://192.168.33.10:

```
$ ./kubectl get pods
POD             IP             CONTAINER(S)          IMAGE(S)                        ...
nginx-127                      controller-manager    gcr.io/google_containers/...
                               apiserver             gcr.io/google_containers/...
                               scheduler             gcr.io/google_containers/...
nginx-461yi     172.17.0.6     nginx                 nginx                           ...
```

Discussion

The *k8s.yml* Compose file shows how this was done:

```
etcd:
  image: kubernetes/etcd:2.0.5.1
  net: "host"
  command: /usr/local/bin/etcd --addr=127.0.0.1:4001 --bind-addr=0.0.0.0:4001 \
  --data-dir=/var/etcd/data
master:
  image: gcr.io/google_containers/hyperkube:v0.14.1
```

```
    net: "host"
    volumes:
      - /var/run/docker.sock:/var/run/docker.sock
    command: /hyperkube kubelet --api_servers=http://localhost:8080 --v=2 \
    --address=0.0.0.0 \
              --enable_server --hostname_override=127.0.0.1 \
              --config=/etc/kubernetes/manifests
proxy:
  image: gcr.io/google_containers/hyperkube:v0.14.1
  net: "host"
  privileged: true
  command: /hyperkube proxy --master=http://127.0.0.1:8080 --v=2
```

Three containers are started by Compose: one container running etcd, one container running the Kubernetes proxy service, and one container running the Kubernetes kubelet. Both the service proxy and the kubelet are running from the same image and using the same binary that is called through the command option. This binary is *hyperkube*, a very nice utility binary that you can use to start all the components of a Kubernetes cluster.

The clever part is that the *master* container calls *hyperkube* by specifying a configuration file in */etc/kubernetes/manifests* located within the container image. You can check what is in this manifest by running a new ephemeral container:

```
$ docker run --rm -it gcr.io/google_containers/hyperkube:v0.14.1 cat /etc/ \
kubernetes/manifests/master.json
{
"apiVersion": "v1beta3",
"kind": "Pod",
"metadata": {"name":"nginx"},
"spec":{
  "hostNetwork": true,
  "containers":[
    {
      "name": "controller-manager",
      "image": "gcr.io/google_containers/hyperkube:v0.14.1",
      "command": [
              "/hyperkube",
              "controller-manager",
              "--master=127.0.0.1:8080",
              "--machines=127.0.0.1",
              "--sync_nodes=true",
              "--v=2"
        ]
    },
    {
      "name": "apiserver",
      "image": "gcr.io/google_containers/hyperkube:v0.14.1",
      "command": [
              "/hyperkube",
              "apiserver",
```

```
        "--portal_net=10.0.0.1/24",
        "--address=127.0.0.1",
        "--etcd_servers=http://127.0.0.1:4001",
        "--cluster_name=kubernetes",
        "--v=2"
      ]
    },
    {
      "name": "scheduler",
      "image": "gcr.io/google_containers/hyperkube:v0.14.1",
      "command": [
        "/hyperkube",
        "scheduler",
        "--master=127.0.0.1:8080",
        "--v=2"
      ]
    }
  ]
 }
}
```

This manifest is given to the kubelet, which starts the containers defined. In this case, it starts the API server, the scheduler, and the controller manager of Kubernetes. These three components form a Kubernetes pod themselves and will be watched over by the kubelet. Indeed, if you list the running pods, you get this:

```
$ ./kubectl get pods
POD         IP  CONTAINER(S)        IMAGE(S)
nginx-127       controller-manager  gcr.io/google_containers/hyperkube:v0.14.1
                apiserver           gcr.io/google_containers/hyperkube:v0.14.1
                scheduler           gcr.io/google_containers/hyperkube:v0.14.1
```

See Also

- Running Kubernetes locally via Docker (*http://kubernetes.io/v1.0/docs/getting-started-guides/docker.html*)

5.10 Compiling Kubernetes to Create Your Own Release

Problem

You want to build the Kubernetes binaries from source instead of downloading the released binaries.

Solution

Kubernetes is written in Go, the build system that uses Docker and builds everything in containers. You can build Kubernetes without using containers and using your local Go environment, but using containers greatly simplifies the setup. Therefore, to build the Kubernetes binaries, you need to install the Go language packages, Docker, and Git to get the source code from GitHub. For instance, on an Ubuntu 14.04 system:

```
$ sudo apt-get update
$ sudo apt-get -y install golang
$ sudo apt-get -y install git
$ sudo curl -sSL https://get.docker.com/ | sudo sh
```

Verify that you have Go and Docker installed:

```
$ go version
go version go1.2.1 linux/amd64
$ docker version
Client version: 1.6.1
Client API version: 1.18
Go version (client): go1.4.2
Git commit (client): 97cd073
OS/Arch (client): linux/amd64
Server version: 1.6.1
Server API version: 1.18
Go version (server): go1.4.2
Git commit (server): 97cd073
OS/Arch (server): linux/amd64
```

Clone the Kubernetes Git repo to get the Go source code:

```
$ git clone https://github.com/GoogleCloudPlatform/kubernetes.git
$ cd kubernetes
```

You are now ready to build the binaries. A build script, *run.sh*, is provided in the */build* directory; just use it. It will ask whether you want to download the Docker image for Golang, then start the build. Here is a snippet of a build run:

```
$ ./build/run.sh hack/build-go.sh
+++ [0513 11:51:46] Verifying Prerequisites....
You don't have a local copy of the golang docker image. This image is 450MB.
Download it now? [y/n] Y
...<snip>
+++ [0513 11:58:08] Placing binaries
+++ [0513 11:58:14] Running build command....
+++ [0513 11:58:16] Output directory is local.  No need to copy results out.
```

The binaries will be in the *_output* directory. If you built on a Linux 64-bit host, they will be in *_output/dockerized/bin/linux/amd64*:

```
~/kubernetes/_output/dockerized/bin/linux/amd64# tree
.
├── e2e
├── genbashcomp
├── gendocs
├── genman
```

```
├── ginkgo
├── hyperkube
├── integration
├── kube-apiserver
├── kube-controller-manager
├── kubectl
├── kubelet
├── kube-proxy
├── kubernetes
├── kube-scheduler
└── web-server
```

Discussion

Similarly, you can also build the complete set of release artifacts. They will be delivered as tarballs with *kubernetes.tar.gz* containing all binaries, examples, add-ons, and deployment scripts. Creating the release will take more time than simply building the binaries; all end-to-end tests will run. To build a full release, do the following and check that the */_output/release-tars/* directory contains all the tarballs:

```
$ ./build/release.sh
$ tree _output/release-tars/
_output/release-tars/
├── kubernetes-client-darwin-386.tar.gz
├── kubernetes-client-darwin-amd64.tar.gz
├── kubernetes-client-linux-386.tar.gz
├── kubernetes-client-linux-amd64.tar
├── kubernetes-client-linux-arm.tar.gz
├── kubernetes-client-windows-amd64.tar.gz
├── kubernetes-salt.tar.gz
├── kubernetes-server-linux-amd64.tar.gz
├── kubernetes.tar.gz
└── kubernetes-test.tar.gz
```

In addition to the tarballs, the release process will create three Docker images for the three main components of a Kubernetes cluster: the API server, the controller, and the scheduler:

```
# docker images
REPOSITORY                                          ...
gcr.io/google_containers/kube-controller-manager    ...
gcr.io/google_containers/kube-scheduler             ...
gcr.io/google_containers/kube-apiserver             ...
```

The release contains a Dockerfile that builds an image containing the *hyperkube* binary. This binary can be used to start all the components of a Kubernetes cluster. This is what was used in Recipe 5.9 to run Kubernetes in a single node using Docker containers. You can use this Dockerfile to build your own Hyperkube image and edit the configuration file *master.json* to your liking:

```
$ tree kubernetes/cluster/images/hyperkube/
kubernetes/cluster/images/hyperkube/
├── Dockerfile
├── Makefile
├── master.json
└── master-multi.json
```

See Also

- Building Kubernetes *README* (*http://bit.ly/build-kub*)
- Development environment using godep (*http://bit.ly/kub-godep*)

5.11 Starting Kubernetes Components with the hyperkube Binary

Problem

A Kubernetes cluster is made of a master node and several worker nodes. Each runs several Kubernetes binaries. To ease deployment, you would like to use a single binary, passing the type of component you want to start as an option to this binary.

Solution

Use *hyperkube*.

As suggested in a tip at the end of Recipe 5.10, a release contains all Kubernetes component binaries: the API server, the controller manager, the scheduler, the service proxy, and the kubelet. The last two run on each worker node, while the first three make up the Kubernetes master together with etcd. *hyperkube* is a single binary that allows you to start all these components.

Assuming you created your own release as shown in Recipe 5.10, you will find *hyperkube* in the *_output/* directory:

```
# tree ~/kubernetes/_output/release-tars/kubernetes/server/kubernetes/server/bin
/root/kubernetes/_output/release-tars/kubernetes/server/kubernetes/server/bin
├── hyperkube
├── kube-apiserver
├── kube-apiserver.docker_tag
```

```
├── kube-apiserver.tar
├── kube-controller-manager
├── kube-controller-manager.docker_tag
├── kube-controller-manager.tar
├── kubectl
├── kubelet
├── kube-proxy
├── kubernetes
├── kube-scheduler
├── kube-scheduler.docker_tag
└── kube-scheduler.tar
```

To use *hyperkube*, you need to specify which component you want to start (i.e., `api server`, `controller-manager`, `scheduler`, `kubelet`, or `proxy`). Once you specify a component, you can pass all the options that you choose. For example, to start the API server, check the *hyperkube* usage:

```
$ ./hyperkube apiserver -h
The main API entrypoint and interface to the storage system. The API server is
also the focal point for all authorization decisions.

Usage:
  apiserver [flags]

Available Flags:
      --address=127.0.0.1: DEPRECATED: see --insecure-bind-address instead
      --admission-control="AlwaysAdmit": Ordered list of plug-ins to do ...
      --admission-control-config-file="": File with admission control ...
      --allow-privileged=false: If true, allow privileged containers.
<snip>
```

5.12 Exploring the Kubernetes API

Problem

Kubernetes exposes a REST API, which you need to learn to be able to manage your Kubernetes cluster and run applications in it.

Solution

Kubernetes exposes a versioned API. With the release of the v1 API, users should expect no breaking changes when targeting that version. Several versions of the API can be served by the API server concurrently, but most users should target the v1 API.

Start a local Kubernetes cluster using Docker, as shown in Recipe 5.9. This is the easiest way to try it out. Once all components are running, you can reach the API served by the API server. If you are on the machine running the API server, you can reach it at `http://localhost:8080` without any authentication. Using `curl` gives you your first Kubernetes raw API experience. Try listing all the API versions available by calling the `http://localhost:8080/api` route like so:

```
$ curl http://localhost:8080/api
{
  "versions": [
    "v1",
  ]
}
```

As you can see here, the server exposes only the v1 API. If you see something like v1beta3, you are running an old version of Kubernetes. If you see something like v2beta1, you are running a bleeding-edge version. To verify which version of Kubernetes you are running, `curl` the `http://localhost:8080/version`. Note that the API version and binary version don't necessarily line up:

```
$ curl http://localhost:8080/version
{
  "major": "1",
  "minor": "0",
  "gitVersion": "v1.0.1",
  "gitCommit": "6a5c06e3d1eb27a6310a09270e4a5fb1afa93e74",
  "gitTreeState": "clean"
}
```

This shows you that in this example I am running the official 1.0.1 build of Kubernetes. This is quite basic and does not give a complete view of the API. Thankfully, Kubernetes uses Swagger (*http://swagger.io*) for API documentation. This means that we have a */swaggerapi/* endpoint that gives all the available API endpoints, like so:

```
$ curl http://localhost:8080/swaggerapi/
{
  "swaggerVersion": "1.2",
  "apis": [
    {
      "path": "/api/v1",
      "description": "API at /api/v1 version v1"
    },
    {
      "path": "/api",
      "description": "get available API versions"
    },
    {
      "path": "/version",
      "description": "git code version from which this is built"
    }
  ],
  "apiVersion": "",
  "info": {
    "title": "",
    "description": ""
```

```
    }
  }
```

You can then retrieve the full JSON specification of each API by using a curl command of this type:

```
$ curl http://localhost:8080/swaggerapi/api/v1
```

This might be useful if you want to write your own Kubernetes client. However, Swagger also exposes a web UI that makes exploring the API straightforward. Assuming you can reach the API server from a web browser, you can open the UI at a http://<KUBE_MASTER_IP>:8080/swagger-ui/, and should be presented with the Swagger UI as shown in Figure 5-3.

Figure 5-3. Swagger UI to explore Kubernetes API

Discussion

Exploring the API with Swagger and curl is useful to get a better understanding of Kubernetes, including the schema used for pods, replication controllers, and services. However, it is more practical to use the kubectl client that comes with every release. The usage is well documented and allows you to perform most API functions:

```
$ ./kubectl
kubectl controls the Kubernetes cluster manager.

Find more information at https://github.com/GoogleCloudPlatform/kubernetes.

Usage:
  kubectl [flags]
  kubectl [command]
```

```
Available Commands:
  get            Display one or many resources
  describe       Show details of a specific resource or group of resources
  create         Create a resource by filename or stdin
  replace        Replace a resource by filename or stdin.
  patch          Update field(s) of a resource by stdin.
  delete         Delete a resource by filename, stdin, resource and name, ...
  namespace      SUPERCEDED: Set and view the current Kubernetes namespace
  logs           Print the logs for a container in a pod.
  rolling-update Perform a rolling update of the given ReplicationController.
  scale          Set a new size for a Replication Controller.
  exec           Execute a command in a container.
  port-forward   Forward one or more local ports to a pod.
  proxy          Run a proxy to the Kubernetes API server
  run            Run a particular image on the cluster.
  stop           Gracefully shut down a resource by name or filename.
  expose         Take a replicated application and expose it as Kubernetes
                 Service
  label          Update the labels on a resource
  config         config modifies kubeconfig files
  cluster-info   Display cluster info
  api-versions   Print available API versions.
  version        Print the client and server version information.
  help           Help about any command

<snip>
```

 As you explore the Kubernetes API, you might enjoy a few interesting routes as well, like /ping/ and /validate:

```
$ curl http://localhost:8080/ping/
{
  "paths": [
    "/api",
    "/api/v1",
    "/healthz",
    "/healthz/ping",
    "/logs/",
    "/metrics",
    "/resetMetrics",
    "/swagger-ui/",
    "/swaggerapi/",
    "/ui/",
    "/version"
  ]
}
```

See Also

- General API documentation (*http://kubernetes.io/v1.0/docs/api.html*)

- Reaching the Kubernetes API (*http://kubernetes.io/v1.0/docs/admin/accessing-the-api.html*)
- Detailed API conventions (*http://kubernetes.io/v1.0/docs/devel/api-conventions.html*)

5.13 Running the Kubernetes Dashboard

Problem

You would like to gain visibility into your Kubernetes cluster in order to gain insight into the various entities that are running (including pods, services, and replication controllers).

Solution

Starting with version 0.16 of Kubernetes, a web user interface is bundled with the API server. Therefore, if you bind your API server to an address that you can access from a browser, you can access the web UI straight away at the `/static/app`.

For example, in an insecure way, you can open the UI at `http://<KUBE_MASTER_IP>:8080/static/app`. Figure 5-4 shows a screenshot.

At this time, the functionality is limited to a set of views, and you cannot manage pods, services, or replication controllers. This should change quickly.

Discussion

The Kubernetes dashboard is under heavy development by folks from Kismatic (*https://kismatic.io*), except frequent changes to the views and added functionality to manage Kubernetes components through the web UI.

The source (*https://github.com/GoogleCloudPlatform/kubernetes/tree/master/www*) contains detailed documentation on bringing up a development environment. It is possible to write your own visualizer (*https://github.com/GoogleCloudPlatform/kubernetes/blob/master/www/master/components/README.md*), referred to as a *component*.

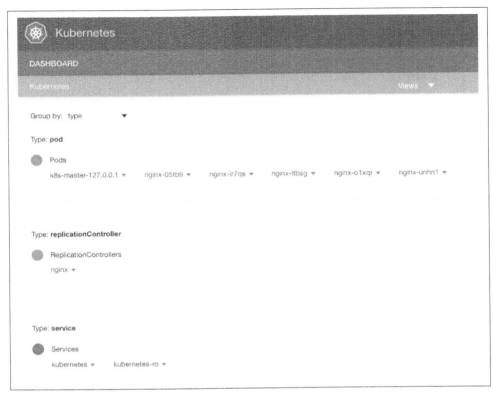

Figure 5-4. Kubernetes dashboard

5.14 Upgrading from an Old API Version

Problem

With the release of the v1 API, you may have configuration files that use an older beta version of the API. You need a tool to simplify the API version migration of all your configuration files.

Solution

This recipe is provided as a helper for developers. It may be deprecated and should not be considered for production work. This tool was used during the development of the API v1 version and may work only with older versions of the source code.

Use the `kube-version-change` Golang program. It is available in the source under the */cmd/* directory.

Assuming you followed Recipe 5.10, you are all set to build the binary for this program. If you have not built Kubernetes from source yet, do so now (see Recipe 5.10).

In the root of the Kubernetes source checked out from GitHub, do the following:

```
$ hack/build-go.sh cmd/kube-version-change
```

This uses your local Golang installation to build the `kube-version-change` program and place it into the */_output/local/bin/* directory. On a 64-bit Linux machine, it will be located precisely in *_output/dockerized/bin/linux/amd64/kube-version-change*.

Discussion

With the version change tool compiled, you are ready to migrate your configuration file to a new API version. Assuming you have a MySQL pod definition file (*mysql.yaml*), use the `v1beta2` API specification like so:

```
apiVersion: v1beta2
desiredState:
  manifest:
    containers:
      - name: mysql
        image: mysql
        env:
        - name: MYSQL_ROOT_PASSWORD
          value: password
        ports:
        - containerPort: 3306
          name: mysql
          protocol: TCP
id: mysql
kind: Pod
labels:
  name: mysql
```

Change the version to `v1`:

```
$ ./kube-version-change -i mysql.yaml -o mysql3.yaml
```

This results in a *mysql3.yaml* pod definition that uses the `v1beta3` API specification:

```
apiVersion: v1beta3
kind: Pod
metadata:
  creationTimestamp: null
  labels:
    name: mysql
  name: mysql
spec:
```

```
  containers:
  - capabilities: {}
    env:
    - name: MYSQL_ROOT_PASSWORD
      value: password
    image: mysql
    imagePullPolicy: IfNotPresent
    name: mysql
    ports:
    - containerPort: 3306
      name: mysql
      protocol: TCP
    resources: {}
    securityContext:
      capabilities: {}
      privileged: false
    terminationMessagePath: /dev/termination-log
  dnsPolicy: ClusterFirst
  restartPolicy: Always
  serviceAccount: ""
  volumes: null
status: {}
```

> You can also migrate from v1beta3 to previous API versions. This
> might be handy to explore the specification. Try this:
>
> ```
> $ ./kube-version-change -i mysql3.yaml -o mysql2.yaml -v v1beta2
> ```

5.15 Configuring Authentication to a Kubernetes Cluster

Problem

You want to set up a Kubernetes cluster with forms of authentication and authorization. This will allow users of the cluster to manage their resources via a Kubernetes client (e.g., kubectl) in a secure manner.

Solution

Start the API server with one of the following options: --token_auth_file, --basic_auth_file, or --client_ca_file. You also need to make sure that you are not binding the API server to an insecure and public IP address.

By default, Kubernetes will serve the API over HTTPS on port 6443 using a self-signed certificate. You can specify your own certificate with the --tls-cert-file and --tls-private-key-file options.

For testing and learning purposes, you might decide to start the API server with the option `--insecure-bind-address=0.0.0.0`, which will bind the so-called *localhost port* to all your network interfaces, including the public IP address of your Kubernetes master node. This is handy, as you can reach your cluster at `http://<KUBE_MASTER_IP>:8080` unauthenticated, but it will be totally insecure.

By default, Kubernetes will expose read-only access on port 7080 on all interfaces. If your firewall opens 7080 to the world, you will offer an unauthenticated view to your cluster. However, this should change prior to Kubernetes v1.0.

Discussion

The format used for the basic authentication and the token-based authentication are straightforward CSV files. The documentation (*https://github.com/GoogleCloudPlat form/kubernetes/blob/master/docs/authentication.md*) also points to the code (*http://bit.ly/kub-auth*). Keeping an eye on these authentication plug-ins will prove useful as authentication mechanisms get deprecated and changes occur. Currently features like expiration of tokens and password reset are not implemented.

For example, create the following file for basic authentication in */tmp/auth*. It follows the convention `password,username,useruid`:

```
foobar,admin,1000
```

Start your API server by using hyperkube (see Recipe 5.11) and the following options:

```
$ hyperkube apiserver --portal_net=10.0.0.1/24
                      --etcd_servers=http://127.0.0.1:4001
                      --cluster_name=kubernetes
                      --basic_auth_file=/tmp/auth
                      --v=2
```

The default options will be used. HTTPS will be served on port 6443, read-only access will be available on port 7080, and the localhost port will bind only to localhost. If you do not open your firewall for port 7080, your Kubernetes cluster will be available only over HTTPS with basic authentication.

Basic authentication will be deprecated in favor of token- and client-based authentication mechanisms. This is available currently as a convenience. The read-only access will also be removed in a future release.

See Also

- Secure access to the API server (*https://github.com/GoogleCloudPlatform/kubernetes/blob/master/docs/accessing_the_api.md*)

- Accessing a cluster (*https://github.com/GoogleCloudPlatform/kubernetes/blob/master/docs/accessing-the-cluster.md*)

- Authentication plug-ins (*https://github.com/GoogleCloudPlatform/kubernetes/blob/master/docs/authentication.md*)

- Authorization roadmap (*https://github.com/GoogleCloudPlatform/kubernetes/blob/master/docs/authorization.md*)

5.16 Configuring the Kubernetes Client to Access Remote Clusters

Problem

You are exposing the API server securely by using an authentication mechanism and you would like your users to access the cluster remotely by using one of the clients (e.g., kubectl).

Solution

Use kubectl configuration to create multiple contexts for accessing your clusters. In each context, specify the cluster API endpoint and the user credentials.

Indeed, kubectl by default communicates with an API server on localhost. But you can define multiple endpoints (useful if using multiple clusters in different regions, for instance) and multiple user profiles (e.g., production, development, service) that may have different authorization policies. The first time you install kubectl, your configuration will be empty. Run kubectl config view to verify it as shown here:

```
$ ./kubectl config view
apiVersion: v1
clusters: []
contexts: []
current-context: ""
kind: Config
preferences: {}
users: []
```

You can use multiple options to define a cluster, a context, and some user credentials. The following is an example of setting up a cluster named k, defined by an HTTPS endpoint with a self-signed certificate; a context kcon is created that uses cluster k and user `superfoobar`. The `superadmin` user has a set of credentials that were set up in Recipe 5.15. At the end of the example, you set the current context: `use-context`. This has the intended results that you can use `kubectl` and that it will properly form the HTTP request and access the remote Kubernetes cluster securely and authenticated:

```
$ ./kubectl config set-cluster k --server=https://<KUBE_MASTER_PUBLIC_IP>:6443 \
                                  --insecure-skip-tls-verify=true
$ ./kubectl config set-context kcon --user=superadmin
$ ./kubectl config set-context kcon --cluster=k
$ ./kubectl config set-credentials superadmin --username=admin --password=foobar
$ ./kubectl config use-context kcon
```

Discussion

Although the `kubectl` client is powerful, remember that you could write your own client because the requests are standard HTTP requests. For example, you can use `curl` to make an authenticated request:

```
$ curl -k -u toto:foobar https://<KUBE_MASTER_PUBLIC_IP>:6443/api
{
  "versions": [
    "v1"
  ]
}
```

See Also

- Kubernetes client libraries (*https://github.com/GoogleCloudPlatform/kubernetes/ blob/master/docs/client-libraries.md*)

## CHAPTER 6

Optimized Operating System Distributions for Docker

6.0 Introduction

In the first chapter we covered several installation scenarios. They showed how to install Docker on traditional operating systems. In this chapter we present a new generation of operating systems (OSes) that are optimized for Docker. These new OSes consider two new trends. First, they consider that everything running in a server will be a container. Second, they try to implement an atomic upgrade mechanism to simplify operation and maintenance of servers in the data center. This means that these new operating systems do not feature a traditional package manager like yum or apt, but instead they assume that you will get your application running in the machine by pulling a Docker image and running a container. These OSes provide just the minimum required to run containers.

The first operation system presented is CoreOS (see Recipe 6.1). CoreOS is available on several public cloud providers. It can be installed on bare-metal and can be tested locally via Vagrant or by building your own ISO. In Recipe 6.2 we show how to configure a CoreOS instance, in Recipe 6.3 we present how to create a cluster of CoreOS machines, and in Recipe 6.4 we see how we can use the native system-based scheduler to launch containers on a CoreOS cluster. We then have a look a Flannel, a network overlay technique that comes bundled in CoreOS. Flannel, as we mentioned in the networking chapter, provides you with a networking solution so that your containers can communicate on a private IP space across multiple hosts.

We then cover three other Docker-optimized OSes. RedHat Atomic is introduced in Recipe 6.6, and Recipe 6.7 shows you how to start an Atomic instance on AWS. Ubuntu Snappy is presented in Recipe 6.8, while Recipe 6.9 shows how to start an

Ubuntu instance on AWS. Showing examples on AWS gives you the option of trying these new OSes on your local machine or in the cloud. Finally, we present RancherOS in Recipe 6.10, which has the unique characteristics of also running system services as containers.

In summary, this chapter gives you some alternatives to running Docker in traditional operating systems and presents a few solutions where everything that runs on the machine is a container. You should also note that there are other choices, like VMware Photon (*https://vmware.github.io/photon/*), and that different approaches which leverage traditional virtualization technologies also exist, like the Clear Linux project (*https://clearlinux.org*) and and hyper.sh (*https://hyper.sh*).

CoreOS is a new Linux distribution available on several public cloud providers. It is part of a new movement that aims to build operating systems that provide just the minimum required to run applications within containers. Philosophically, it tries to simplify operation of the infrastructure, through a scalable, easily manageable OS that provides a clear separation of concerns between operations and applications.

6.1 Discovering the CoreOS Linux Distribution with Vagrant

Problem

You want to use the CoreOS Linux distribution to run your Docker containers, but first you want to try CoreOS on your local machine.

Solution

Use Vagrant (*http://vagrantup.com*) to start a virtual machine in VirtualBox that will use CoreOS. Official documentation that describes the entire process is available (*https://coreos.com/docs/running-coreos/platforms/vagrant/*). This recipe is a summary of this documenation.

To run your first CoreOS virtual machine via Vagrant, you start by cloning a Git repository (*https://github.com/coreos/coreos-vagrant.git*) and then use `vagrant up`. You will be able to `ssh` to the started instance and use Docker:

```
$ git clone https://github.com/coreos/coreos-vagrant.git
$ cd coreos-vagrant/
$ tree
.
├── CONTRIBUTING.md
├── MAINTAINERS
├── README.md
├── Vagrantfile
├── config.rb.sample
```

```
└── user-data.sample

0 directories, 6 files
$ vagrant up
$ vagrant ssh
Last login: Mon Jan 12 10:39:30 2015 from 10.0.2.2
CoreOS alpha (557.0.0)
core@core-01 ~ $ docker ps
CONTAINER ID    IMAGE    COMMAND    CREATED    STATUS    PORTS    NAMES
```

CoreOS uses `systemd` (*http://www.freedesktop.org/wiki/Software/systemd/*) as a Linux init system and aims to be a minimal distribution with rolling upgrades that can be easily rolled back. Core packages should be installed in the distribution directly, and applications should be fully contained in containers. As such, there is no package manager in CoreOS. All services running in a CoreOS instance are running as `sys temd` unit files, and you can interact (*https://coreos.com/docs/launching-containers/launching/getting-started-with-systemd*) with them using commands like `systemctl` or `journalctl`:

```
$ systemctl list-units | grep docker |awk {'print $1'}
sys-devices-virtual-net-docker0.device
sys-subsystem-net-devices-docker0.device
var-lib-docker-btrfs.mount
docker.service
docker.socket
early-docker.target

$ journalctl -u docker.service
-- Logs begin at Mon 2015-01-12 10:39:15 UTC, ... --
Jan 12 10:39:34 core-01 systemd[1]: Starting Docker ...
Jan 12 10:39:34 core-01 systemd[1]: Started Docker ...
Jan 12 10:39:34 core-01 dockerd[876]: ... msg="+job serveapi(fd://)"
Jan 12 10:39:34 core-01 dockerd[876]: ... msg="+job init_networkdriver()"
Jan 12 10:39:34 core-01 dockerd[876]: ... msg="Listening for HTTP on fd ()"
Jan 12 10:39:34 core-01 dockerd[876]: ... msg="-job init_networkdriver() = OK (0)"
Jan 12 10:39:34 core-01 dockerd[876]: ... msg="Loading containers: start."
Jan 12 10:39:34 core-01 dockerd[876]: ... msg="Loading containers: done."
Jan 12 10:39:34 core-01 dockerd[876]: ... msg="docker daemon: 1.4.1 ..."
Jan 12 10:39:34 core-01 dockerd[876]: ... msg="+job acceptconnections()"
Jan 12 10:39:34 core-01 dockerd[876]: ... msg="-job acceptconnections() = OK (0)"
Jan 12 10:39:34 core-01 dockerd[876]: ... msg="GET /v1.16/containers/json"
Jan 12 10:39:34 core-01 dockerd[876]: ... msg="+job containers()"
Jan 12 10:39:34 core-01 dockerd[876]: ... msg="-job containers() = OK (0)"
```

Discussion

Although you can start a single instance of CoreOS via Vagrant by cloning the Git repository and using `vagrant up`, you will notice two files, *config.rb.sample* and *user-data.sample*. These files allow you to configure a cluster of CoreOS instances (see

Recipe 6.3) and set up services at boot time. They are read by Vagrant in the Vagrant-file:

```
CLOUD_CONFIG_PATH = File.join(File.dirname(__FILE__), "user-data")
CONFIG = File.join(File.dirname(__FILE__), "config.rb")
```

For example, to allow you to connect remotely to the Docker service running in the CoreOS instance started, copy *config.rb.sample* to *config.rb* and copy *user-data.sample* to *user-data*. Then edit *config.rb* to uncomment the $expose_docker_tcp=2375 line:

```
$ cp config.rb.sample config.rb
$ cp user-data.sample user-data
$ tree
.
├── CONTRIBUTING.md
├── MAINTAINERS
├── README.md
├── Vagrantfile
├── config.rb
├── config.rb.sample
├── user-data
└── user-data.sample

0 directories, 8 files
$ vi config.rb #uncomment $expose_docker_tcp=2375
$ vagrant up
```

 If you still have the CoreOS instance running from the instructions in the solution section of this recipe, provision the instance again with the vagrant reload --provision command or destroy it with vagrant destroy and bring it back up again with vagrant up.

Vagrant, which configures a NAT and a host-only interface for the CoreOS instance, will forward port 2375 on the NAT interface, which will allow you to access Docker on your localhost:

```
$ docker -H tcp://127.0.0.1:2375 ps
CONTAINER ID    IMAGE    COMMAND    CREATED    STATUS    PORTS    NAMES
```

See Also

- CoreOS documentation (*https://coreos.com/docs/*)

Discussion of Docker containers versus the CoreOS-specific Rocket (*https://coreos.com/blog/rocket/*) is beyond the scope of this cookbook. Rocket is an implementation of the App Container specification (*https://github.com/appc/spec/blob/master/SPEC.md*) proposed by CoreOS. Recipe 4.6 discusses the effort of the Open Container Initiative, which brings these two container formats together.

6.2 Starting a Container on CoreOS via cloud-init

Problem

Knowing how to start a CoreOS instance via Vagrant, you would like to use `cloud-init` (*https://cloudinit.readthedocs.org/en/latest/*) to start a container at boot time.

Solution

You know how to start a CoreOS instance via Vagrant (see Recipe 6.1). You now need to add a `systemd` unit within the *user-data* file. CoreOS will automatically launch this unit during the boot process.

Create a new *user-data* file that contains only the following:

```
#cloud-config

coreos:
  units:
    - name: es.service
      command: start
      content: |
        [Unit]
        After=docker.service
        Requires=docker.service
        Description=starts Elastic Search container

        [Service]
        TimeoutStartSec=0
        ExecStartPre=/usr/bin/docker pull dockerfile/elasticsearch
        ExecStart=/usr/bin/docker run -d -p 9200:9200 -p 9300:9300 \
              dockerfile/elasticsearch
```

If you still have a CoreOS instance running from Recipe 6.1, destroy it with `vagrant destroy` and bring up a new one with `vagrant up`.

The `docker.service` unit starts automatically in CoreOS, so there is no need to specify it in the *user-data* file.

The virtual machine will boot quickly and start the es.service defined in the cloud config file. Docker will start by pulling the *dockerfile/elasticsearch* image. This could take some time, so be patient and monitor the download via docker images. Once the image is downloaded, the container will get started (see the ExecStart command in the *user-data* file):

```
$ docker ps
CONTAINER ID    IMAGE                        COMMAND                ...
fa9ff4f2234c    dockerfile/elasticsearch:latest "/elasticsearch/bin/  ...
```

Find the IP address of the virtual machine on the host-only interface (i.e., eth1) and open your browser or curl at that address on port 9200:

```
$ curl -s http://172.17.8.101:9200 | python -m json.tool
{
    "cluster_name": "elasticsearch",
    "name": "Wyatt Wingfoot",
    "status": 200,
    "tagline": "You Know, for Search",
    "version": {
        "build_hash": "89d3241d670db65f994242c8e8383b169779e2d4",
        "build_snapshot": false,
        "build_timestamp": "2014-10-26T15:49:29Z",
        "lucene_version": "4.10.2",
        "number": "1.4.1"
    }
}
```

Congratulations—you are running one Elasticsearch (*http://www.elasticsearch.com*) container on a CoreOS instance, specifying it as a systemd unit file via cloud-init.

Discussion

The *user-data* file present in the coreos-vagrant repository is used by CoreOS to configure the instance using the CoreOS version of cloud-init (*https://cloudinit.read thedocs.org/en/latest/*). cloud-init is used by most public cloud providers and supported by most infrastructure as a service software solution to contextualize the virtual machine instances started in the cloud at boot time. The interesting part in this recipe is that a container is defined as a systemd unit file and started on boot. CoreOS has some official documentation (*https://coreos.com/docs/launching-containers/launch ing/getting-started-with-systemd/*) about this.

 CoreOS has its own implementation of cloud-init (*http://bit.ly/ cloud-init*). Some cloud-init operations may not be supported, and others are valid for only CoreOS (e.g., fleet, etcd, flannel).

6.3 Starting a CoreOS Cluster via Vagrant to Run Containers on Multiple Hosts

Problem

You want to become familiar with some of the CoreOS features and add-ons (e.g., etcd, fleet) to manage a cluster of Docker hosts.

Solution

If you have not done so already, clone the CoreOS Vagrant project from GitHub and set the configuration files:

```
$ git clone https://github.com/coreos/coreos-vagrant.git
$ cd coreos-vagrant/
$ cp config.rb.sample config.rb
$ cp user-data.sample user-data
```

You will use the same Vagrantfile as in Recipe 6.1 but specify the number of instances you want in your cluster in the *config.rb* file. This cluster will be made of a set of CoreOS instances started by Vagrant in VirtualBox or potentially VMware Fusion.

In Recipe 6.2, you saw how to modify the user data to run a container at boot time. In Recipe 6.1, you modified the *config.rb* file to expose port 2375 and access the Docker daemon remotely. To bootstrap a CoreOS cluster with Vagrant, you need to edit the *config.rb* file to specify the number of instances in the cluster. For example, $num_instances=4 will start four CoreOS instances.

In addition, at the top of the *config.rb* file you will see some Ruby code that edits the *user-data* file to set a discovery key in this YAML file. This uses a discovery service run by the CoreOS team to help you run etcd on your cluster instances. etcd (*https:// github.com/coreos/etcd*) is a highly available key-value store for shared configuration and discovery that can be used in conjunction with CoreOS. It is similar to other service-discovery solutions like Apache ZooKeeper (*http://zookeeper.apache.org*) or Consul (*https://consul.io*). You could run etcd on a different machine, but in this recipe you will take advantage of the Vagrantfile definition to run it in a multimachine configuration on the cluster nodes that you will start. etcd will allow the Docker hosts to discover themselves and help scheduling of the containers.

 Discussion on etcd is outside the scope of this cookbook. CoreOS provides a convenient etcd-based discovery (*https://coreos.com/ docs/cluster-management/setup/cluster-discovery*) service to help with bootstrapping your CoreOS cluster. This is used in this Vagrant setup but is not recommended in production.

In the *config.rb* file, uncomment the beginning of the script and set your number of instances so that it looks like this:

```
if File.exists?('user-data') && ARGV[0].eql?('up')
  require 'open-uri'
  require 'yaml'

  token = open('https://discovery.etcd.io/new').read

  data = YAML.load(IO.readlines('user-data')[1..-1].join)
  data['coreos']['etcd']['discovery'] = token

  yaml = YAML.dump(data)
  File.open('user-data', 'w') { |file| file.write("#cloud-config\n\n#{yaml}") }
end
...
$num_instances=4
```

 If you have followed Recipe 6.1 and Recipe 6.2, destroy any existing CoreOS instances before booting your cluster with vagrant destroy.

With your number of instances set to four, make sure you have copied the original *user-data.sample* to a *user-data* file and then simply vagrant up and wait for the provisioning to finish. You can then ssh to one of the nodes and use a new tool, fleet, to list the machines that have joined the cluster:

```
$ cp user-data.sample user-data
$ vagrant up
$ vagrant status
Current machine states:

core-01                    running (virtualbox)
core-02                    running (virtualbox)
core-03                    running (virtualbox)
core-04                    running (virtualbox)
$ vagrant ssh core-01
CoreOS (stable)
core@core-01 ~ $ fleetctl list-machines
MACHINE    IP     METADATA
01efec94... 172.17.8.102  -
3602cd04... 172.17.8.104  -
cd3de202... 172.17.8.103  -
e4c0e706... 172.17.8.101  -
```

Discussion

The `etcd` discovery service provided by CoreOS is used to boostrap the cluster (i.e., defining a leader). In the *user-data* file, you can now see a line that defines the `discovery` key and contains a token (your token will be different than the one listed here):

```
discovery: https://discovery.etcd.io/61297b379e5024f33b57bd7e7225d7d7
```

If you curl this URL (curl -s https://discovery.etcd.io/ 61297b379e5024f33b57bd7e7225d7d7 | python -m json.tool), you will see the IPs of the nodes in your cluster. Anyone who obtains access to your token could obtain a list of your cluster nodes and try to add one of his nodes in your cluster, so handle with care:

```
{
    "action": "get",
    "node": {
        "createdIndex": 279743993,
        "dir": true,
        "key": "/_etcd/registry/61297b379e5024f33b57bd7e7225d7d7",
        "modifiedIndex": 279743993,
        "nodes": [
            {
                "createdIndex": 279744808,
                "expiration": "2015-01-19T17:50:15.797821504Z",
                "key": "/_etcd/registry/61297b379e5024f33b57bd7.../e4c0...",
                "modifiedIndex": 279744808,
                "ttl": 599113,
                "value": "http://172.17.8.101:7001"
            },
            {
                "createdIndex": 279745601,
                "expiration": "2015-01-19T17:59:49.196184481Z",
                "key": "/_etcd/registry/61297b379e5024f33b57bd7.../01ef...",
                "modifiedIndex": 279745601,
                "ttl": 599687,
                "value": "http://172.17.8.102:7001"
            },
            {
                "createdIndex": 279746380,
                "expiration": "2015-01-19T17:51:41.963086657Z",
                "key": "/_etcd/registry/61297b379e5024f33b57bd7.../cd3d...",
                "modifiedIndex": 279746380,
                "ttl": 599199,
                "value": "http://172.17.8.103:7001"
            },
            {
                "createdIndex": 279747319,
                "expiration": "2015-01-19T17:52:33.315082679Z",
                "key": "/_etcd/registry/61297b379e5024f33b57bd7.../3602...",
                "modifiedIndex": 279747319,
```

```
                "ttl": 599251,
                "value": "http://172.17.8.104:7001"
            }
        ]
    }
}
```

Your nodes have now formed an etcd cluster that can be used as a fully working highly available key-value store. Using the `etcdctl` command, you can set and get keys:

```
core@core-01 ~ $ etcdctl set foobar "Docker"
Docker
core@core-01 ~ $ etcdctl get foobar
Docker
core@core-01 ~ $ etcdctl ls
/foobar
/coreos.com
```

To launch containers on the cluster, you can define `systemd` units as you did in Recipe 6.2 and start them with the `fleetctl` CLI (see Recipe 6.4).

See Also

- CoreOS clustering with Vagrant (*https://coreos.com/blog/coreos-clustering-with-vagrant/*)

- Introduction to `etcd` (*https://coreos.com/docs/distributed-configuration/getting-started-with-etcd/*)

- Getting started with `fleet` (*https://coreos.com/docs/launching-containers/launching/launching-containers-fleet/*)

6.4 Using fleet to Start Containers on a CoreOS Cluster

Problem

You have a working CoreOS cluster and would like to start containers on it.

Solution

With a CoreOS cluster in hand (see Recipe 6.3), use the `fleetctl` CLI to start your containers. You write `systemd` units describing those running containers and use `fleetctl start` to schedule them on the cluster.

For example, consider how you started a container via `cloud-init` in Recipe 6.2. You can extract the following `systemd` unit to start an Elasticsearch container on a cluster (let's call it `es.service`):

```
[Unit]
After=docker.service
Requires=docker.service
Description=starts Elastic Search container

[Service]
TimeoutStartSec=0
ExecStartPre=-/usr/bin/docker kill es
ExecStartPre=-/usr/bin/docker rm es
ExecStartPre=/usr/bin/docker pull dockerfile/elasticsearch
ExecStart=/usr/bin/docker run --name es -p 9200:9200 \
                                         -p 9300:9300 \
                                         dockerfile/elasticsearch

ExecStop=/usr/bin/docker stop es
```

Start this container with `fleetctl`:

```
$ vagrant ssh core-01
$ fleetctl start es.service
$ fleetctl list-units
UNIT     MACHINE        ACTIVE      SUB
es.service  01efec94.../172.17.8.102  activating  start-pre
$ fleetctl list-units
UNIT     MACHINE        ACTIVE  SUB
es.service  01efec94.../172.17.8.102  active  running
```

`fleet` will schedule the unit on one of the nodes in your cluster. `systemd` will run the `es.service` unit, which will start by downloading the image. Once the image is downloaded, it will run the container defined in the `ExecStart` step of the unit file.

Discussion

The `fleet` CLI `fleetctl` comes with some nice commands to check the journal of the unit, destroy it, and `ssh` to the nodes that have been tasked with running the unit. These commands can come in handy during debugging steps:

```
$ fleetctl list-units
UNIT     MACHINE        ACTIVE  SUB
es.service  01efec94.../172.17.8.102  active  running
$ fleetctl ssh es.service
Last login: Mon Jan 12 22:03:29 2015 from 172.17.8.101
CoreOS (stable)
core@core-02 ~ $ docker ps
CONTAINER ID    IMAGE                          COMMAND         ...
6fc661ba2153    dockerfile/elasticsearch:latest  "/elasticsearch/bin/ ...
core@core-02 ~ $ exit
$ fleetctl journal es.service
```

```
-- Logs begin at Mon 2015-01-12 17:50:47 UTC, end at Mon 2015-01-12 22:13:20 UTC
Jan 12 22:06:13 core-02 ...[node          ] [Wendigo] initializing ...
Jan 12 22:06:13 core-02 ...[plugins       ] [Wendigo] loaded [], sites []
Jan 12 22:06:17 core-02 ...[node          ] [Wendigo] initialized
Jan 12 22:06:17 core-02 ...[node          ] [Wendigo] starting ...
Jan 12 22:06:17 core-02 ...[transport      ] [Wendigo] bound_address ...
Jan 12 22:06:17 core-02 ... discovery      ] [Wendigo] elasticsearch/_NcgQa...
Jan 12 22:06:21 core-02 ...[cluster.service ] [Wendigo] new_master [Wendigo]...
Jan 12 22:06:21 core-02 ...[http          ] [Wendigo] bound_address ...
Jan 12 22:06:21 core-02 ...[node          ] [Wendigo] started
Jan 12 22:06:21 core-02 ...[gateway       ] [Wendigo] recovered [0] ...
```

See Also

- Launching containers with `fleet` (*https://coreos.com/docs/launching-containers/launching/launching-containers-fleet/*)

6.5 Deploying a flannel Overlay Between CoreOS Instances

Contributed by Eugene Yakubovich

Problem

You have a CoreOS cluster and would like Docker containers to communicate using overlay networking instead of port forwarding.

Solution

Set up `flannel` on all of the CoreOS instances. Include the following snippet in your *cloud-config* as part of CoreOS provisioning:

```
#cloud-config

coreos:
  units:
    - name: flanneld.service
      drop-ins:
        - name: 50-network-config.conf
          content: |
            [Service]
            ExecStartPre=/usr/bin/etcdctl set \
              /coreos.com/network/config \
              '{ "Network": "10.1.0.0/16" }'
      command: start
```

Make sure to pick an IP address range that is unused by your organization. `flannel` uses `etcd` for coordination. Be sure that you also follow the recipe to set up an `etcd` cluster.

Make sure your security policy allows traffic on UDP port 8285. Start three CoreOS instances and wait for `flannel` to initialize. You can use the `ifconfig` utility to check that the `flannel0` interface is up:

```
$ ifconfig

flannel0: flags=81<UP,POINTOPOINT,RUNNING>  mtu 1472
        inet 10.1.77.0  netmask 255.255.0.0  destination 10.1.77.0
        unspec 00-00-00-00-00-00-00-00-00-00-00-00-00-00-00-00  txqueuelen ...
        RX packets 0  bytes 0 (0.0 B)
        RX errors 0  dropped 0  overruns 0  frame 0
        TX packets 0  bytes 0 (0.0 B)
        TX errors 0  dropped 0 overruns 0  carrier 0  collisions 0
```

Next, run a container to print out its IP address and listen on TCP port 8000:

```
$ docker run -it --rm busybox /bin/sh -c \
    "ifconfig eth0 && nc -l -p 8000"
eth0      Link encap:Ethernet  HWaddr 02:42:0A:01:4D:03
          inet addr:10.1.77.3  Bcast:0.0.0.0  Mask:255.255.255.0
          UP BROADCAST  MTU:1472  Metric:1
          RX packets:3 errors:0 dropped:0 overruns:0 frame:0
          TX packets:1 errors:0 dropped:0 overruns:0 carrier:0
          collisions:0 txqueuelen:0
          RX bytes:234 (234.0 B)  TX bytes:90 (90.0 B)
```

Take note of the IP address reported by `ifconfig`. Other containers that are part of the `flannel` network can use this IP to reach this container. On a different host, run a container to send a string to the listener:

```
$ docker run -it --rm busybox /bin/sh -c \
    "echo Hello, container | nc 10.1.77.3 8000"
```

The first container will print out "Hello, container" and exit.

When you add more items to the `units` section of *cloud-config*, be sure that any services that start Docker containers are listed after `flanneld.service`. Since units are processed in order, this will ensure that `flannel` is ready prior to containers starting.

Discussion

`flannel`'s configuration is stored in `etcd` (*/coreos.com/network/config*) and needs to be set prior to `flanneld` starting. The easiest way to ensure this is by using the Exe cStartPre directive in the `flanneld.service` via a `systemd` drop-in. As illustrated previously, it can be written out to disk via *cloud-config.*

For real-world cases, an automatic method is needed to distribute the IP information of the server container. When creating a unit file for your service, you can utilize `etcd` to register the IP of the server for clients to query:

```
[Service]
ExecStartPre=/usr/bin/docker create --name=netcat-server busybox \
/usr/bin/nc -l -p 8000
ExecStart=/usr/bin/docker start -a netcat-server
ExecStartPost=/bin/bash -c 'etcdctl set /services/netcat-server \
$(docker inspect --format="{{.NetworkSettings.IPAddress}}" netcat-server)'

ExecStop=/usr/bin/docker stop netcat-server
ExecStopPost=/usr/bin/docker rm netcat-server
```

An alternative to the `ExecStartPost` entry is to create a separate sidekick unit (*http://bit.ly/fleetunit*). You can also use the SkyDNS (*https://github.com/skynetservices/skydns*) project to expose a DNS interface for the clients.

With the default configuration, `flannel` uses a TUN device to send packets to user space for UDP encapsulation. It is a robust solution, as the TUN device has been part of the Linux kernel for many years. However, the cost of moving every packet in and out of the `flannel` daemon can have significant impact on performance. Modern Linux kernels have support for a new type of encapsulation called VXLAN. VXLAN also wraps packets in network-friendly UDP but with the advantage of performing this task in the kernel. CoreOS always ships the latest kernel, making it a great candidate for taking advantage of VXLAN. Enabling VXLAN is as easy as selecting a different backend in the `flannel` config:

```
ExecStartPre=/usr/bin/etcdctl set /coreos.com/network/config \
    '{ "Network": "10.1.0.0/16", "Backend": { "Type": "vxlan" } }'
```

When running in nonsecure environments, it is best to use TLS for `flannel`-to-`etcd` communication. TLS client certificates can be used to restrict access to `etcd`. See `etcd` and `flannel` documentation for details.

6.6 Using Project Atomic to Run Docker Containers

Problem

You are looking for an operating system alternative to CoreOS, Ubuntu, Snappy, and RancherOS.

Solution

Use Project Atomic (*http://www.projectatomic.io*). Atomic is sponsored by Red Hat and inspired by the RHEL and CentOS distribution. It is based on CentOS 7, and like CoreOS, Ubuntu, Snappy, and RancherOS, it is aimed at providing a Docker-optimized Linux distribution, where applications are deployed as containers. Atomic upgrades are done through a system called `rpm-ostree` (*http://www.projectatomic.io/docs/os-updates/*). Once an upgrade is available, a reboot installs the new upgrade, which can also be rolled back.

You can try Atomic by using the CentOS builds (*http://buildlogs.centos.org/rolling/7/isos/x86_64/*). You have the choice of downloading an ISO, a *qcow2* image for use in a kernel-based virtual machine (KVM), or a Vagrant box. (The Vagrant box for Virtual-Box may not be the latest Atomic build and will require an upgrade.)

As usual in this book, to make things easy, I prepared a Vagrantfile for you:

```
$bootstrap=<<SCRIPT
gpasswd -a vagrant root
SCRIPT

# Vagrantfile API/syntax version. Don't touch unless you know what you're doing!
VAGRANTFILE_API_VERSION = "2"

Vagrant.configure(VAGRANTFILE_API_VERSION) do |config|
  # Every Vagrant virtual environment requires a box to build off of.
  config.vm.box = "atomic"
  config.vm.box_url = "http://buildlogs.centos.org/rolling/7/isos/x86_64/\
                      CentOS-7-x86_64-AtomicHost-Vagrant-VirtualBox.box"

  config.vm.provider "virtualbox" do |vb, override|
     vb.customize ["modifyvm", :id, "--memory", "2048"]
  end

  config.vm.network :forwarded_port, host: 9090, guest: 9090
  config.vm.provision :shell, inline: $bootstrap

end
```

With Vagrant (*http://vagrantup.com*) installed, you can just `vagrant up` and you will be able to `ssh` into an atomic host. Clone the repository that comes with this book and you will have the preceding Vagrantfile:

```
$ git clone https://github.com/how2dock/docbook
$ cd dockbook/ch06/atomic
$ vagrant up
$ vagrant ssh
```

Once on the Atomic machine, you will have Docker already installed. You can explore the host with the `atomic` command and perform an upgrade with `sudo atomic host upgrade`.

See Also

- The project Atomic documentation (*http://www.projectatomic.io/docs/*)

6.7 Starting an Atomic Instance on AWS to Use Docker

Problem

You do not want to use Vagrant to try Atomic (see Recipe 6.6) and do not want to use an ISO image either.

Solution

Start an Atomic instance on Amazon EC2. Atomic AMIs are available on AWS EC2. You can open your AWS management console and go through the instance launch wizard. Search for a community AMI named *atomic*; several AMIs are available, most based on the Fedora 22 release. After having created an SSH key pair, you can launch the instance, and once it is running, you can connect to it. As an example, here you connect to an Atomic instance with IP address 52.18.234.151. You will have access to Docker right away:

```
$ ssh -i ~/.ssh/<SSH_PRIVATE_KEY> fedora@52.18.234.151
[fedora@ip-172-31-46-186 ~]$ sudo docker ps
CONTAINER ID    IMAGE        COMMAND      CREATED      STATUS      PORTS      NAMES
[fedora@ip-172-31-46-186 ~]$ sudo docker version | version
Client version: 1.5.0-dev
...
Server version: 1.5.0-dev
```

Such an instance comes with the `atomic` command, which you can use to upgrade the host. Check the instance status and launch an upgrade. It will download the new Atomic version. You will then need to reboot to get on the new version:

```
[fedora@ip-172-31-46-186 ~]$ atomic host status
    TIMESTAMP (UTC)       VERSION    ID          OSNAME          REFSPEC
* 2015-05-12 18:53:06   22.66      cd414cba85  fedora-atomic  fedora-atomic:...
[fedora@ip-172-31-46-186 ~]$ atomic host upgrade
```

```
Updating from: fedora-atomic:fedora-atomic/f22/x86_64/docker-host
[fedora@ip-172-31-46-186 ~]$ sudo systemctl reboot
```

After reboot, you will see that your host has automatically upgraded to a new version of Docker, which ships in the latest version of Atomic:

```
[fedora@ip-172-31-46-186 ~]$ sudo docker version
Client version: 1.7.1.fc22
...
Server version: 1.7.1.fc22
...
```

Discussion

To start an instance, you can use the AWS command-line tools or use the script provided in this recipe. The script has the advantage of being based on Apache Libcloud and can be easily adapted to other cloud providers that may provide an Atomic template:

```python
#!/usr/bin/env python

import os
from libcloud.compute.types import Provider
from libcloud.compute.providers import get_driver

ACCESS_ID = os.getenv('AWSAccessKeyId')
SECRET_KEY = os.getenv('AWSSecretKey')

IMAGE_ID = 'ami-dd3fb0aa'
SIZE_ID = 'm3.medium'

cls = get_driver(Provider.EC2_EU_WEST)
driver = cls(ACCESS_ID, SECRET_KEY)

sizes = driver.list_sizes()
images = driver.list_images()
size = [s for s in sizes if s.id == SIZE_ID][0]
image = [i for i in images if i.id == IMAGE_ID][0]

# Reads cloud config file
userdata = "\n".join(open('./cloud.cfg').readlines())

# Replace the name of the ssh key pair with yours
# You will need to open SSH port 22 on your default security group
# This also assumes a keypair named 'atomic'
name = "atomic"
node = driver.create_node(name=name, image=image,size=size,ex_keyname='atomic', \
                          ex_userdata=userdata)
snap, ip = driver.wait_until_running(nodes=[node])[0]
print ip[0]
```

As mentioned as comments in the script, you will need to have a security group with port 22 open, an SSH key pair called *atomic*, and a *cloud.cfg* file that contains your user data.

6.8 Running Docker on Ubuntu Core Snappy in a Snap

Problem

You would like to take the new Ubuntu Core Snappy for a test drive. You do not want to mess with connecting to a public cloud, do not want to install an ISO by hand, and want to avoid reading as much documentation as possible. You want Snappy in a snap.

Solution

I provide a Vagrantfile for starting an Ubuntu Core Snappy virtual machine on your local host. Clone the repository accompanying this book if you have not done so already. Then head to the *ch06/snappy* directory and `vagrant up`. Finally, `ssh` to the VM and use Docker:

```
$ git clone https://github.com/how2dock/docbook.git
$ cd docbook/ch06/snappy
$ vagrant up
$ vagrant ssh
$ snappy info
release: ubuntu-core/devel
frameworks: docker
apps:
$ docker ps
CONTAINER ID    IMAGE   COMMAND    CREATED    STATUS    PORTS    NAMES
```

This process downloads a public Vagrant box from Atlas `komljen/ ubuntu-snappy` (*https://vagrantcloud.com/komljen/boxes/ubuntu-snappy*). If you do not trust this box, do not use it.

Ubuntu Snappy is in alpha release and should be considered a technical preview.

Discussion

On December 9, 2014, Canonical announced (*http://bit.ly/snappy-core*) *Snappy*, a new Linux distribution based on Ubuntu Core, with transactional updates. It is a significant departure from the package and application management model used thus far in mainstream Ubuntu server and desktop.

Ubuntu Core (*https://wiki.ubuntu.com/Core*) is a minimal root filesystem that provides enough operating system capabilities to install packages. With Snappy, you get transactional updates and rollback on Ubuntu Core. This is achieved through an image-based workflow inherited from the Ubuntu phone application management system. This means (among other things) that `apt-get` does not work on `snappy`.

This makes Docker the perfect application framework on Snappy. Docker is installed as a *framework* that can be updated and rolled back as atomic transactions.

Follow this walk-through:

```
$ apt-get update
Ubuntu Core does not use apt-get, see 'snappy --help'!
$ snappy --help
...
Commands:
  {info,versions,search,update-versions,update,
   rollback,install,uninstall,tags,build,chroot,
   framework,fake-version,nap}
    info
    versions
    search
    update-versions
    update
    rollback              undo last system-image update.
    install
    uninstall
    tags
    build
    chroot
    framework
...
$ snappy versions
Part          Tag    Installed  Available  Fingerprint     Active
ubuntu-core   edge   140        142        184ad1e863e947  *
```

To get Docker running, you need to install a so-called `snappy` framework. Search for the Docker framework and install it like so:

```
$ snappy search docker
Part     Version    Description
docker   1.3.2.007  The docker app deployment mechanism
$ sudo snappy install docker
docker     4 MB    [===============]    OK
Part    Tag    Installed  Available  Fingerprint     Active
docker  edge   1.3.2.007  -          b1f2f85e77adab  *
$ snappy versions
Part          Tag      Installed  Available  Fingerprint     Active
```

```
ubuntu-core   edge  140       142        184ad1e863e947  *
docker        edge  1.3.2.007  -         b1f2f85e77adab  *
```

You can now use Docker on Ubuntu Snappy:

```
$ docker ps
CONTAINER ID    IMAGE    COMMAND    CREATED    STATUS    PORTS    NAMES
```

Enjoy running Docker on Ubuntu Snappy.

See Also

- Snappy announcement (*http://bit.ly/snappy-core*)
- Command-line walk-through (*http://blog.dustinkirkland.com/2014/12/its-a-snap.html*)

6.9 Starting an Ubuntu Core Snappy Instance on AWS EC2

Problem

You have a taste of Ubuntu Snappy with Vagrant (see Recipe 6.8), but you would like to start a Snappy instance in a public cloud, especially AWS EC2.

Solution

This is an advanced recipe that assumes some knowledge of Amazon AWS. Although all steps are provided, you might want to read *Programming Amazon Web Services* (*http://bit.ly/prog-aws*) by James Murty before trying this recipe out.

As prerequisites, you will need the following:

- An account on AWS (*http://aws.amazon.com*)
- A set of access and secret API keys (*http://docs.aws.amazon.com/general/latest/gr/getting-aws-sec-creds.html*)
- A default AWS security group with in-bound SSH allowed
- An SSH key pair called `snappy`
- A host with Apache Libcloud (*http://libcloud.apache.org*) installed (`sudo pip install apache-libcloud`)

To make this as easy as possible, I am providing a Python script that uses Apache Libcloud to start an instance on Amazon EC2. Libcloud is an API wrapper that abstracts the differences in API in various cloud providers. The same script can be slightly modified to start Snappy instances on most cloud providers. Assuming you have all the prerequisites, you should be able to do the following:

```
$ git clone https://github.com/how2dock/docbook
$ cd ch06/snappy-cloud
$ ./ec2snappy.py
54.154.68.31
```

Once the instance is running, you can ssh to it and check the Snappy version:

```
$ ssh -i ~/.ssh/id_rsa_snappy ubuntu@54.154.68.31
$ snappy versions
Part          Tag    Installed  Available  Fingerprint    Active
ubuntu-core   edge   141        142        7f068cb4fa876c  *
```

All that is left is to install the Docker Snappy framework and you can start running containers:

```
$ snappy search docker
Part     Version     Description
docker   1.3.2.007   The docker app deployment mechanism
$ sudo snappy install docker
docker     4 MB    [================]    OK
Part     Tag    Installed  Available  Fingerprint    Active
docker   edge   1.3.2.007  -          b1f2f85e77adab  *
$ docker pull ubuntu:14.04
ubuntu:14.04: The image you are pulling has been verified
511136ea3c5a: Pull complete
3b363fd9d7da: Pull complete
607c5d1cca71: Pull complete
f62feddc05dc: Pull complete
8eaa4ff06b53: Pull complete
Status: Downloaded newer image for ubuntu:14.04
$ docker images
REPOSITORY      TAG        IMAGE ID        CREATED       VIRTUAL SIZE
ubuntu          14.04      8eaa4ff06b53    9 days ago    192.7 MB
```

The script used is a simple Python script that uses Libcloud. It assumes you have set your AWS keys as environment variables in AWSAccessKeyId and AWSSecretKey. It starts an instance in the eu_west_1 availability zone with the m3.medium instance type. The user data is made of the content of the *cloud.cfg* file, which allows SSH access. Finally, the script sets the SSH key pair to snappy (you will need to have created this key ahead of running the script, and stored the private key in *~/.ssh/ id_rsa_snappy*):

```
#!/usr/bin/env python

import os
from libcloud.compute.types import Provider
from libcloud.compute.providers import get_driver
```

```
ACCESS_ID = os.getenv('AWSAccessKeyId')
SECRET_KEY = os.getenv('AWSSecretKey')

IMAGE_ID = 'ami-20f34b57'
SIZE_ID = 'm3.medium'

cls = get_driver(Provider.EC2_EU_WEST)
driver = cls(ACCESS_ID, SECRET_KEY)

sizes = driver.list_sizes()
images = driver.list_images()

size = [s for s in sizes if s.id == SIZE_ID][0]
image = [i for i in images if i.id == IMAGE_ID][0]

#Reads cloud config file
userdata = "\n".join(open('./cloud.cfg').readlines())

#Replace the name of the ssh key pair with yours
#You will need to open SSH port 22 on your default security group
name = "snappy"
node = driver.create_node(name=name, image=image,size=size, \
                          ex_keyname='snappy',ex_userdata=userdata)
print node.extra['network_interfaces']
```

 If you want to use a different availability zone than EU_WEST, you will need to check the announcement (*http://www.ubuntu.com/cloud/tools/snappy*) for the correct AMI ID in your preferred zone.

Discussion

Snappy is available in Beta on Amazon AWS, Google GCE, and Microsoft Azure, as shown in Figure 6-1.

Figure 6-1. Snappy Beta on public clouds

Follow the documentation (*http://www.ubuntu.com/cloud/tools/snappy*) to start an instance in these clouds by using the command-line tools for each provider, or modify the Libcloud-based script provided.

For instance on Google GCE, once you have created an account (*https://cloud.google.com/compute/*) and installed the Cloud SDK (*https://cloud.google.com/sdk/*), you can start a Snappy instance with the GCE Cloud SDK:

```
$ gcloud compute instances create snappy-test \
        --image-project ubuntu-snappy \
        --image ubuntu-core-devel-v20141215 \
        --metadata-from-file user-data=cloud.cfg
Created [https://www.googleapis.com/compute/v1/projects/runseb/zones/\
        europe-west1-c/instances/snappy-test2].
NAME         ZONE          MACHINE_TYPE  INTERNAL_IP   EXTERNAL_IP   STATUS
snappy-test2 europe-west1-c n1-standard-1 10.240.250.42 130.211.103.14 RUNNING
$ ssh -i ~/.ssh/id_rsa_snappy ubuntu@130.211.103.14
...
$ snappy info
release: ubuntu-core/devel
frameworks:
apps:
```

Happy Cloud snapping!

See Also

- Detailed command-line instructions (*http://www.ubuntu.com/cloud/tools/snappy*) with EC2 tools

- Announcement (*http://bit.ly/snappy-aws*) of Snappy available on AWS

6.10 Running Docker Containers on RancherOS

Problem

You are looking for an operating system alternative to CoreOS, Ubuntu Snappy, and Project Atomic.

Solution

Try the newly announced RancherOS (*http://rancher.com/rancher-os/*) from Rancher Labs (*http://rancher.com*). RancherOS is a minimalist Linux distribution that fits in about 20MB. Everything in RancherOS is a Linux container; it removes the need for a `systemd` init system by running a so-called `system-docker` daemon as PID 1 and running Linux services directly within containers. The `system-docker` then launches the Docker daemon used to run application containers.

 RancherOS was announced recently (*http://rancher.com/announcing-rancher-os/*) and should be considered a work in progress.

In order to test it, Rancher has made a convenient Vagrant project available (*https://github.com/rancherio/os-vagrant*). The following four lines of bash will get you up and running:

```
$ git clone https://github.com/rancherio/os-vagrant
$ cd os-vagrant
$ vagrant up
$ vagrant ssh
```

You can then use the latest Docker on the machine:

```
[rancher@rancher ~]$ docker ps
CONTAINER ID    IMAGE    COMMAND    CREATED    STATUS    PORTS    NAMES
[rancher@rancher ~]$ docker version
Client version: 1.7.0
...
Server version: 1.7.0
...
```

As `root`, you will be able to see the `system-docker` and the system services running within containers:

```
[rancher@rancher ~]$ sudo system-docker ps
CONTAINER ID     IMAGE                         COMMAND               ... NAMES
bde437da2059     rancher/os-console:v0.3.3     "/usr/sbin/entry.sh       console
2113b2e191ea     rancher/os-ntp:v0.3.3         "/usr/sbin/entry.sh       ntp
a7795940ec89     rancher/os-docker:v0.3.3      "/usr/sbin/entry.sh       docker
b0266396e938     rancher/os-acpid:v0.3.3       "/usr/sbin/entry.sh       acpid
aa8e18e59e67     rancher/os-udev:v0.3.3        "/usr/sbin/entry.sh       udev
f7145dfd21c9     rancher/os-syslog:v0.3.3      "/usr/sbin/entry.sh       syslog
```

Discussion

RancherOS is also available as an AMI (*https://github.com/rancherio/os*) on Amazon EC2.

See Also

- The RancherOS GitHub (*https://github.com/rancherio/os*) page

## CHAPTER 7

The Docker Ecosystem: Tools

7.0 Introduction

Docker in itself is extremely powerful and you now have covered all the topics to get you to a new way of writing distributed applications. However, Docker is even more powerful because of its large and vibrant ecosystem. This chapter presents a large set of tools in the Docker ecosystem.

To get started in this ecosystem we cover some tools that also come from Docker, Inc. If you have installed the Docker toolbox described in the first chapter you will have those tools already installed. Otherwise, each recipe shows you how to install them separately. First we show you how to use `docker-compose` in Recipe 7.1. Compose is way to describe a multicontainer application in a single YAML file. We look at our first example in this book, WordPress, and describe a compose file that allows you to run a WordPress site with two containers. We extend our look at Compose with a more complex example that shows you how to deploy a single-node Mesos (*http://mesos.apache.org*) cluster in Recipe 7.2. After Compose, we introduce Swarm in Recipe 7.3. A cluster manager for Docker, Swarm allows you to expose several Docker hosts behind a single Docker API endpoint. From the client side everything looks identical to a single-host setup, but Swarm can manage multiple hosts and schedule the containers on them. In Recipe 7.4, we illustrate how you can easily create your own Docker swarm cluster using `docker-machine`, which we introduced in the first chapter. This has the nice twist that you can use `docker-machine` to create multiple Docker hosts in a public cloud and configure them automatically as a Swarm cluster. To wrap up the list of Docker, Inc. tools, we give a brief introduction to Kitematic, the Docker desktop user interface, in Recipe 7.5.

Aside from Docker Inc., a large number of projects make up the Docker ecosystem, and the rest of the chapter presents a few of them. First, a basic web interface to

Docker is presented in Recipe 7.6, then an interactive shell based on docker-py is shown in Recipe 7.7. System administrators who are familiar with configuration management will find Recipe 7.8 interesting; it shows how you can use Ansible to manage the deployment of your containers using an Ansible playbook.

An area of great interest is container orchestrators. Docker Swarm, which we cover in this chapter, is an example of container orchestrator, but there exist many. Recipe 7.9 introduces Rancher, an orchestrator that has very interesting capabilities like multi-data-center networking, load-balancing and an integration with Docker Compose. CloudFoundry Lattice is introduced in Recipe 7.10. It is a great way to start learning how Cloudfoundry treats microservices applications and is Docker compatible. We also dive deeper into Mesos, with a single-node Mesos sandbox example in Recipe 7.11 and a cluster setup shown in Recipe 7.12.

To wrap up this chapter we present a self-discovery mechanism based on registrator in Recipe 7.13. With a large number of ephemeral containers running on a cluster, you want to have a system that detects these containers and registers them in a data store. This data store can then be queried to locate services and make sure your application keeps on running. Some of the orchestrators presented earlier in the chapter offer a discovery mechanism, but if you have to build your own, using registrator is a good solution.

7.1 Using Docker Compose to Create a WordPress Site

Problem

You have created a WordPress site using Recipe 1.16, but you would like to describe the multicontainer setup in a clear manifest and bring up the containers in a single command.

Solution

Use Docker Compose (*https://docs.docker.com/compose/*), a command-line utility to define and run multicontainer applications with Docker. With Compose, you define the services that need to run in a YAML file. Then bring up the services by using the docker-compose command.

The first thing to do is to install (*https://docs.docker.com/compose/*) Compose. You can install it via the Python index or via a single curl command.

If you are starting on your own Docker host, install Compose manually via the Python package index using pip:

```
$ sudo apt-get install python-pip
$ sudo pip install -U docker-compose
```

Or via `curl`:

```
$ curl -L https://github.com/docker/compose/releases/download/1.4.0/\
        docker-compose-`uname -s`-`uname -m` > /usr/local/bin/docker-compose
```

If you are using my examples, you are just a `vagrant up` away from using Compose:

```
$ git clone https://github.com/how2dock/docbook.git
$ cd docbook/ch07/compose/
$ vagrant up
$ vagrant ssh
$ docker-compose --version
docker-compose 1.4.0
```

The next step is to define the two containers that compose your WordPress installation in a YAML file. Each service will run via a container. You give them a name. In this case, you will call the WordPress service `wordpress` and the MySQL service `db`. Each service will then be defined by an image. The various arguments given at the command line in Recipe 1.16 need to be set in this YAML config file: the exposed ports, the environment variables, and the mounted volumes.

Create the following *docker-compose.yml* text file (if you are using my Vagrant machine, the file is already in */vagrant/docker-compose.yml*):

```
wordpress:
  image: wordpress
  links:
   - mysql
  ports:
   - "80:80"
  environment:
   - WORDPRESS_DB_NAME=wordpress
   - WORDPRESS_DB_USER=wordpress
   - WORDPRESS_DB_PASSWORD=wordpresspwd
mysql:
  image: mysql
  volumes:
   - /home/docker/mysql:/var/lib/mysql
  environment:
   - MYSQL_ROOT_PASSWORD=wordpressdocker
   - MYSQL_DATABASE=wordpress
   - MYSQL_USER=wordpress
   - MYSQL_PASSWORD=wordpresspwd
```

To bring up the two containers, type `docker-compose up -d` at the command line, in the directory where you have your *docker-compose.yml* file. The two linked containers will start, and you will be able to access the WordPress site by opening your browser at `http://<ip_of_host>`:

```
$ docker-compose up -d
Creating vagrant_mysql_1...
Creating vagrant_wordpress_1...
```

```
$ docker-compose ps
        Name                     Command            State        Ports
-------------------------------------------------------------------------------
vagrant_mysql_1        /entrypoint.sh mysqld         Up     3306/tcp
vagrant_wordpress_1    /entrypoint.sh apache2-for ...  Up     0.0.0.0:80->80/tcp
```

Discussion

 Docker Compose was originally developed by Orchard and was called Fig (*http://www.fig.sh*). After acquisition of Orchard by Docker Inc., Fig was renamed *Docker Compose*. You can expect a tight integration of Compose with the Docker CLI even though the current Compose is a separate binary. The source can be found on GitHub (*https://github.com/docker/compose*).

Compose has the following commands to manage a container environment:

```
Fast, isolated development environments using Docker.
...

Commands:
  build     Build or rebuild services
  help      Get help on a command
  kill      Kill containers
  logs      View output from containers
  port      Print the public port for a port binding
  ps        List containers
  pull      Pulls service images
  rm        Remove stopped containers
  run       Run a one-off command
  scale     Set number of containers for a service
  start     Start services
  stop      Stop services
  restart   Restart services
  up        Create and start containers
```

The usage of each command is obtained by specifying `--help` after the command— for example, `docker-compose kill --help`. Most commands take `SERVICE` as a parameter. A service in Compose is the name given to the running container in the *docker-compose.yml* file. For example, you could stop the WordPress service and start it again:

```
$ docker-compose stop wordpress
Stopping vagrant_wordpress_1...
$ docker-compose ps
        Name                     Command            State        Ports
-------------------------------------------------------------------------------
vagrant_mysql_1        /entrypoint.sh mysqld         Up     3306/tcp
vagrant_wordpress_1    /entrypoint.sh apache2-for ...  Exit 0
$ docker-compose start wordpress
```

```
Starting vagrant_wordpress_1...
$ docker-compose ps
       Name               Command            State        Ports
-----------------------------------------------------------------------
vagrant_mysql_1      /entrypoint.sh mysqld        Up      3306/tcp
vagrant_wordpress_1  /entrypoint.sh apache2-for ... Up    0.0.0.0:80->80/tcp
```

7.2 Using Docker Compose to Test Apache Mesos and Marathon on Docker

Problem

You are interested in Apache Mesos (*http://mesos.apache.org*), the data center resource-allocation system used by companies like Twitter. Mesos allows multilevel scheduling to share resources between different types of workloads while maximizing utilization of your servers. Before going into production with Mesos, you would like to experiment with it on a single server.

Solution

With Docker Compose (seen in Recipe 7.1), deploying Mesos on a single Docker host with one command is straightforward.

You need to start four containers: one for ZooKeeper (*http://zookeeper.apache.org*), one for the Mesos master, one for the Mesos slave, and one for the Mesos framework Marathon (*https://github.com/mesosphere/marathon*). Starting these four containers can be simplified by describing their start-up options in a YAML file that is read by Compose. Here is a sample YAML manifest to deploy Mesos using Compose:

```
zookeeper:
  image: garland/zookeeper
  ports:
   - "2181:2181"
   - "2888:2888"
   - "3888:3888"
mesosmaster:
  image: garland/mesosphere-docker-mesos-master
  ports:
   - "5050:5050"
  links:
   - zookeeper:zk
  environment:
   - MESOS_ZK=zk://zk:2181/mesos
   - MESOS_LOG_DIR=/var/log/mesos
   - MESOS_QUORUM=1
   - MESOS_REGISTRY=in_memory
   - MESOS_WORK_DIR=/var/lib/mesos
marathon:
```

```
    image: garland/mesosphere-docker-marathon
    links:
      - zookeeper:zk
      - mesosmaster:master
    command: --master zk://zk:2181/mesos --zk zk://zk:2181/marathon
    ports:
      - "8080:8080"
mesosslave:
    image: garland/mesosphere-docker-mesos-master:latest
    ports:
      - "5051:5051"
    links:
      - zookeeper:zk
      - mesosmaster:master
    entrypoint: mesos-slave
    environment:
      - MESOS_HOSTNAME=192.168.33.10
      - MESOS_MASTER=zk://zk:2181/mesos
      - MESOS_LOG_DIR=/var/log/mesos
      - MESOS_LOGGING_LEVEL=INFO
```

 To access the Marathon sandbox, we started the Mesos slave with the environment variable `MESOS_HOSTNAME=192.168.33.10`. Replace this IP with the IP of your Docker host.

Copy this file into *docker-compose.yml* and launch Compose:

```
$ ./docker-compose up -d
Recreating vagrant_zookeeper_1...
Recreating vagrant_mesosmaster_1...
Recreating vagrant_marathon_1...
Recreating vagrant_mesosslave_1...
...
```

Once the images have been downloaded and the containers started, you will be able to access the Mesos UI at *http://<IP_OF_HOST>:5050*. The Marathon UI will be available on port 8080 of the same host.

Discussion

If you have cloned the online repository that comes with this book, you are only a `vagrant up` away from running Mesos with Docker:

```
$ git clone https://github.com/how2dock/docbook.git
$ cd dockbook/ch07/compose
$ vagrant up
$ vagrant ssh
$ cd /vagrant
$ docker-compose -f mesos.yml up -d
```

You can then manage the containers with the `docker-compose` command.

See Also

- Deploying Mesos in seven commands (*http://bit.ly/mesos-7*)
- Mesos frameworks (*http://mesos.apache.org/documentation/latest/mesos-frameworks/*)

7.3 Starting Containers on a Cluster with Docker Swarm

Problem

You know how to use Docker with a single host. You would like to start containers on a cluster of hosts while keeping the user experience of the Docker CLI you are accustomed to on a single machine.

Solution

Use Docker Swarm (*https://github.com/docker/swarm*). Docker Swarm, the native clustering tool for Docker, allows a user to access a pool of Docker hosts as if it were a single host. Docker Swarm was announced at DockerCon (*http://blog.docker.com/tag/docker-swarm/*) Europe in December 2014. The first beta release of Swarm was announced (*http://blog.docker.com/2015/02/scaling-docker-with-swarm/*) on February 26, 2015. As of this writing, Docker Swarm is still in Beta.

To ease testing of Docker *Swarm*, I provide a Vagrant setup and bootstrap scripts that set up a four-node Swarm cluster. The cluster is composed of one head node and three compute nodes, all running Ubuntu 14.04. To get the cluster up, clone the Git repository accompanying this book (if you have not done so already), and head to the *ch07* directory and the *swarm* subdirectory. Use Vagrant to boot the cluster:

```
$ git clone https://github.com/how2dock/docbook.git
$ cd docbook/ch07/swarm/
$ vagrant up
```

You should see four virtual machines being started by Vagrant. The machines will be bootstrapped via bash scripts defined in the Vagrantfile:

```
...
$bootstrap=<<SCRIPT
apt-get update
curl -sSL https://get.docker.com/ | sudo sh
gpasswd -a vagrant docker
echo "DOCKER_OPTS=\"-H tcp://0.0.0.0:2375\"" >> /etc/default/docker
service docker restart
SCRIPT
```

```
$swarm=<<SCRIPT
apt-get update
curl -sSL https://get.docker.com/ | sudo sh
gpasswd -a vagrant docker
docker pull swarm
SCRIPT
...
```

Once the nodes are up and Vagrant has returned, ssh to the head node and start a Swarm container by using the *swarm* image that was pulled during the bootstrap process:

```
$ vagrant ssh swarm-head
$ docker run -v /vagrant:/tmp/vagrant -p 1234:1234 -d swarm manage \
        file://tmp/vagrant/swarm-cluster.cfg -H=0.0.0.0:1234
72acd5bc00de0b411f025ef6f297353a1869a3cc8c36d687e1f28a2d8f422a06
```

 The Swarm server setup uses a file-based discovery mechanism. The *swarm-cluster.cfg* file contains the hardcoded lists of the Swarm nodes started by Vagrant. Additional discovery services (*http:// docs.docker.com/swarm/discovery/*) are available for Swarm. You can use a service hosted by Docker Inc., Consul (*https://consul.io*), Etcd (*https://github.com/coreos/etcd*), or ZooKeeper (*http:// zookeeper.apache.org*). You can also write your own discovery interface.

With the Swarm server running and the worker nodes discovered, you will be able to use the local Docker client to get information about the cluster and start containers. You will need to use the -H option of the Docker CLI to target the Swarm server running in a container instead of the local Docker daemon:

```
$ docker -H 0.0.0.0:1234 info
Containers: 0
Nodes: 3
 swarm-2: 192.168.33.12:2375
  └ Containers: 0
  └ Reserved CPUs: 0 / 1
  └ Reserved Memory: 0 B / 490 MiB
 swarm-3: 192.168.33.13:2375
  └ Containers: 0
  └ Reserved CPUs: 0 / 1
  └ Reserved Memory: 0 B / 490 MiB
 swarm-1: 192.168.33.11:2375
  └ Containers: 0
  └ Reserved CPUs: 0 / 1
  └ Reserved Memory: 0 B / 490 MiB
```

Using the local Docker client and specifying the Swarm server as a Docker daemon endpoint, you can start containers on the entire cluster. For example, let's start Nginx:

```
$ docker -H 0.0.0.0:1234 run -d -p 80:80 nginx
8399c544b61953fd5610b01be787cb3802e2e54f220673b94d78160d0ee35b33
$ docker -H 0.0.0.0:1234 run -d -p 80:80 nginx
1b2c4634fc6d9f2c3fd63dd48a2580f466590ddff7405f889ada885746db3cbd
$ docker -H 0.0.0.0:1234 ps
CONTAINER ID  IMAGE      ... PORTS                          NAMES
1b2c4634fc6d  nginx:1.7  ... 443/tcp, 192.168.33.11:80->80/tcp  swarm-1...
8399c544b619  nginx:1.7  ... 443/tcp, 192.168.33.12:80->80/tcp  swarm-2...
```

You just started two Nginx containers. Swarm scheduled them on two of the nodes in the cluster. You can open your browser at *http://192.168.33.11* and *http://192.168.33.12* and you will see the default Nginx page.

 The docker run command can take some time to return. Swarm needs to schedule the container on a node in the cluster, and that node needs to pull the Nginx image.

Discussion

In this setup, the Docker Swarm server is running within a local container on the Swarm head node. You can see it with docker ps and you can check the logs with docker logs. In the logs, you see the requests made to start the Nginx containers. It is interesting to see that you are using the Docker client on the Swarm head node to communicate with the local Docker daemon and the Swarm server running in a local container:

```
$ docker ps
CONTAINER ID  IMAGE          COMMAND        ... PORTS
72acd5bc00de  swarm:latest   swarm manage   ... 2375/tcp, 0.0.0.0:1234->1234/tcp

$ docker logs 72acd5bc00de
... msg="Listening for HTTP" addr="0.0.0.0:1234" proto=tcp
... msg="HTTP request received" method=GET uri="/v1.17/info"
... msg="HTTP request received" method=GET uri="/v1.17/containers/json"
... msg="HTTP request received" method=POST uri="/v1.17/containers/create"
... msg="HTTP request received" method=POST uri="/v1.17/containers/.../start"
... msg="HTTP request received" method=GET uri="/v1.17/containers/json"
... msg="HTTP request received" method=POST uri="/v1.17/containers/create"
... msg="HTTP request received" method=POST uri="/v1.17/containers/.../start"
... msg="HTTP request received" method=GET uri="/v1.17/containers/json"
```

In these logs, you clearly see the API calls being made to the Swarm server to launch the Nginx containers in the cluster.

See Also

- Introduction to Swarm (*https://docs.docker.com/swarm/*)

- Swarm installation documentation (*https://docs.docker.com/swarm/install-manual/*)

7.4 Using Docker Machine to Create a Swarm Cluster Across Cloud Providers

Problem

You understand how to create a Swarm cluster manually (see Recipe 7.3), but you would like to create one with nodes in multiple public cloud providers and keep the user experience of the local Docker CLI.

Solution

Use *Docker Machine* (see Recipe 1.9) to start Docker hosts in several cloud providers and bootstrap them automatically to create a Swarm cluster.

The first thing to do is to obtain a swarm discovery token. This will be used during the bootstrapping process when starting the nodes of the cluster. As explained in Recipe 7.3, Swarm features multiple discovery processes. In this recipe, you use the service hosted by Docker, Inc. A discovery token is obtained by running a container based on the *swarm* image and running the create command. Assuming you do not have access to a Docker host already, you use docker-machine to create one solely for this purpose:

```
$ ./docker-machine create -d virtualbox local
INFO[0000] Creating SSH key...
...
INFO[0042] To point your Docker client at it, run this in your shell: \
$(docker-machine env local)
$ eval "$(docker-machine env local)"
$ docker run swarm create
31e61710169a7d3568502b0e9fb09d66
```

With the token in hand, you can use docker-machine and multiple public cloud drivers to start worker nodes. You can start a Swarm head node on VirtualBox, a worker on DigitalOcean (see Figure 1-7), and another one on Azure (see Recipe 8.6).

 Do not start a Swarm head in a public cloud and a worker on your localhost with VirtualBox. Chances are the head will not be able to route network traffic to your local worker node. It is possible to do, but you would have to open ports on your local router.

```
$ docker-machine create -d virtualbox --swarm --swarm-master \
--swarm-discovery token://31e61710169a7d3568502b0e9fb09d66 head
INFO[0000] Creating SSH key...
...
INFO[0069] To point your Docker client at it, run this in your shell: \
$(docker-machine env head)
$ docker-machine create -d digitalocean --swarm --swarm-discovery \
token://31e61710169a7d3568502b0e9fb09d66 worker-00
...
$ docker-machine create -d azure --swarm --swarm-discovery \
token://31e61710169a7d3568502b0e9fb09d66 swarm-worker-01
...
```

Your Swarm cluster is now ready. Your Swarm head node is running locally in a Virtual-Box VM, one worker node is running in DigitalOcean, and another one in Azure. You can set the local *docker-machine* binary to use the head node running in Virtual-Box and start using the Swarm subcommands:

```
$ eval "$(docker-machine env --swarm head)"
$ docker info
Containers: 4
Nodes: 3
 head: 192.168.99.103:2376
  └ Containers: 2
  └ Reserved CPUs: 0 / 4
  └ Reserved Memory: 0 B / 999.9 MiB
 worker-00: 45.55.160.223:2376
  └ Containers: 1
  └ Reserved CPUs: 0 / 1
  └ Reserved Memory: 0 B / 490 MiB
 swarm-worker-01: swarm-worker-01.cloudapp.net:2376
  └ Containers: 1
  └ Reserved CPUs: 0 / 1
  └ Reserved Memory: 0 B / 1.639 GiB
```

Discussion

If you start a container, Swarm will schedule it in round-robin fashion on the cluster. For example, you can start three Nginx containers in a for loop:

```
$ for i in `seq 1 3`;do docker run -d -p 80:80 nginx;done
```

This leads to three Nginx containers on the three nodes in your cluster. Remember that you will need to open port 80 on the instances running in the cloud to access the container (e.g., see Recipe 8.6):

```
$ docker ps
... IMAGE     ... PORTS                              NAMES
... nginx:1.7 ... 443/tcp, 104.210.33.180:80->80/tcp swarm-worker-01/
                                                      loving_torvalds
... nginx:1.7 ... 443/tcp, 45.55.160.223:80->80/tcp  worker-00/drunk_swartz
... nginx:1.7 ... 443/tcp, 192.168.99.103:80->80/tcp head/condescending_galileo
```

Do not forget to remove the machine you started in the cloud.

See Also

- Using (*https://docs.docker.com/swarm/install-w-machine/*) Docker Machine with Docker Swarm

7.5 Managing Containers Locally Using the Kitematic UI

Problem

Instead of using the command line to manage your containers locally, you would like to use a graphical interface.

Solution

Use Kitematic (*https://kitematic.com*). It is available for OS X 10.9+ and Windows 7+. As of Docker 1.8, Kitematic is now bundled in the Docker Toolbox (see Recipe 1.6).

After installing Kitematic by downloading it from the website (*https://kitematic.com*) or after installing Docker Toolbox, you can start it. It will automatically create a local Docker host using Docker Machine and VirtualBox. After the host has booted, you will be presented with the Kitematic dashboard (see Figure 7-1).

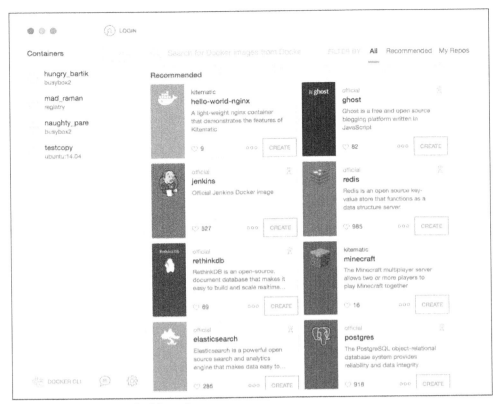

Figure 7-1. Kitematic dashboard

Kitematic presents you with default container images, and also lets you search the Docker Hub. In the left gutter in Figure 7-1 you can also see containers that are on your Docker host. You can start, stop, and manage their settings all through the UI.

Let's say you want to start Nginx. You can search for an *nginx_* image in the search box at the top of the dashboard and then simply click the Create icon. Docker automatically downloads the image and starts the container. You can then enter the Settings window (see Figure 7-2) and check the settings. You could stop the container, change the settings, and restart the container.

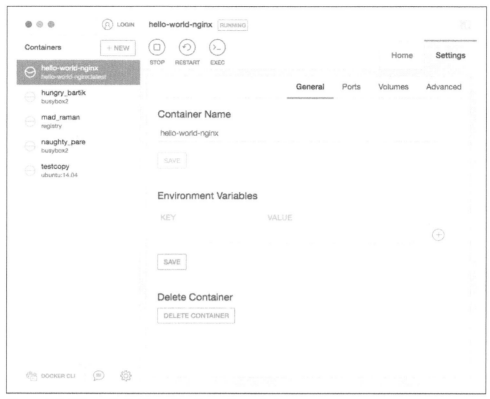

Figure 7-2. Kitematic Settings Configuration window

Kitematic is useful for local work and simple container tasks. It will certainly be integrated with Docker Compose and Swarm, which will make it a powerful graphical interface for managing production deployments.

See Also

- Kitematic official website (*https://kitematic.com*)

7.6 Managing Containers Through Docker UI

Problem

You have access to a Docker host and know how to manage images and containers, but you would like to use a simple web interface.

Solution

Use the Docker UI (*https://github.com/crosbymichael/dockerui*). Although you can create your own image (*https://github.com/crosbymichael/dockerui/wiki/Ways-to-run-dockerui*) from source, the Docker UI is also available on Docker Hub (*https://regis try.hub.docker.com/u/dockerui/dockerui/*), which makes running it in a container straightforward.

On your Docker host, start the Docker UI container:

```
$ docker run -d -p 9000:9000
            --privileged
            -v /var/run/docker.sock:/var/run/docker.sock
            dockerui/dockerui
```

You can then open your browser at *http://<IP_OF_DOCKER_HOST>:9000* and you will have access to the UI. Figure 7-3 shows an example.

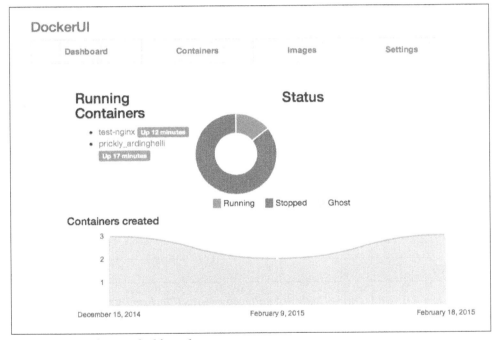

Figure 7-3. Docker UI dashboard

The Docker UI is not part of the official Docker release and is a community-maintained project (*https://github.com/crosbymichael/dockerui*).

Discussion

Once you have access to the UI, you can start a container. Go to the Images tab, select an image, and click the Create button. You will be able to specify all the container start-up options through the UI. Do not miss the HostConfig options, where you can set port mappings. Figure 7-4 shows you a preview of this screen.

Figure 7-4. Starting a container through the Docker UI

See Also

- Docker UI wiki (*https://github.com/crosbymichael/dockerui/wiki*) that contains additional documentation

7.7 Using the Wharfee Interactive Shell

Problem

You know how to use the Docker CLI but would like to use a more powerful interactive shell with autocompletion and history.

Solution

Use Wharfee (*http://wharfee.com*), a Python-based interactive CLI. Wharfee is based on docker-py (see Recipe 4.10) and uses a few Python modules to create the interactive shell.

On a Docker host, install Python and the package index command line installed pip. Then install Wharfee. For example, on an Ubuntu system:

```
$ sudo apt-get install python python-pip
$ sudo pip install wharfee
```

You are now ready to use this new powerful command-line interface. You launch Wharfee and you enter the interactive shell. The commands that you use are the exact same Docker commands, except that you do not need to use the docker prefix. As you type, you will get autocompletion suggestions and some syntax highlighting.

```
$ wharfee
Version: 0.6.5
Home: http://wharfee.com
wharfee> images
There are no images to list.
wharfee> ps
There are no containers to list.
```

To start a container, you need to pull an image explicitly:

```
wharfee> pull nginx:latest
Pulling from library/nginx latest
...
wharfee> run -d -p 80:80 nginx:latest
bf96488c76d617b6d3d2f8aea0ff928eff7fe05e61219eb23f865f60631d9f83
wharfee> ps
Status         Created  Image        ... Command                 Ports
-----------    -------  -----------  ... ---------------------   --------------
Up 2 seconds   now      nginx:latest ... nginx -g 'daemon off;'  443/tcp, 80/tcp
```

Wharfee is a nice CLI that comes in handy with its autocompletion feature and highlighting.

See Also

- Wharfee source code (*https://github.com/j-bennet/wharfee*)
- Wharfee official website (*http://wharfee.com*)

7.8 Orchestrating Containers with Ansible Docker Module

Problem

You have developed some expertise with Ansible (*http://www.ansible.com/home*) to configure your servers and orchestrate application deployment. You would like to take advantage of this expertise and use Ansible to manage Docker containers.

Solution

Use the Ansible Docker module (*http://docs.ansible.com/docker_module.html*). This module is part of the Ansible core, so after installing Ansible, no additional packages need to be installed.

Ansible will run from your local machine, connect over SSH to your Docker hosts, and use the docker-py API client to issue calls to the Docker daemon.

For example, to start an Nginx container in detached mode with a port mapping, you would write an Ansible playbook (*http://docs.ansible.com/playbooks.html*) like this:

```
- hosts: nginx
  tasks:
  - name: Run nginx container
    docker: image=nginx:latest detach=true ports=80:80
```

 Discussion about how to use Ansible is beyond the scope of this recipe. See the Ansible documentation (*http://docs.ansible.com*).

Discussion

To get you up and running with the Ansible Docker module, you can use the Vagrantfile accompanying this recipe. This will start a virtual machine acting as a Docker host with the docker-py client installed. Two playbooks, an inventory file, and some Ansible configurations are also available to make it turnkey.

The first task is to install Ansible on your local machine:

```
$ sudo pip install ansible
```

Then to test the Nginx playbook, follow these instructions:

```
$ git clone https://github.com/how2dock/docbook.git
$ cd ch07/ansible
$ tree
.
├── README.md
```

```
├── Vagrantfile
├── ansible.cfg
├── dock.yml
├── inventory
├── solo
│   ├── Vagrantfile
│   └── dock.yml
└── wordpress.yml
$ vagrant up
```

The Nginx playbook shown in the solution section is in the *dock.yml* file. To start this container using Ansible, run the playbook. Once it finishes, open your browser at *http://192.168.33.10* and you will see the welcome screen of Nginx. You can also connect to the VM with `vagrant ssh` and check the running container with the usual `docker ps` command.

```
$ ansible-playbook -u vagrant dock.yml
PLAY [nginx] **********************************************************

GATHERING FACTS ******************************************************
ok: [192.168.33.10]

TASK: [Run nginx container] ****************************************
changed: [192.168.33.10]

PLAY RECAP ***********************************************************
192.168.33.10              : ok=2    changed=1    unreachable=0    failed=0
```

You can kill this Nginx container with `docker kill` within the virtual machine or run a playbook that sets the state of the container to `killed`:

```
- hosts: nginx
  tasks:
  - name: Kill nginx container
    docker: image=nginx:latest detach=true ports=80:80 state=killed
```

If you want to try a more complex example, check the WordPress playbook *wordpress.yml*. You have deployed WordPress several times already (see Recipe 1.15 or Recipe 1.16). Run the playbook and open your browser at *http://192.168.33.10* and enjoy WordPress once again. (You will need to have killed any container using port 80 on the host; otherwise, you will get a port conflict error).

```
$ ansible-playbook -u vagrant wordpress.yml

PLAY [wordpress] *****************************************************

GATHERING FACTS ****************************************************
ok: [192.168.33.10]

TASK: [Docker pull mysql] *****************************************
changed: [192.168.33.10]
```

```
TASK: [Docker pull wordpress] **************************************************
changed: [192.168.33.10]

TASK: [Run mysql container] ****************************************************
ok: [192.168.33.10]

TASK: [Run wordpress container] ************************************************
changed: [192.168.33.10]

PLAY RECAP *********************************************************************
192.168.33.10                : ok=5    changed=3    unreachable=0    failed=0
```

Because Ansible playbooks are written in YAML, you will notice some similarities with the WordPress compose example in Recipe 7.1:

```
- hosts: wordpress
  tasks:

  - name: Docker pull mysql
    command: docker pull mysql:latest

  - name: Docker pull wordpress
    command: docker pull wordpress:latest

  - name: Run mysql container
    docker:
      name=mysql
      image=mysql
      detach=true
      env="MYSQL_ROOT_PASSWORD=wordpressdocker,MYSQL_DATABASE=wordpress, \
          MYSQL_USER=wordpress,MYSQL_PASSWORD=wordpresspwd"

  - name: Run wordpress container
    docker:
      image=wordpress
      env="WORDPRESS_DB_NAME=wordpress,WORDPRESS_DB_USER=wordpress, \
          WORDPRESS_DB_PASSWORD=wordpresspwd"
      ports="80:80"
      detach=true
      links="mysql:mysql"
```

You have run the playbooks directly from the local machine, but Vagrant has an Ansible provisioner. This means that you can run the playbook when the VM is started. Go to *ch07/ansible/solo* and `vagrant up`. The Nginx container will automatically start.

See Also

- *Ansible: Up and Running* (*http://bit.ly/ansible-up-and-running*), which has a section on the Docker module

7.9 Using Rancher to Manage Containers on a Cluster of Docker Hosts

Problem

You want to manage containers in production through a system that supports multi-host networking, an overlay network that allows containers to reach each other without complex port-forwarding rules, group management, and a powerful dashboard.

Solution

Consider Rancher (*http://rancher.com/rancher-io/*) from Rancher Labs (*http://rancher.com*), the makers of Rancher OS (see Recipe 6.10). It is straightforward to set up with a management server running as a container and a worker agent running as a container as well.

To easily test Rancher and see whether it suits your needs, clone the project repository on GitHub (*https://github.com/rancherio/rancher*) and start a virtual machine locally through Vagrant, as shown here:

```
$ git clone https://github.com/rancherio/rancher.git
$ cd rancher
$ vagrant up
```

The virtual machine started is based on CoreOS (see Recipe 6.1), but you could use any other OS that runs Docker. The Vagrantfile contains two provisioning steps that install the management server and the worker agent from Docker images. You can use these commands almost identically to start Rancher on your own machines.

 Once in the Rancher dashboard, if you navigate to the Add Host button, you will be presented with the exact Docker command to run on another host to join this Rancher deployment.

```
$ docker run -d -p 8080:8080 rancher/server:latest
$ docker run -e CATTLE_AGENT_IP=172.17.8.100 --privileged -e WAIT=true \
         -v /var/run/docker.sock:/var/run/docker.sock \
    rancher/agent:latest http://localhost:8080
```

Once the Vagrant machine is up and the Rancher images have been downloaded, two containers will start and you will be able to access the Rancher dashboard at `http://localhost:8080`.

> If you already have a server running on port 8080 in your local machine, Vagrant will pick a different port to serve the Rancher UI on. You can always access it by using the host-only network at `http://172.17.8.100:8080`.

The dashboard will show only one host and no running containers. By clicking Add Container, you will be redirected to a page where you can set the container run parameters (see Figure 7-5). You can expand the *Advanced Options* area to set parameters such as environment variables, volumes, networking, and capabilities of the containers (e.g., memory, privileged mode). By default, the networking will be a so-called managed network, which will use a network overlay. You can still use the default Docker networking.

> Considering the changes that will happen with Docker networking, this recipe does not expand on the Rancher overlay itself. See Chapter 3 for more information.

Rancher will build a network overlay, even though in this case you are using a single host, and start the container within the IP range of the overlay. If you map the exposed port of the container to a port on the host, you will be able to access it through your browser. For example, if you start Nginx and map it to port 80 of the host, you will enjoy the welcome screen of Nginx. The container creation screen looks like Figure 7-6.

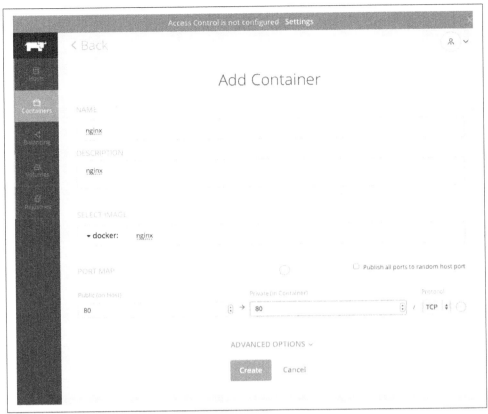

Figure 7-5. Starting a container via the Rancher UI

At this stage, you have a working Rancher test bed. You can explore the dashboard. The Containers tab lists all your running containers. You can open a shell into a container, and start/stop it. The Volumes tab lists the volumes currently being used; volume manipulation through the dashboard is limited at this time. Finally, you can define an existing private registry, or define load-balancers.

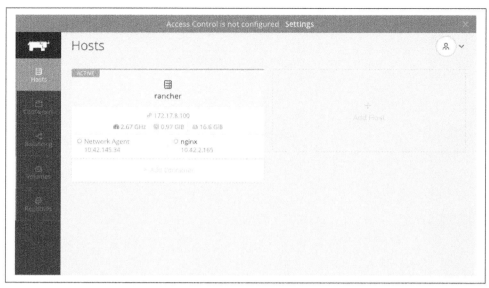

Figure 7-6. Rancher dashboard with running container

Discussion

So far, you've done everything by using the dashboard. Rancher also exposes a REST API to manage all its resources. To use the API, you need to generate a set of API access and secret keys. This is done by clicking the user icon at the top right of the dashboard and selecting the API & Keys option. The API is not documented on the GitHub page, but the dashboard offers a nice API explorer.

You can manage a running container through the dashboard. By clicking the container, you will see an option to View in API. This redirects you to the API explorer. This explorer features the JSON object describing the container as well as a set of actions that can be performed (green boxes in the UI). Selecting one of the actions opens a new window that will show you the API request that you can make. This is a perfect way to learn the API and possibly write your own client. Figure 7-7 is a snapshot of a request to stop a container.

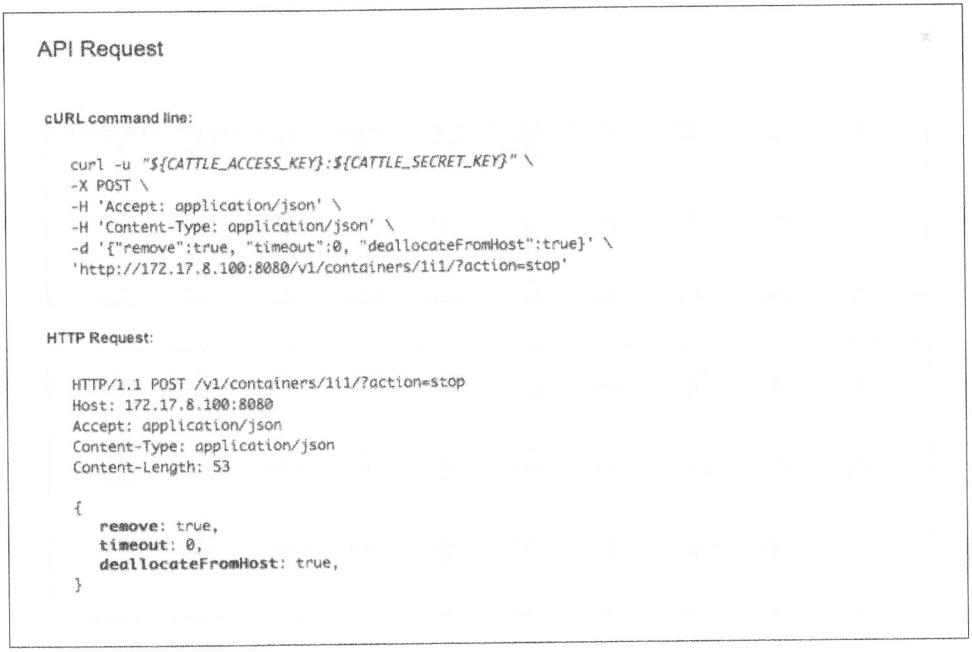

Figure 7-7. Rancher API request example

7.10 Running Containers on a Cluster Using Lattice

Problem

You are looking for a container orchestration system to schedule containers on a cluster of machines. Additionally, you may have experience with Cloud Foundry and are interested in its approach to containers.

Solution

Use Lattice (*http://lattice.cf*). Lattice, a cluster scheduler for container-based applications, includes an HTTP load-balancing feature, log aggregation, health management, and dynamic scaling of the applications. This lightweight container scheduler gives developers the experience of working with native cloud applications and gives them a taste of the Cloud Foundry (*https://www.cloudfoundry.org*) PaaS.

To get started quickly, you can follow the Getting Started guide from the Lattice website (*http://lattice.cf/docs/getting-started/*). It uses a Vagrant box to deploy a *Lattice cell* on your local machine. After installing the Lattice client ltc, you can communicate with your Lattice setup and deploy Docker images.

Let's clone the Lattice project, check out the latest release, and boot the Vagrant box:

```
$ git clone https://github.com/cloudfoundry-incubator/lattice.git
$ cd lattice
$ git checkout v0.3.0
$ vagrant up
...
==> default: Lattice is now installed and running.
==> default: You may target it using: ltc target 192.168.11.11.xip.io
==> default:
```

Download the ltc CLI and make the file executable. For example, to get the CLI in your PATH, you could do the following:

```
$ sudo wget https://lattice.s3.amazonaws.com/releases/latest/darwin-amd64/ltc \
-O /usr/local/bin/ltc
$ sudo chmod +x /usr/local/bin/ltc
```

You are now ready to configure the CLI to point to your local Lattice deployment done via Vagrant. Follow the last message of the Vagrant deployment and use ltc:

```
$ ltc target 192.168.11.11.xip.io
Blob store is targeted.
Api Location Set
```

All that is left now is to start a container with the ltc create command, specifying the Docker image from the Docker Hub that you want to run. As a quick test, let's run nginx in Lattice:

```
$ ltc create nginx-app nginx -r
...
nginx-app is now running.
App is reachable at:
http://nginx-app.192.168.11.11.xip.io
```

Once the application is created, you can reach it at the URL returned by ltc. The URL uses *xip.io*, a wildcard DNS service that makes reaching services on your local network by DNS names easy. In this example, if you open your browser at *http://nginx-app.192.168.11.11.xip.io*, you will see the Nginx welcome screen.

You can easily scale the number of instances of an application with ltc scale, terminate an application with ltc rm, and many other operational tasks. See ltc help for more information.

Discussion

The Lattice cell started via Vagrant does not run the Docker engine. However, you specified a Docker image and Lattice accepted it. In fact, the Lattice runtime extracts the filesystem of the Docker image and executes the application in its own container runtime.

This had a side effect in the example: you needed to specify to run the application as root for Nginx to be deployed successfully. This was achieved with the -r option of ltc create.

Although this basic setup was done with Vagrant, Lattice can be deployed in various cloud providers by using Terraform (*https://github.com/cloudfoundry-incubator/lattice/tree/master/terraform*).

See Also

- Using buildpacks (*http://www.chipchilders.com/blog/2015/8/12/buildpacks-in-lattice.html*) with Lattice

7.11 Running Containers via Apache Mesos and Marathon

Problem

You are looking for a cluster scheduler to launch containers on a Docker host in your data center. You might also already be running Apache Mesos to schedule long-running jobs, cron jobs, or even Hadoop or parallel computing workloads, and would like to use it to run containers.

Solution

Use Apache Mesos (*http://mesos.apache.org*) and the Docker containerizer. Mesos is a cluster resource allocator that leverages multiple scheduling frameworks to maximize utilization of your data-center resources. Mesos is used by large companies like eBay, Twitter, Netflix, Airbnb, and more (*http://mesos.apache.org/documentation/latest/powered-by-mesos/*).

The Mesos architecture (*http://mesos.apache.org/documentation/latest/mesos-architecture/*) is based on one or several master nodes, worker nodes (or Mesos slaves), one or more scheduling frameworks that are deployed in Mesos, and a service-discovery system that uses ZooKeeper (*http://zookpeeper.apache.org*). In Recipe 7.2, you already saw how to use Docker Compose to start a testing Mesos infrastructure on a single node.

Marathon (*http://mesos.apache.org/documentation/latest/mesos-frameworks/*) is one of the Mesos frameworks that can allow you to run tasks on a Mesos cluster. Mesos supports Docker (i.e., Docker containerizer). This means that you can launch Marathon tasks that are made of Docker containers.

Amazon ECS service (see Recipe 8.11) can also use Mesos to schedule containers on AWS. Docker Swarm (see Recipe 7.3) is also scheduled to add support for Mesos-based scheduling.

This recipe uses Mesos Playa (*https://github.com/mesosphere/playa-mesos*), a Mesos sandbox, to show you how to run Docker containers with Mesos.

To get started, clone the `playa-mesos` repository from GitHub, start the virtual machine via Vagrant, and `ssh` to it:

```
$ git clone https://github.com/mesosphere/playa-mesos.git
$ vagrant up
$ vagrant ssh
```

Once the machine is up, you can access the Mesos web interface at *http://10.141.141.10:5050* and the Marathon web interface at *http://10.141.141.10:8080*.

Discussion on how to use Mesos (*http://mesos.apache.org*) and Marathon (*http://https://mesosphere.github.io/marathon/*) are beyond the scope of this book. Refer to the two websites for more information.

Marathon exposes a REST API that you can use to start tasks. Tasks are defined in a JSON file and can be submitted to the API endpoint via `curl`. Here is an example task described in JSON:

```
{
  "id": "http",
  "cmd": "python -m SimpleHTTPServer $PORT0",
  "mem": 50,
  "cpus": 0.1,
  "instances": 1,
  "constraints": [
    ["hostname", "UNIQUE"]
  ],
  "ports": [0]
}
```

The `id` is the name of the task (also called Application in Marathon). The `cmd` is what the application will run (here, a simple HTTP server via Python). What is important to note is the use of `ports`, which is set to a list containing 0. This means that Marathon will dynamically allocate a port that this application will use. This dynamic port is passed to the `cmd` argument as `$PORT0`.

Save this JSON description in a file called *test.json* and submit this application via `curl`:

```
$ curl -is -H "Content-Type: application/json"
         -d @test.json 10.141.141.10:8080/v2/apps
HTTP/1.1 201 Created
...
```

Once the application starts, you will see it in the UI (Figure 7-8) and be able to access the URL that points to the HTTP server that was just started. Note the port that was dynamically allocated.

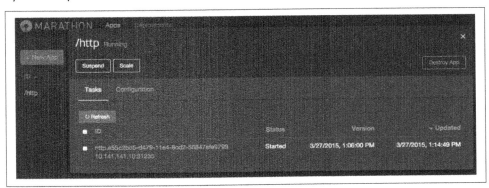

Figure 7-8. Marathon UI for HTTP server

Let's now move on to starting an application that is made of a Docker container. By default, the VM started by Playa Mesos will contain Docker, but the Mesos slave is not configured to use it. Therefore, you need to do a few configurations and restart mesos-slave. In the virtual machine, do the following:

```
vagrant@mesos:~$ sudo su
root@mesos:/home/vagrant# cd /etc/mesos-slave
root@mesos:/etc/mesos-slave# echo 'docker,mesos' > containerizers
root@mesos:/etc/mesos-salve# echo '5mins' > executor_registration_timeout
root@mesos:/etc/mesos-slave# service mesos-slave restart
mesos-slave stop/waiting
mesos-slave start/running, process 2581
```

Create the following JSON file (e.g., *docker.json*) that describes running an Nginx container with a dynamic port allocation on the host:

```
{
  "container": {
    "type": "DOCKER",
    "docker": {
      "image": "nginx",
      "network": "BRIDGE",
      "portMappings": [
        { "containerPort": 80, "hostPort": 0 }
      ]
    }
  },
```

```
    "id": "nginx",
    "instances": 1,
    "cpus": 0.5,
    "mem": 512
}
```

Create this application via the Marathon API by using `curl` and check the list of running applications:

```
$ curl -si -H 'Content-Type: application/json'
         -d @docker.json 10.141.141.10:8080/v2/apps
$ curl -sX GET -H "Content-Type: application/json" 10.141.141.10:8080/v2/tasks
         | python -m json.tool

{
    "tasks": [
        {
            "appId": "/nginx",
            "host": "10.141.141.10",
            "id": "nginx.404b7376-d47b-11e4-8cd2-56847afe9799",
            "ports": [
                31236
            ],
            "servicePorts": [
                10001
            ],
            "stagedAt": "2015-03-27T12:17:35.285Z",
            "startedAt": null,
            "version": "2015-03-27T12:17:29.312Z"
        },
        {
            "appId": "/http",
            "host": "10.141.141.10",
            "id": "http.a55c2bd5-d479-11e4-8cd2-56847afe9799",
            "ports": [
                31235
            ],
            "servicePorts": [
                10000
            ],
            "stagedAt": "2015-03-27T12:06:05.873Z",
            "startedAt": "2015-03-27T12:14:49.986Z",
            "version": "2015-03-27T12:06:00.485Z"
        }
    ]
}
```

You see the `http` application that you started earlier. And you also see the new `nginx` application, which uses Docker. The application will take a little bit of time to deploy, just enough time to `docker pull nginx`. To take into account the time it may take to download an image from a registry, you define the `executor_registration_timeout` before restarting the `mesos-slave`. Marathon also allocates a port dynamically to bind port 80 of the Nginx container to the host, and in this case it chooses 31236. If you open your browser at *http://10.141.141.10:31236*, you will see the familiar web page of Nginx.

Discussion

The Docker application definition specified in JSON format can contain volume mounts, can specify arguments that will overwrite the CMD arguments defined in a Dockerfile, can specify docker run parameters, and can also run in privileged mode. The Docker containerizer (*https://mesosphere.github.io/marathon/docs/native-docker.html*) documentation has detailed information. But as a quick reference, you could also define an application with all those extra functionalities, like so:

```
{
    "id": "privileged-job",
    "container": {
        "docker": {
            "image": "mesosphere/inky"
            "privileged": true,
            "parameters": [
                { "key": "hostname", "value": "a.corp.org" },
                { "key": "volumes-from", "value": "another-container" },
                { "key": "lxc-conf", "value": "..." }
            ]
        },
        "type": "DOCKER",
        "volumes": []
    },
    "args": ["hello"],
    "cpus": 0.2,
    "mem": 32.0,
    "instances": 1
}
```

Finally, running Mesos on a single host defeats the purpose of this recipe, and you will want to create a Mesos cluster with the Docker containerizer enabled on all Mesos slaves.

See Also

- Mesosphere documentation (*https://mesosphere.github.io/marathon/docs/native-docker.html*) for the Docker containerizer

- Marathon example (*https://github.com/mesosphere/marathon/tree/master/examples*) JSON files

- Original post (*http://frankhinek.com/deploy-docker-containers-on-mesos-0-20/*) this recipe is based on

7.12 Using the Mesos Docker Containerizer on a Mesos Cluster

Problem

In Recipe 7.11, you saw how to test the Mesos Docker containerizer to run containers on a Mesos sandbox. You would like to do the same but on a Mesos cluster.

Solution

Build a Mesos cluster using containers and the images prepared by Mesosphere (*https://mesosphere.com*) on the Docker Hub. Configure the Mesos slave to use the Docker containerizer.

To facilitate testing this recipe, use the online material accompanying this book. This recipe uses a Vagrantfile that sets up a local three-node Mesos cluster and uses Ansible to start the container that runs the Mesos software components (i.e., ZooKeeper, Mesos master, Marathon framework, and Mesos slave).

Clone the repository if you have not done so already, head to *ch07/mesos*, and use Vagrant to bring up the three-node cluster:

 If you have enough memory on your local machine, you can add more nodes to this setup or change the memory allocated to each node (see the Vagrantfile).

```
$ git clone https://github.com/how2dock/docbook.git
$ cd dockbook/ch07/mesos
$ vagrant up
$ vagrant status
Current machine states:

mesos-head              running (virtualbox)
mesos-1                 running (virtualbox)
mesos-2                 running (virtualbox)
```

If you have followed along recipe by recipe, you will have read Recipe 7.8. If not, read that recipe first to configure Ansible (*http://ansible.com*) on your machine. You will use an Ansible playbook to start a few containers on the VM. The playbook is *mesos.yml*. To start all containers, run the playbook:

```
$ ansible-playbook -u vagrant mesos.yml
```

Once the play is done, the Mesos head node will have three containers running (i.e., ZooKeeper, Mesos master, and the Marathon framework). The two slaves will have one container running (i.e., the Mesos slave). All images come from Docker Hub.

Open your browser at `http://192.168.33.10:5050` to access the Mesos UI, and then open your browser at `http://192.168.33.10:8080` to access the Marathon UI.

To start an Nginx container in that Mesos cluster, create a Mesos application in the Marathon framework using the API:

```
$ curl -si -H 'Content-Type: application/json' \
        -d @docker.json 192.168.33.10:8080/v2/apps
```

Once the image has been downloaded, you can access the Nginx welcome screen in a similar fashion as described in Recipe 7.11.

 The *docker.json* application definition specifies 128 MB of RAM. If your slaves do not have enough memory, the application could be stuck in *deploying* stage. Make sure that your slaves have enough RAM or reduce the memory constraints of your application.

Discussion

The inventory used by Ansible is harcoded in the *inventory* file. If you change the IP address of the nodes or add more nodes, make sure to update the inventory as well.

The current play executes `docker run` commands remotely over SSH. If you want to use the Ansible Docker module, comment the `command` tasks and uncomment the `docker` tasks.

You will notice that the Mesos slave runs as a container. When starting the container, you pass the environment variable `MESOS_CONTAINERIZERS=docker,mesos`, which configures the slave to use Docker. The slave will start other containers on the host itself. This is achieved by mounting */var/run/docker.sock*, */usr/bin/docker*, and */sys* from the host to the container. Although it works in the testing scenario, the Mesos containerizer is not made to do this. You should consider running the slave on the hosts themselves until Mesos development recommends running the slave in containers for production.

See Also

- Apache Mesos configuration (*http://mesos.apache.org/documentation/latest/configuration/*)

7.13 Discovering Docker Services with Registrator

Problem

You are building a distributed application with services based on containers started on multiple hosts. You need to automatically discover these services to configure your application. This is needed when services migrate from one host to another or when they are started automatically.

Solution

Use *registrator* (*https://github.com/gliderlabs/registrator*). It runs as a container on the hosts in your system. By mounting the Docker socket */var/run/docker.sock*, it listens to containers that come and go, and registers or unregisters them on a data store backend. Several backend data stores are available (e.g., etcd (*https://github.com/ coreos/etcd*), Consul (*https://www.consul.io*), and SkyDNS 2), and registrator can possibly support more. These service registries are not specific to Docker even though etcd comes bundled in the CoreOS distribution (see Recipe 6.3).

To use *registrator*, you first need to set up one backend for service registries. Since these are available as static binaries, you can download them and run them in the foreground for testing. For example, to use etcd:

```
$ curl -L  https://github.com/coreos/etcd/releases/download/v0.4.6/\
          etcd-v0.4.6-linux-amd64.tar.gz
       -o etcd-v0.4.6-linux-amd64.tar.gz
$ tar xzvf etcd-v0.4.6-linux-amd64.tar.gz
$ cd etcd-v0.4.6-linux-amd64
$ sudo ./etcd
2015/03/26 14:02:21 no data-dir provided, using default data-dir ./default.etcd
2015/03/26 14:02:21 etcd: listening for peers on http://localhost:2380
2015/03/26 14:02:21 etcd: listening for peers on http://localhost:7001
2015/03/26 14:02:21 etcd: listening for client requests on http://localhost:2379
2015/03/26 14:02:21 etcd: listening for client requests on http://localhost:4001
...
```

Leave etcd running. In another terminal session, create a directory in the etcd key-value store (e.g., *cookbook* in the following code). This directory will hold the services when they are discovered:

```
$ cd etcd-v0.4.6-linux-amd64
$ ./etcdctl mkdir cookbook
$ ./etcdctl ls
/cookbook
```

Then download the *registrator* image from Docker Hub and run it:

```
$ docker pull gliderlabs/registrator
$ docker run -d -v /var/run/docker.sock:/tmp/docker.sock
```

```
-h 192.168.33.10
gliderlabs/registrator
-ip 192.168.33.10
etcd://192.168.33.10:4001/cookbook
```

 You define the registry service backend as an argument to the *gliderlabs/registrator* image. Do not forget the name of the directory that you created with `etcdctl`. It completes the URI of your backend endpoint.

 Replace `192.168.33.10` with the IP address of your own setup. In this example, I ran everything on the same host. But you will most likely want to run an `etcd` cluster separate from your cluster of Docker hosts where you will run registrator.

You can now start any container, expose ports to the host, and you will see the registration in your `etcd` key-value store:

```
$ docker run -d -p 80:80 nginx
$ ./etcdctl ls /cookbook
/cookbook/nginx-80
$ ./etcdctl ls /cookbook/nginx-80
/cookbook/nginx-80/192.168.33.10:pensive_franklin:80
$ ./etcdctl get /cookbook/nginx-80/192.168.33.10:pensive_franklin:80
192.168.33.10:80
```

If you look at the logs of the registrator container, you will see that it is listening to Docker events and registering the ports exposed to the host:

```
$ docker logs <CONTAINER_ID>
2015/03/26 ... registrator: Forcing host IP to 192.168.33.10
2015/03/26 ... registrator: Using etcd registry backend at \
                            etcd://192.168.33.10:4001/cookbook
2015/03/26 ... registrator: ignored: 6f8043d9973f no published ports
2015/03/26 ... registrator: Listening for Docker events...
2015/03/26 ... registrator: ignored 8c033ca03a82 port 443 not published on host
2015/03/26 ... registrator: added: 8c033ca03a82 192.168.33.10:pensive_franklin:80
```

In these logs, `6f8043d9973f` is the container ID of the registrator container, and `8c033ca03a82` is the container ID of the Nginx container that you started.

Discussion

The naming convention for the keys stored in `etcd` is based on the `Service` object created by registrator and passed to the registry backend. From the GitHub repo (*https://github.com/gliderlabs/registrator*), the `Service` structure is defined like this:

```
type Service struct {
    ID      string                    // <hostname>:<container-name>:<internal-port>
                                       //[:udp if udp]
    Name    string                    // <basename(container-image)>
                                       //[-<internal-port> if >1 published ports]
    Port    int                       // <host-port>
    IP      string                    // <host-ip> || <resolve(hostname)> if 0.0.0.0
    Tags    []string                  // empty, or includes 'udp' if udp
    Attrs   map[string]string         // any remaining service metadata from environment
}
```

The key for the service is defined by the following:

```
<registry-uri-path>/<service-name>/<service-id>
```

In this example, it is then (see the ID definition in the Service object):

```
cookbook/nginx-80/192.168.33.10:pensive_franklin:80
```

and set to `<ip>:<port>` or in this example `192.168.33.10:80` (see the Port and IP definitions in the Service object).

If you do not want to use etcd but rather use consul (*http://consul.io*), you can switch the registry backend. You can easily try this on a single host, by using the *progrium/consul* image from Docker Hub. Pull the image and run the consul agent in one terminal session (the Consul container is not detached in this example):

```
$ docker pull progrium/consul
$ docker run -p 8400:8400 -p 8500:8500 -p 8600:53/udp
            -h cookbook progrium/consul -server
            -bootstrap -ui-dir /ui
```

In another session, start registrator but change the registry URI to *consul://192.168.33.10:8500/foobar*:

```
$ docker run -d -v /var/run/docker.sock:/tmp/docker.sock
            -h 192.168.33.10 gliderlabs/registrator
            -ip 192.168.33.10 consul://192.168.33.10:8500/foobar
```

You can now start an Nginx container:

```
$ docker run -d -p 80:80 nginx
```

And now, if you check the Consul UI at `http://192.168.33.10:8500/ui`, you will see that a *foobar* directory has been created with several keys in them: the keys for the Consul container itself and the key for your Nginx container. See Figure 7-9.

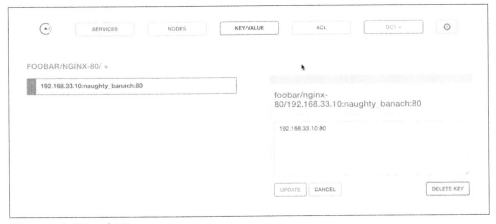

Figure 7-9. Consul UI

With Docker service registration under control, you can start thinking about dynamically reconfiguring other services (see Recipe 10.3).

See Also

- GitHub repository of registrator (*https://github.com/gliderlabs/registrator*)
- Original blog post from Jeff Lindsay (*http://progrium.com/blog/2014/09/10/automatic-docker-service-announcement-with-registrator/*)

## CHAPTER 8

Docker in the Cloud

8.0 Introduction

With the advent of public and private clouds, enterprises have moved an increasing number of workloads to the clouds. A significant portion of IT infrastructure is now provisioned on public clouds like Amazon Web Services (*http://aws.amazon.com*) (AWS), Google Compute Engine (*https://cloud.google.com*) (GCE), and Microsoft Azure (*http://azure.microsoft.com/en-us/*) (Azure). In addition, companies have deployed private clouds to provide a self-service infrastructure for IT needs.

Although Docker, like any software, runs on bare-metal servers, running a Docker host in a public or private cloud (i.e., on virtual machines) and orchestrating containers started on those hosts is going to be a critical part of new IT infrastructure needs. Figure 8-1 depicts a simple setup where you are accessing a remote Docker host in the cloud using your local Docker client.

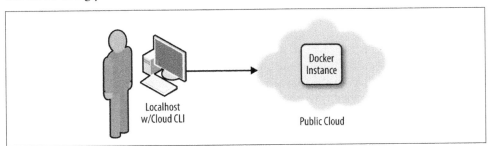

Figure 8-1. Docker in the cloud

This chapter covers the top three public clouds (i.e., AWS, GCE, and Azure) and some of the Docker services they offer. If you have never used a public cloud, now is the time and Recipe 8.1 will cover some basics to get you started. Then you will see how to use the CLI of these clouds to start instances and install Docker in Recipe 8.2, Recipe 8.3, and Recipe 8.4. To avoid installing the CLI we show you a trick in Recipe 8.7, where all the cloud clients can actually run in a container.

While Docker Machine (see Recipe 1.9) will ultimately remove the need to use these provider CLIs, learning how to start instances with them will help you use the other Docker-related cloud services. That being said, in Recipe 8.5 we show you how to start a Docker host in AWS EC2 using docker-machine and we do the same with Azure in Recipe 8.6.

We then present some Docker-related services on GCE and EC2. First on GCE, we look at the Google container registry, a hosted Docker registry that you can use with your Google account. It works like the Docker Hub but has the advantage of leveraging Google's authorization system to give access to your images to team members and the public if you want to. Google container virtual machines (VM) are then introduced in Recipe 8.9; they represent a nice short introduction to some of the concepts of Kubernetes while dealing with a single host. The hosted Kubernetes service, Google Container Engine (i.e., GKE), is presented in Recipe 8.10. GKE is the fastest way to experiment with Kubernetes if you already have a Google cloud account.

To finish this chapter, we look at two services on AWS that allow you to run your containers. First we look at the Amazon Container Service (*https://aws.amazon.com/ ecs/*) (i.e., ECS) in Recipe 8.11. We show you how to create an ECS cluster in Recipe 8.12 and how to run containers by defining tasks in Recipe 8.13. We wrap up with a walkthrough of using AWS Beanstalk to deploy your containers in Recipe 8.14.

In this chapter we show you how to use public clouds to create Docker hosts, and we also introduce some container-based services that have reached general availability recently: the AWS container service and the Google container engine. Both services mark a new trend in public cloud providers who need to embrace Docker as a new way to package, deploy and manage distributed applications. We can expect more services like these to come out and extend the capabilities of Docker and containers in general.

 AWS, GCE, and Azure are the recognized top-three public cloud providers in the world. However, Docker can be installed on any public cloud where you can run a Linux distribution supported by Docker (e.g., Ubuntu, CentOS, CoreOS).

8.1 Accessing Public Clouds to Run Docker

Problem

You need access to a public cloud to run Docker in cloud instances. You have never used a public cloud and need to quick walk-through to get you started.

Solution

If you do not already have access, create an account on your public cloud provider of choice:

- For GCE, you can start with a free trial (*https://cloud.google.com/*). You need a Google account. You can then log in to the console (*https://cloud.google.com/console*).

- For Azure, you can start with a free trial (*http://azure.microsoft.com/en-us/pricing/free-trial/*).

- For AWS, you can have access to a free tier (*http://aws.amazon.com/free/*). Once you create an account, you can log in to the console (*https://aws.amazon.com/console*).

Log into the web console of the provider that you want to use and go through the launch instance wizard. Make sure you can start an instance that you can connect to via `ssh`. Figure 8-2 shows the AWS console, Figure 8-3 shows the GCE console, and Figure 8-4 shows the Azure console.

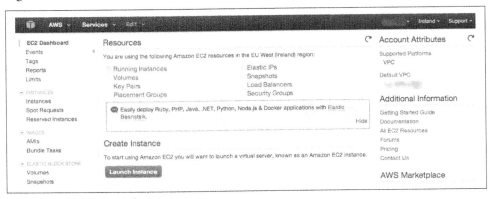

Figure 8-2. AWS console

Figure 8-3. GCE console

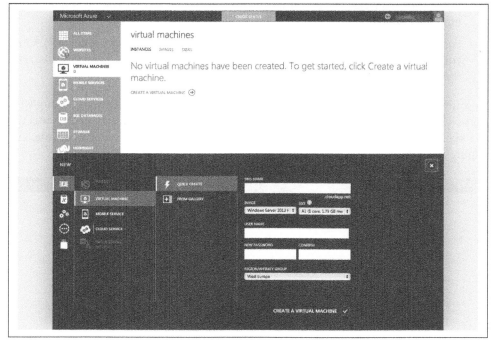

Figure 8-4. Azure console

Discussion

If you are not familiar with one of these clouds and have not completed this setup, you will not be able to follow the recipes in this chapter. However, a complete step-by-step walk-through of using these clouds is beyond the scope of this cookbook.

These instructions are not Docker-specific. Once you create an account on one of these clouds, you will have access to any of the cloud services provided.

On AWS, the recipes in this chapter will use the Elastic Compute Cloud (*http://aws.amazon.com/documentation/ec2/*) (EC2) service. To start instances, you need to become familiar with four basic principles:

- AWS API keys (*http://docs.aws.amazon.com/cli/latest/userguide/cli-chap-getting-set-up.html*) to use with the AWS command-line interface (CLI)
- SSH key pairs (*http://docs.aws.amazon.com/AWSEC2/latest/UserGuide/ec2-key-pairs.html*) to connect to your instances via ssh
- Security groups (*http://docs.aws.amazon.com/AWSEC2/latest/UserGuide/using-network-security.html*) to control traffic to and from EC2 instances
- Instance user data (*http://bit.ly/aws-instance*) to configure your instances at start-up time

On GCE, you will use the Google Compute Engine service (*https://cloud.google.com/compute/docs/*). The AWS principles also apply to GCE:

- GCE authentication (*https://cloud.google.com/compute/docs/authentication*). The rest of the chapter uses the gcloud CLI, which uses OAuth2 for authentication. Other types of authentication and authorization mechanisms are available for GCE.
- Using an SSH key to connect (*https://cloud.google.com/compute/docs/instances#sshkeys*) to an instance.
- Instance firewall (*https://cloud.google.com/compute/docs/networking#addingafirewall*).
- Instance metadata (*https://cloud.google.com/compute/docs/metadata#updatinginstancemetadata*).

See Also

- *Programming Amazon Web Services (http://bit.ly/prog-aws)*
- AWS Getting Started guide (*http://aws.amazon.com/documentation/gettingstar ted/*)
- *Automating Microsoft Azure Infrastructure Services* (*http://bit.ly/automat ing_azure_infrastructure*)
- GCE Getting Started guide (*https://cloud.google.com/compute/docs/signup*)

8.2 Starting a Docker Host on AWS EC2

Problem

You want to start a VM instance on the AWS EC2 cloud and use it as a Docker host.

Solution

Although you can start an instance and install Docker in it via the EC2 web console, you will use the AWS command-line interface (CLI). First, as mentioned in Recipe 8.1, you should obtain a set of API keys. In the web console, select your account name at the top right of the page and go to the Security Credentials page, shown in Figure 8-5. You will be able to create a new access key. The secret key corresponding to this new access key will be given to you only once, so make sure that you store it securely.

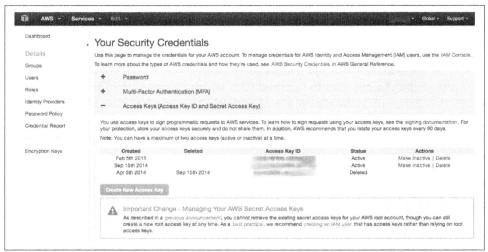

Figure 8-5. AWS Security Credentials page

You can then install the AWS CLI and configure it to use your newly generated keys. Select an AWS region (*http://bit.ly/aws-zone*) where you want to start your instances by default.

The AWS CLI, `aws`, is a Python package that can be installed via the Python Package Index (`pip`). For example, on Ubuntu:

```
$ sudo apt-get -y install python-pip
$ sudo pip install awscli
$ aws configure
AWS Access Key ID [****************n-mg]: AKIAIEFDGHQRTW3MNQ
AWS Secret Access Key [****************UjEg]: b4pWYhMUosg976arg9869Qd+Yg1qo22wC
Default region name [eu-east-1]: eu-west-1
Default output format [table]:
$ aws --version
aws-cli/1.7.4 Python/2.7.6 Linux/3.13.0-32-generic
```

To access your instance via `ssh`, you need to have an SSH key pair set up in EC2. Create a key pair via the CLI, copy the returned private key into a file in your *~/.ssh* folder, and make that file readable and writable only by you. Verify that the key has been created, either via the CLI or by checking the web console:

```
$ aws ec2 create-key-pair --key-name cookbook
$ vi ~/.ssh/id_rsa_cookbook
$ chmod 600 ~/.ssh/id_rsa_cookbook
$ aws ec2 describe-key-pairs
---------------------------------------------------------------------------
|                          DescribeKeyPairs                               |
+-------------------------------------------------------------------------+
||                            KeyPairs                                   ||
|+--------------------------------------------------------+------------+|
||                      KeyFingerprint                    |  KeyName   ||
|+--------------------------------------------------------+------------+|
||  69:aa:64:4b:72:50:ee:15:9a:da:71:4e:44:cd:db:c0:a1:72:38:36  | cookbook ||
|+--------------------------------------------------------+------------+|
```

You are ready to start an instance on EC2. The standard Linux images from AWS now contain a Docker repository. Hence when starting an EC2 instance from an Amazon Linux AMI, you will be one step away from running Docker (`sudo yum install docker`):

 Use a paravirtualized (PV) Amazon Linux AMI, so that you can use a `t1.micro` instance type. In addition, the default security group allows you to connect via `ssh`, so you do not need to create any additional rules in the security group if you only need to `ssh` to it.

```
$ aws ec2 run-instances --image-id ami-7b3db00c
                        --count 1
                        --instance-type t1.micro
```

```
                     --key-name cookbook
$ aws ec2 describe-instances
$ ssh -i ~/.ssh/id_rsa_cookbook ec2-user@54.194.31.39
The authenticity of host '54.194.31.39 (54.194.31.39)' can't be established.
RSA key fingerprint is 9b:10:32:10:ac:46:62:b4:7a:a5:94:7d:4b:2a:9f:61.
Are you sure you want to continue connecting (yes/no)? yes
Warning: Permanently added '54.194.31.39' (RSA) to the list of known hosts.

     __|  __|_  )
     _|  (     /   Amazon Linux AMI
    ___|\___|___|

https://aws.amazon.com/amazon-linux-ami/2014.09-release-notes/
[ec2-user@ip-172-31-8-174 ~]$
```

Install the Docker package, start the Docker daemon, and verify that the Docker CLI
is working:

```
[ec2-user@ip-172-31-8-174 ~]$ sudo yum update
[ec2-user@ip-172-31-8-174 ~]$ sudo yum install docker
[ec2-user@ip-172-31-8-174 ~]$ sudo service docker start
[ec2-user@ip-172-31-8-174 ~]$ sudo docker ps
CONTAINER ID    IMAGE       COMMAND     CREATED     STATUS      PORTS       NAMES
```

Do not forget to terminate the instance or you might get charged for it:

```
$ aws ec2 terminate-instances --instance-ids <instance id>
```

Discussion

You spent some time in this recipe creating API access keys and installing the CLI.
Hopefully, you see the ease of creating Docker hosts in AWS. The standard AMIs are
now ready to go to install Docker in two commands.

The Amazon Linux AMI also contains cloud-init (*https://
cloudinit.readthedocs.org/en/latest/*), which has become the standard for configuring
cloud instances at boot time. This allows you to pass *user data* at instance creation.
cloud-init parses the content of the user data and executes the commands. Using
the AWS CLI, you can pass some user data to automatically install Docker. The small
downside is that it needs to be base64-encoded.

Create a small bash script with the two commands from earlier:

```
#!/bin/bash
yum -y install docker
service docker start
```

Encode this script and pass it to the instance creation command:

```
$ udata="$(cat docker.sh | base64 )"
$ aws ec2 run-instances --image-id ami-7b3db00c \
                        --count 1 \
```

```
                    --instance-type t1.micro \
                    --key-name cookbook \
                    --user-data $udata
$ ssh -i ~/.ssh/id_rsa_cookbook ec2-user@<public IP of the created instance>
$ sudo docker ps
CONTAINER ID    IMAGE        COMMAND      CREATED      STATUS       PORTS        NAMES
```

With the Docker daemon running, if you wanted to access it remotely, you would need to set up TLS access (see Recipe 4.9), and open port 2376 in your security group.

Using this CLI is not Docker-specific. This CLI gives you access to the complete set of AWS APIs. However, using it to start instances and install Docker in them significantly streamlines the provisioning of Docker hosts.

See Also

- Installing the AWS CLI (*http://docs.aws.amazon.com/cli/latest/userguide/instal ling.html*)

- Configuring the AWS CLI (*http://docs.aws.amazon.com/cli/latest/userguide/cli-chap-getting-started.html*)

- Launching an instance via the AWS CLI (*http://docs.aws.amazon.com/cli/latest/userguide/cli-ec2-launch.html*)

8.3 Starting a Docker Host on Google GCE

Problem

You want to start a VM instance on the Google GCE cloud and use it as a Docker host.

Solution

Install the gcloud (*https://cloud.google.com/sdk/gcloud/*) CLI (you will need to answer a few questions), and then log in to the Google cloud. If the CLI can open a browser, you will be redirected to a web page and asked to sign in and accept the terms of use. If your terminal cannot launch a browser, you will be given a URL to open in a browser. This will give you an access token to enter at the command prompt:

```
$ curl https://sdk.cloud.google.com | bash
$ gcloud auth login
```

```
Your browser has been opened to visit:
    https://accounts.google.com/o/oauth2/auth?redirect_uri=...
...
$ gcloud compute zones list
NAME            REGION        STATUS  NEXT_MAINTENANCE TURNDOWN_DATE
asia-east1-c    asia-east1    UP
asia-east1-a    asia-east1    UP
asia-east1-b    asia-east1    UP
europe-west1-b  europe-west1  UP
europe-west1-c  europe-west1  UP
us-central1-f   us-central1   UP
us-central1-b   us-central1   UP
us-central1-a   us-central1   UP
```

If you have not set up a project, set one up in the web console (*https://cloud.google.com/storage/docs/projects*). Projects allow you to manage team members and assign specific permission to each member. It is roughly equivalent to the Amazon Identity and Access Management (IAM) service.

To start instances, it is handy to set some defaults for the region and zone (*https://cloud.google.com/compute/docs/zones*) that you would prefer to use (even though deploying a robust system in the cloud will involve instances in multiple regions and zones). To do this, use the gcloud config set command; for example:

```
$ gcloud config set compute/region europe-west1
$ gcloud config set compute/zone europe-west1-c
$ gcloud config list --all
```

To start an instance, you need an image name (*https://cloud.google.com/sdk/gcloud/reference/compute/instances/create*) and an instance type (*https://cloud.google.com/compute/docs/machine-types*). Then the gcloud tool does the rest:

```
$ gcloud compute instances create cookbook \
                --machine-type n1-standard-1 \
                --image ubuntu-14-04 \
                --metadata startup-script=\
                            "sudo wget -qO- https://get.docker.com/ | sh"
...
$ gcloud compute ssh cookbook
sebastiengoasguen@cookbook:~$ sudo docker ps
CONTAINER ID    IMAGE    COMMAND    CREATED    STATUS    PORTS    NAMES
...
$ gcloud compute instances delete cookbook
```

In this example, you created an Ubuntu 14.04 instance, of machine type n1-standard-1 and passed metadata specifying that it was to be used as a start-up script. The bash command specified installed the *docker.io* package from the standard Ubuntu repository. This led to a running instance with Docker running. The GCE metadata is relatively equivalent to the AWS EC2 user data and is processed by cloud-init in the instance.

Discussion

If you list the images available in a zone, you will see that some are interesting for Docker-specific tasks:

```
$ gcloud compute images list
NAME                                       PROJECT             ALIAS           ... STATUS
...
centos-7-v20150710                         centos-cloud        centos-7            READY
...
coreos-alpha-774-0-0-v20150814             coreos-cloud                            READY
...
container-vm-v20150806                     google-containers   container-vm        READY
...
ubuntu-1404-trusty-v20150805               ubuntu-os-cloud     ubuntu-14-04        READY
...
windows-server-2012-r2-dc-v20150813        windows-cloud       windows-2012-r2     READY
...
```

Indeed, GCE provides CoreOS (*http://coreos.com*) images, as well as container VMs (*https://cloud.google.com/compute/docs/containers/container_vms*). CoreOS is discussed in Chapter 6. Container VMs are Debian 7–based instances that contain the Docker daemon and the Kubernetes (*http://kubernetes.io*) kubelet. Kubernetes is discussed in Chapter 5, and Recipe 8.9 provides more detail about the container VM.

If you want to start a CoreOS instance, you can use the image alias. You do not need to specify any metadata to install Docker:

```
$ gcloud compute instances create cookbook --machine-type n1-standard-1 \
                                  --image coreos
$ gcloud compute ssh cookbook
...
CoreOS (stable)
sebastiengoasguen@cookbook ~ $ docker ps
CONTAINER ID    IMAGE    COMMAND    CREATED    STATUS    PORTS    NAMES
```

 Using the `gcloud` CLI is not Docker-specific. This CLI gives you access to the complete set of GCE APIs. However, using it to start instances and install Docker in them significantly streamlines the provisioning of Docker hosts.

8.4 Starting a Docker Host on Microsoft Azure

Problem

You want to start a VM instance on the Microsoft Azure cloud and use it as a Docker host.

Solution

First you need an account on Azure (see Figure 8-1). If you do not want to use the Azure portal (*https://manage.windowsazure.com*), you need to install the Azure CLI. On a fresh Ubuntu 14.04 machine, you would do this:

```
$ sudo apt-get update
$ sudo apt-get -y install nodejs-legacy
$ sudo apt-get -y install npm
$ sudo npm install -g azure-cli
$ azure -v
0.8.14
```

Then you need to set up your account for authentication from the CLI. Several methods are available (*http://azure.microsoft.com/en-us/documentation/articles/xplat-cli/*). One is to download your account settings from the portal and import them on the machine you are using the CLI from:

```
$ azure account download
$ azure account import ~/Downloads/Free\
Trial-2-5-2015-credentials.publishsettings
$ azure account list
```

You are now ready to use the Azure CLI to start VM instances. Pick a location and an image:

```
$ azure vm image list | grep Ubuntu
$ azure vm location list
info:     Executing command vm location list
+ Getting locations
data:     Name
data:     ----------------
data:     West Europe
data:     North Europe
data:     East US 2
data:     Central US
data:     South Central US
data:     West US
data:     East US
data:     Southeast Asia
data:     East Asia
data:     Japan West
info:     vm location list command OK
```

To create an instance with `ssh` access using password authentication, use the `azure vm create` command:

```
$ azure vm create cookbook --ssh=22 \
                     --password #@$#%#@$ \
                     --userName cookbook \
                     --location "West Europe" \
                     b39f27a8b8c64d52b05eac6a62ebad85__Ubuntu-14_04_1-LTS \
```

```
                           -amd64-server-20150123-en-us-30GB
...
$ azure vm list
...
data:   Name      Status      Location      DNS Name               IP Address
data:   --------  ---------   -----------   ---------------------  -------------
data:   cookbook  ReadyRole   West Europe   cookbook.cloudapp.net  100.91.96.137
info:   vm list command OK
```

You can then ssh to the instance and set up Docker as you did in Recipe 1.1.

Discussion

The Azure CLI is still under active development (*https://msopentech.com/blog/
2014/10/08/latest-updates-to-azure-cli/*). The source can be found on GitHub (*https://
github.com/Azure/azure-xplat-cli*), and a Docker Machine driver is available (*https://
github.com/docker/machine#microsoft-azure*).

The Azure CLI also allows you to create a Docker host automatically by using the
azure vm docker create command:

```
$ azure vm docker create goasguen -l "West Europe" \
                          b39f27a8b8c64d52b05eac6a62ebad85__Ubuntu \
                          -14_04_1-LTS-amd64-server-20150123-en-us \
                          -30GB cookbook @#$%@#$%$
info:   Executing command vm docker create
warn:   --vm-size has not been specified. Defaulting to "Small".
info:   Found docker certificates.
...
info:   vm docker create command OK
$ azure vm list
info:   Executing command vm list
+ Getting virtual machines
data:   Name      Status      Location      DNS Name               IP Address
data:   --------  ---------   -----------   ---------------------  -------------
data:   goasguen  ReadyRole   West Europe   goasguen.cloudapp.net  100.112.4.136
```

The host started will automatically have the Docker daemon running, and you can
connect to it by using the Docker client and a TLS connection:

```
$ docker --tls -H tcp://goasguen.cloudapp.net:4243 ps
CONTAINER ID    IMAGE      COMMAND      CREATED      STATUS      PORTS      NAMES
$ docker --tls -H tcp://goasguen.cloudapp.net:4243 images
REPOSITORY   TAG    IMAGE ID    CREATED      VIRTUAL SIZE
```

 Using this CLI is not Docker-specific. This CLI gives you access to
the complete set of Azure APIs. However, using it to start instances
and install Docker in them significantly streamlines the provisioning of Docker hosts.

See Also

- The Azure command-line interface (*http://azure.microsoft.com/en-us/documenta tion/articles/xplat-cli/*)
- Starting a CoreOS (*https://coreos.com/docs/running-coreos/cloud-providers/azure/ #via-the-cross-platform-cli*) instance on Azure
- Using Docker Machine with Azure (*https://github.com/chanezon/azure-linux/ blob/master/docker/machine.md*)

8.5 Starting a Docker Host on AWS Using Docker Machine

Problem

You understand how to use the AWS CLI to start an instance in the cloud and know how to install Docker (see Recipe 8.2). But you would like to use a streamlined process integrated with the Docker user experience.

Solution

Use Docker Machine (*https://github.com/docker/machine*) and its AWS EC2 driver.

Download the release candidate binaries for Docker Machine. Set some environment variables so that Docker Machine knows your AWS API keys and your default VPC in which to start the Docker host. Then use Docker Machine to start the instance. Docker automatically sets up a TLS connection, and you can use this remote Docker host started in AWS. On a 64-bit Linux machine, do the following:

```
$ sudo su
# curl -L https://github.com/docker/machine/releases/\
        download/v0.4.0/docker-machine_linux-amd64 > \
                /usr/local/bin/docker-machine
# chmod +x docker-machine
# exit
$ export AWS_ACCESS_KEY_ID=<your AWS access key>
$ export AWS_SECRET_ACCESS_KEY_ID=<your AWS secret key>
$ export AWS_VPC_ID=<the VPC ID you want to start the instance in>
$ docker-machine create -d amazonec2 cookbook
INFO[0000] Launching instance...
INFO[0023] Waiting for SSH ...
...
INFO[0129] "cookbook" has been created and is now the active machine
INFO[0129] To connect: docker $(docker-machine config cookbook) ps
```

Once the machine has been created, you can use your local Docker client to communicate with it. Do not forget to kill the machine after you are finished:

```
$ eval "$(docker-machine env cookbook)" ps
CONTAINER ID    IMAGE       COMMAND     CREATED     STATUS      PORTS       NAMES
$ docker-machine ls
NAME        ACTIVE   DRIVER      STATE       URL
cookbook    *        amazonec2   Running     tcp://<IP_Docker_Machine_AWS>:2376
$ docker-machine kill cookbook
```

You can manage your machines directly from the Docker Machine CLI:

```
$ docker-machine -h
...
COMMANDS:
    active Get or set the active machine
    create Create a machine
    config Print the connection config for machine
    inspect  Inspect information about a machine
    ip   Get the IP address of a machine
    kill   Kill a machine
    ls   List machines
    restart  Restart a machine
    rm    Remove a machine
    env    Display the commands to set up the environment for
           the Docker client
    ssh    Log into or run a command on a machine with SSH
    start  Start a machine
    stop   Stop a machine
    upgrade  Upgrade a machine to the latest version of Docker
    url    Get the URL of a machine
    help, h  Shows a list of commands or help for one command
```

Discussion

Docker Machine contains drivers for several cloud providers (*https://github.com/docker/machine/tree/master/drivers*). We already showcased the Digital Ocean driver (see Recipe 1.9), and you can see how to use it for Azure in Recipe 8.6.

The AWS driver takes several command-line options to set your keys, VPC, key pair, image, and instance type. You can set them up as environment variables as you did previously or directly on the machine command line:

```
$ docker-machine create -h
...
OPTIONS:
    --amazonec2-access-key              AWS Access Key [$AWS_ACCESS_KEY_ID]
    --amazonec2-ami                     AWS machine image [$AWS_AMI]
    --amazonec2-instance-type 't2.micro'  AWS instance type [$AWS_INSTANCE_TYPE]
    --amazonec2-region 'us-east-1'      AWS region [$AWS_DEFAULT_REGION]
    --amazonec2-root-size '16'          AWS root disk size (in GB) ...
    --amazonec2-secret-key              AWS Secret Key [$AWS_SECRET_ACCESS_KEY]
```

```
--amazonec2-security-group          AWS VPC security group ...
--amazonec2-session-token           AWS Session Token [$AWS_SESSION_TOKEN]
--amazonec2-subnet-id               AWS VPC subnet id [$AWS_SUBNET_ID]
--amazonec2-vpc-id                  AWS VPC id [$AWS_VPC_ID]
--amazonec2-zone 'a'                AWS zone for instance ... [$AWS_ZONE]
```

Finally, machine will create an SSH key pair and a security group for you. The security group will open traffic on port 2376 to allow communications over TLS from a Docker client. Figure 8-6 shows the rules of the security group in the AWS console.

Figure 8-6. Security group for machine

8.6 Starting a Docker Host on Azure with Docker Machine

Problem

You know how to start a Docker host on Azure by using the Azure CLI, but you would like to unify the way you start Docker hosts in multiple public clouds by using Docker Machine.

Solution

Use the Docker Machine Azure driver. In Figure 1-7, you saw how to use *Docker Machine* to start a Docker host on DigitalOcean. The same thing can be done on Microsoft Azure. You will need a valid subscription to Azure (*http://azure.micro soft.com/en-us/pricing/free-trial/*).

You need to download the *docker-machine* binary. Go to the documentation site (*https://docs.docker.com/machine/*) and choose the correct binary for your local computer architecture. For example, on OS X:

```
$ wget https://github.com/docker/machine/releases/download/v0.4.0/ \
docker-machine_darwin-amd64
$ mv docker-machine_darwin-amd64 docker-machine
$ chmod +x docker-machine
$ ./docker-machine --version
docker-machine version 0.3.0
```

With a valid Azure subscription, create an X.509 certificate and upload it through the Azure portal (*https://manage.windowsazure.com*). You can create the certificate with the following commands:

```
$ openssl req -x509 -nodes -days 365 -newkey rsa:1024 \
        -keyout mycert.pem -out mycert.pem
$ openssl pkcs12 -export -out mycert.pfx -in mycert.pem -name "My Certificate"
$ openssl x509 -inform pem -in mycert.pem -outform der -out mycert.cer
```

Upload *mycert.cer* and define the following environment variables:

```
$ export AZURE_SUBSCRIPTION_ID=<UID of your subscription>
$ export AZURE_SUBSCRIPTION_CERT=mycert.pem
```

You can then use `docker-machine` and set your local Docker client to use this remote Docker daemon:

```
$ ./docker-machine create -d azure goasguen-foobar
INFO[0002] Creating Azure machine...
INFO[0061] Waiting for SSH...
INFO[0360] "goasguen-foobar" has been created and is now the active machine.
INFO[0360] To point your Docker client at it, run this in your shell: \
$(docker-machine env goasguen-foobar)
$ ./docker-machine ls
NAME        ACTIVE   DRIVER   STATE     URL                                     SWARM
toto1111    *        azure    Running   tcp://goasguen-foobar.cloudapp.net:2376
$ $(docker-machine env goasguen-foobar)
$ docker ps
CONTAINER ID    IMAGE    COMMAND    CREATED    STATUS    PORTS    NAMES
```

In this example, `goasguen-foobar` is the name that I gave to my Docker machine. This needs to be a globally unique name. Chances are that names like *foobar* and *test* have already been taken.

Discussion

With your local Docker client set up to use the remote Docker daemon running in this Azure virtual machine, you can pull images from your favorite registries and start containers.

For example, let's start an Nginx container:

```
$ docker pull nginx
$ docker run -d -p 80:80 nginx
```

To expose port 80 of this remote host in Azure, you need to add an endpoint to the VM that was created. Head over to the Azure portal, select the VM (here, goasguen-foobar), and add an endpoint for the HTTP request, as in Figure 8-7. Once the endpoint is created, you can access Nginx at http://<unique_name>.cloudapp.net.

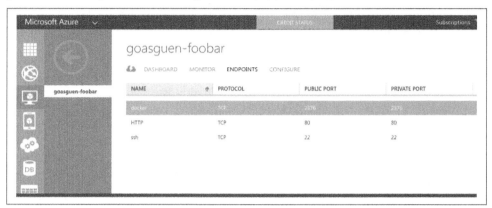

Figure 8-7. Azure endpoint for a virtual machine

See Also

- Docker Machine Azure driver documentation (*http://docs.docker.com/machine/#microsoft-azure*)

8.7 Running a Cloud Provider CLI in a Docker Container

Problem

You want to take advantage of containers and run your cloud provider CLI of choice within a container. This gives you more portability options and avoids having to install the CLI from scratch. You just need to download a container image from the Docker Hub.

Solution

For the Google GCE CLI, there is a public image (*https://registry.hub.docker.com/u/google/cloud-sdk/*) maintained by Google. Download the image via docker pull and run your GCE commands through interactive ephemeral containers.

For example, using boot2docker on an OS X machine:

```
$ boot2docker up
$ $(boot2docker shellinit)
$ docker pull google/cloud-sdk
$ docker images | grep google
google/cloud-sdk    latest    a7e7bcdfdc16    10 days ago    1.263 GB
```

You can then log in and issue commands as described in Recipe 8.3. The only difference is that the CLI is running within containers. The login command is issued
through a named container. That named container is used as a data volume container
(i.e., --volumes-from cloud-config) in subsequent CLI calls. This allows you to use
the authorization token that is stored in it:

```
$ docker run -t -i --name gcloud-config google/cloud-sdk gcloud auth login
Go to the following link in your browser:
...
$ docker run --rm \
            -ti \
            --volumes-from gcloud-config google/cloud-sdk \
            gcloud compute zones list
NAME             REGION        STATUS    NEXT_MAINTENANCE TURNDOWN_DATE
asia-east1-c     asia-east1    UP
asia-east1-a     asia-east1    UP
asia-east1-b     asia-east1    UP
europe-west1-b   europe-west1  UP
europe-west1-c   europe-west1  UP
us-central1-f    us-central1   UP
us-central1-b    us-central1   UP
us-central1-a    us-central1   UP
```

Using an alias makes things even better:

```
$ alias magic='docker run --rm \
               -ti \
               --volumes-from gcloud-config \
               google/cloud-sdk gcloud'
$ magic compute zones list
NAME             REGION        STATUS    NEXT_MAINTENANCE TURNDOWN_DATE
asia-east1-c     asia-east1    UP
asia-east1-a     asia-east1    UP
asia-east1-b     asia-east1    UP
europe-west1-b   europe-west1  UP
europe-west1-c   europe-west1  UP
us-central1-f    us-central1   UP
us-central1-b    us-central1   UP
us-central1-a    us-central1   UP
```

Discussion

A similar process can be used for AWS. If you search for an *awscli* image on Docker
Hub, you will see several options. The Dockerfile (*https://registry.hub.docker.com/u/
nathanleclaire/awscli/dockerfile/*) provided shows you how the image was constructed

and the CLI installed within the image. If you take the *nathanleclaire/awscli* image, you notice that no volumes are mounted to keep the credentials from container to container. Hence you need to pass the AWS access keys as environment variables when you launch a container:

```
$ docker pull nathanleclaire/awscli
$ docker run --rm \
          -ti \
          -e AWS_ACCESS_KEY_ID="AKIAIUCASDLGFIGDFGS" \
          -e AWS_SECRET_ACCESS_KEY="HwQdNnAIqrwy9797arghqQERfrgot" \
          nathanleclaire/awscli \
          --region eu-west-1 \
          --output=table \
          ec2 describe-key-pairs
-------------------------------------------------------------------------------
|                               DescribeKeyPairs                              |
+-----------------------------------------------------------------------------+
||                                 KeyPairs                                  ||
|+-------------------------------------------------------------+-----------+|
||                       KeyFingerprint                         |  KeyName  ||
|+-------------------------------------------------------------+-----------+|
||  69:aa:64:4b:72:50:ee:15:9a:da:71:4e:44:cd:db:c0:a1:72:38:36 |  cookbook ||
|+-------------------------------------------------------------+-----------+|
```

Also notice that `aws` was set up as an entry point in this image. Therefore, there you don't need to specify it and should only pass arguments to it.

 You can build your own AWS CLI image that allows you to handle API keys more easily.

See Also

- Official documentation (*https://registry.hub.docker.com/u/google/cloud-sdk/*) on the containerized Google SDK

8.8 Using Google Container Registry to Store Your Docker Images

Problem

You have used a Docker private registry hosted on your own infrastructure (see Recipe 2.11) but you would like to take advantage of a hosted service. Specifically, you would like to take advantage of the newly announced Google container registry (*https://cloud.google.com/tools/container-registry/*).

 Other hosted private registry solutions exist, including Docker Hub Enterprise (*https://www.docker.com/enterprise/hub/*) and Quay.io (*https://quay.io*). This recipe does not represent an endorsement of one versus another.

Solution

If you have not done so yet, go through Recipe 8.1 to sign up on Google Cloud Platform. Then download the Google Cloud CLI and create a project (see Recipe 8.3). Make sure that you update your `gcloud` CLI on your Docker host to load the preview components. You will have access to `gcloud docker`, which is a wrapper around the docker client:

```
$ gcloud components update
$ gcloud docker help
Usage: docker [OPTIONS] COMMAND [arg...]

A self-sufficient runtime for linux containers.
...
```

This example creates a *cookbook* project (*https://cloud.google.com/storage/docs/projects*) on Google Cloud with the project ID *sylvan-plane-862*. Your project name and project ID will differ.

As an example, on the Docker host that we are using, we have a *busybox* image that we uploaded to the Google Container Registry (GCR). You need to tag the image you want to push to the GCR so that it follows the namespace naming convention of the GCR (i.e., `gcr.io/project_id/image_name`). You can then upload the image with `gcloud docker push`:

```
$ docker images | grep busybox
busybox     latest      a9eb17255234     8 months ago     2.433 MB
$ docker tag busybox gcr.io/sylvan_plane_862/busybox
$ gcloud docker push gcr.io/sylvan_plane_862/busybox
The push refers to a repository [gcr.io/sylvan_plane_862/busybox] (len: 1)
Sending image list
Pushing repository gcr.io/sylvan_plane_862/busybox (1 tags)
511136ea3c5a: Image successfully pushed
42eed7f1bf2a: Image successfully pushed
120e218dd395: Image successfully pushed
a9eb17255234: Image successfully pushed
Pushing tag for rev [a9eb17255234] on \
{https://gcr.io/v1/repositories/sylvan_plane_862/busybox/tags/latest}
```

The naming convention of the GCR namespace is such that if you have dashes in your project ID, you need to replace them with underscores.

If you navigate to your storage browser in your Google Developers console, you will see that a new bucket has been created and that all the layers making your image have been uploaded (see Figure 8-8).

Figure 8-8. Google container registry image

Discussion

Automatically, Google compute instances that you started in the same project that you used to push the images to, will have the correct privileges to pull that image. If you want other people to be able to pull that image, you need to add them as members to that project. You can set your project by default with `gcloud config set project <project_id>` so you do not have to specify it on subsequent `gcloud` commands.

Let's start an instance in GCE, `ssh` to it, and pull the *busybox* image from GCR:

```
$ gcloud compute instances create cookbook-gce --image container-vm \
                                              --zone europe-west1-c \
                                              --machine-type f1-micro
$ gcloud compute ssh cookbook-gce
Updated [https://www.googleapis.com/compute/v1/projects/sylvan-plane-862].
...
$ sudo gcloud docker pull gcr.io/sylvan_plane_862/busybox
Pulling repository gcr.io/sylvan_plane_862/busybox
a9eb17255234: Download complete
511136ea3c5a: Download complete
42eed7f1bf2a: Download complete
120e218dd395: Download complete
```

```
Status: Downloaded newer image for gcr.io/sylvan_plane_862/busybox:latest
sebastiengoasguen@cookbook:~$ sudo docker images | grep busybox
gcr.io/sylvan_plane_862/busybox    latest    a9eb17255234    ...
```

To be able to push from a GCE instance, you need to start it with the correct scope: `--scopes https://www.googleapis.com/auth/devstorage.read_write`.

8.9 Using Docker in GCE Google-Container Instances

Problem

You know how to start instances in Google GCE and configure Docker to be set up at boot time, but you would like to use an image that is already configured with Docker.

Solution

As mentioned in Recipe 8.3, GCE offers *container-optimized images.*

Make sure that you set your project to the project ID with `gcloud config set project <project_id>`.

```
$ gcloud compute images list
NAME                                PROJECT            ALIAS         DEPRECATED STATUS
...
container-vm-v20141208              google-containers  container-vm             READY
container-vm-v20150112              google-containers  container-vm             READY
container-vm-v20150129              google-containers  container-vm             READY
...
```

These images (*https://cloud.google.com/compute/docs/containers/container_vms*), which are based on Debian 7, contain the Docker daemon and the Kubernetes (*http://kubernetes.io*) `kubelet` service.

Kubernetes is discussed in more detail in Chapter 5.

The `kubelet` service running in instances based on these images allows the user to pass a manifest (known as a *pod* (*https://github.com/kubernetes/kubernetes/blob/*

master/docs/user-guide/pods.md)) that describes the set of containers that need to run in the instance. The `kubelet` will start the containers and monitor them. A pod manifest is a YAML file like so:

```
version: v1
kind: Pod
metadata:
  name: nginx
spec:
  containers:
    - name: nginx
      image: nginx
      ports:
        - name: nginx
          hostPort: 80
          containerPort: 80
```

 Your image in the pod manifest can reference an image in the Google Container Registry (see Recipe 8.8)—for instance, `gcr.io/<your_project_name>/busybox`.

This simple manifest describes a single container based on the *nginx* image and an exposed port. You can pass this manifest to the `gcloud` instance creation command. Save the preceding YAML file in *nginx.yml* to start the instance:

```
$ gcloud compute instances create cookbook-gce \
        --image container-vm \
        --metadata-from-file google-container-manifest=nginx.yml \
        --zone europe-west1-c \
        --machine-type f1-micro
```

In your Google GCE console, you can browse to the started instance (see Figure 8-9). You can allow HTTP traffic as well as see the container manifest you passed. If the API version has been updated, you will see a `v1` instead of a `v2`. Once the containers defined in the pod manifest have started, open your browser at the IP of the instance on port 80 and you will see the Nginx welcome page.

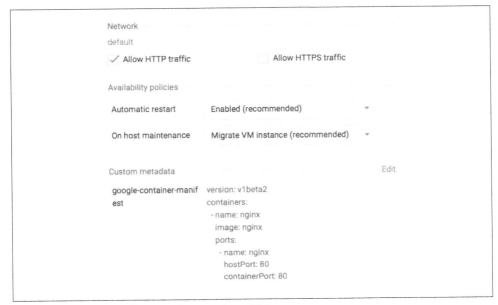

Network

default

✓ Allow HTTP traffic   ☐ Allow HTTPS traffic

Availability policies

Automatic restart   Enabled (recommended)   ▾

On host maintenance   Migrate VM instance (recommended)   ▾

Custom metadata   Edit

google-container-manif   version: v1beta2
est   containers:
                            - name: nginx
                              image: nginx
                              ports:
                                - name: nginx
                                  hostPort: 80
                                  containerPort: 80

Figure 8-9. Pod manifest in GCE container VM

Discussion

If you connect to the instance directly via `ssh`, you can list the containers that are running. You will see a *google/cadvisor* container used for monitoring and two *kubernetes/pause:go* containers. The last two act as network proxy to the *cadvisor* monitoring container and to the pod exposed ports.

```
$ gcloud compute ssh cookbook-gce
...
sebastiengoasguen@cookbook-gce:~$ sudo docker ps
CONTAINER ID      IMAGE                  COMMAND                    ...
1f83bb1197c9      nginx:latest           "nginx -g 'daemon of       ...
b1e6fed3ee20      google/cadvisor:0.8.0  "/usr/bin/cadvisor"        ...
79e879c48e9e      kubernetes/pause:go    "/pause"                   ...
0c1a51ab2f94      kubernetes/pause:go    "/pause"                   ...
```

Chapter 9 covers `cadvisor` (*https://github.com/google/cadvisor*).

8.10 Using Kubernetes in the Cloud via GCE

Problem

You want to use a group of Docker hosts and manage containers on them. You like the Kubernetes (*https://kubernetes.io*) container orchestration engine but would like to use it as a hosted cloud service.

Solution

Use the Google Container Engine (*https://cloud.google.com/container-engine/*) service. This new service allows you to create a Kubernetes cluster on-demand using the Google API. A cluster will be composed of a master node and a set of compute nodes that act as container VMs, similar to what was described in Recipe 8.9.

 Google Container Engine is in Beta. Kubernetes is under heavy development. Expect frequent changes to the API and use it in production at your own risk. For details on Kubernetes, see Chapter 5.

Update your gcloud SDK to use the container engine preview. If you have not yet installed the Google SDK, see Recipe 8.3.

```
$ gcloud components update
```

Starting a Kubernetes cluster using the Google Container Engine service requires a single command:

```
$ gcloud container clusters create cook --num-nodes 1 --machine-type g1-small
Creating cluster cook...done.
Created [https://container.googleapis.com/v1/projects/sylvan-plane-862/zones/ \
us-central1-f/clusters/cook].
kubeconfig entry generated for cook.
NAME   ZONE            MASTER_VERSION   MASTER_IP       MACHINE_TYPE   STATUS
cook   us-central1-f   1.0.3            104.197.33.61   g1-small       RUNNING
```

Your cluster IP addresses, project name, and zone will differ from what is shown here. What you do see is that a Kubernetes configuration file, *kubeconfig*, was generated for you. It is located at *~/.kube/config* and contains the endpoint of your container cluster as well as the credentials to use it.

You could also create a cluster through the Google Cloud web console (see Figure 8-10).

Google Developers Console   +Sebastien

App Engine

Compute Engine

   VM instances

   Instance groups

   Instance templates

   Disks

   Snapshots

   Images

   Networks

   Network load balancing

   HTTP load balancing

   Metadata

   Zones

   Operations

   Quotas

Container Engine

Click to Deploy

Container Engine ALPHA
Container clusters.

Containers package an application so it can be easily deployed to run in its own isolated environment. Containers are managed in clusters that automate VM creation and maintenance. Learn more

Create a container cluster

Figure 8-10. Container Engine Wizard

Once your cluster is up, you can submit containers to it—meaning that you can inter‐ act with the underlying Kubernetes master node to launch a group of containers on the set of nodes in your cluster. Groups of containers are defined as *pods*. This is the same concept introduced in Recipe 8.9. The gcloud CLI gives you a convenient way to define simple pods and submit them to the cluster. Next you are going to launch a container using the *tutum/wordpress* image, which contains a MySQL database. When you installed the gcloud CLI, it also installed the Kubernetes client kubectl. You can verify that kubectl is in your path. It will use the configuration that was autogener‐ ated when you created the cluster. This will allow you to launch containers from your local machine on the remote container cluster securely:

```
$ kubectl run wordpress --image=tutum/wordpress --port=80
$ kubectl get pods
NAME              READY    STATUS    RESTARTS    AGE
wordpress-0d58l   1/1      Running   0           1m
```

Once the container is scheduled on one of the cluster nodes, you need to create a Kubernetes service to expose the application running in the container to the outside world. This is done again with kubectl:

```
$ kubectl expose rc wordpress --create-external-load-balancer=true
NAME        LABELS           SELECTOR        IP(S)      PORT(S)
wordpress   run=wordpress    run=wordpress              80/TCP
```

The `expose` command creates a Kubernetes service (one of the three Kubernetes primitives with pods and replication controllers) and it also obtains a public IP address from a load-balancer. The result is that when you list the services in your container cluster, you can see the *wordpress* service with an internal IP and a public IP where you can access the WordPress UI from your laptop:

```
$ kubectl get services
NAME          LABELS          SELECTOR        IP(S)          PORT(S)
wordpress     run=wordpress1  run=wordpress   10.95.252.182  80/TCP
                                              104.154.82.185
```

You will then be able to enjoy WordPress.

Discussion

The `kubectl` CLI can be used to manage all resources in a Kubernetes cluster (i.e., pods, services, replication controllers, nodes). As shown in the following snippet of the `kubectl` usage, you can create, delete, describe, and list all of these resources:

```
$ kubectl -h
kubectl controls the Kubernetes cluster manager.

Find more information at https://github.com/GoogleCloudPlatform/kubernetes.

Usage:
  kubectl [flags]
  kubectl [command]

Available Commands:
  get            Display one or many resources
  describe       Show details of a specific resource or group of resources
  create         Create a resource by filename or stdin
  replace        Replace a resource by filename or stdin.
  patch          Update field(s) of a resource by stdin.
  delete         Delete a resource by filename, stdin, resource and name, or ...
  ...
```

Although you can launch simple pods consisting of a single container, you can also specify a more advanced pod defined in a JSON or YAML file by using the `-f` option:

```
$ kubectl create -f /path/to/pod/pod.json
```

In Recipe 8.9, you saw an example of a pod in YAML. Here let's write your pod in a JSON file, using the newly released Kubernetes *v1* API version. This pod will start Nginx:

```
{
  "kind": "Pod",
  "apiVersion": "v1",
  "metadata": {
    "name": "nginx",
```

```
    "labels": {
      "app": "nginx"
    }
  },
  "spec": {
    "containers": [
      {
        "name": "nginx",
        "image": "nginx",
        "ports": [
          {
            "containerPort": 80,
            "protocol": "TCP"
          }
        ]
      }
    ]
  }
}
```

Start the pod and check its status. Once it is running and you have a firewall with port 80 open for the cluster nodes, you will be able to see the Nginx welcome page. Additional examples are available on the Kubernetes GitHub page (*https://github.com/ GoogleCloudPlatform/kubernetes/tree/master/examples*).

```
$ kubectl create -f nginx.json
pods/nginx
$ kubectl get pods
NAME            READY    STATUS    RESTARTS    AGE
nginx           1/1      Running   0           20s
wordpress       1/1      Running   0           17m
```

To clean things up, remove your pods, exit the master node, and delete your cluster:

```
$ kubectl delete pods nginx
$ kubectl delete pods wordpress
$ gcloud container clusters delete cook
```

See Also

- Cluster operations (*https://cloud.google.com/container-engine/docs/clusters/opera tions*)

- Pod operations (*https://cloud.google.com/container-engine/docs/pods/operations*)

- Service operations (*https://cloud.google.com/container-engine/docs/services/opera tions*)

- Replication controller operations (*https://cloud.google.com/container-engine/docs/ services/operations*)

8.11 Setting Up to Use the EC2 Container Service

Problem

You want to try the new Amazon AWS EC2 container service (ECS).

Solution

ECS is a generally available service of Amazon Web Services. Getting set up to test ECS involves several steps. This recipe summarizes the main steps, but you should refer to the official documentation (*http://bit.ly/ecs-setup*) for all details:

1. Sign up (*http://aws.amazon.com*) for AWS if you have not done so.

2. Log in to the AWS console. Review Recipe 8.1 and Recipe 8.2 if needed. You will launch ECS instances within a security group associated with a VPC. Create a VPC and a security group, or ensure that you have default ones present.

3. Go to the IAM console and create a role for ECS. If you are not familiar with IAM, this step is a bit advanced and can be followed step by step on the AWS documentation for ECS (*http://bit.ly/ecs-setup*).

4. For the role that you just created, create an inline policy (*http://bit.ly/ecs-setup*). If successful, when you select the Show Policy link, you should see Figure 8-11. See the discussion section of this recipe for an automated way of creating this policy using Boto (*http://docs.pythonboto.org/en/latest/*).

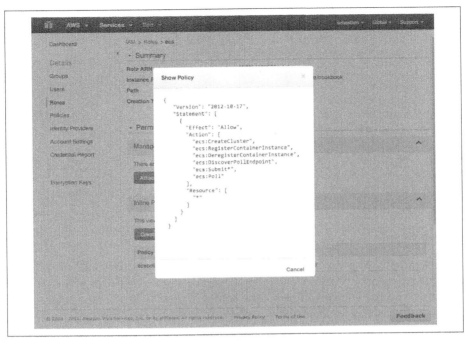

Figure 8-11. ECS policy in IAM role console

5. Install the latest AWS CLI (*http://aws.amazon.com/cli/*). The ECS API is available in version 1.7.0 or greater. You can verify that the `aws ecs` commands are now available:

```
$ sudo pip install awscli
$ aws --version
aws-cli/1.7.8 Python/2.7.9 Darwin/12.6.0
$ aws ecs help


ECS()                                                                    ECS()


NAME
       ecs -


DESCRIPTION
       Amazon  EC2  Container Service (Amazon ECS) is a highly scalable,
       fast, container management service that makes it easy to run,
       stop, and  manage  Docker containers on a cluster of Amazon
       EC2 instances. Amazon ECS lets you launch and stop
       container-enabled applications with simple API calls,  allows
       you to get the state of your cluster from a centralized service,
       and gives you access to many familiar Amazon EC2 features like
       security groups, Amazon EBS volumes, and IAM roles.

...
```

6. Create an AWS CLI configuration file that contains the API keys of the IAM user you created. Note the region being set is us-east-1, which is the Northern Virginia region where ECS is currently available:

```
$ cat ~/.aws/config
[default]
output = table
region = us-east-1
aws_access_key_id = <your AWS access key>
aws_secret_access_key = <your AWS secret key>
```

Once you have completed all these steps, you are ready to use ECS. You need to create a cluster (see Recipe 8.12), define tasks corresponding to containers, and run those tasks to start the containers on the cluster (see Recipe 8.13).

Discussion

Creating the IAM profile and the ECS policy for the instances that will be started to form the cluster can be overwhelming if you have not used AWS before. To facilitate this step, you can use the online code accompanying this book, which uses the Python Boto (*http://docs.pythonboto.org/en/latest/*) client to create the policy.

Install Boto, copy */.aws/config* to */.aws/credentials*, clone the repository, and execute the script:

```
$ git clone https://github.com/how2dock/docbook.git
$ sudo pip install boto
$ cp ~/.aws/config ~/.aws/credentials
$ cd ch08/ecs
$ ./ecs-policy.py
```

This script creates an ecs role, an ecspolicy policy, and a cookbook instance profile. You can edit the script to change these names. After completion, you should see the role and the policy in the IAM console (*https://console.aws.amacon.con/iam/home#roles*).

See Also

- Video of an ECS demo (*https://aws.amazon.com/blogs/compute/amazon-ecs-video-demo/*)

- ECS documentation (*http://docs.aws.amazon.com/AmazonECS/latest/developer guide/get-set-up-for-amazon-ecs.html*)

8.12 Creating an ECS Cluster

Problem

You are set up to use ECS (see Recipe 8.11). Now you want to create a cluster and some instances in it to run containers.

Solution

Use the AWS CLI that you installed in Recipe 8.11 and explore the new ECS API. In this recipe, you will learn to use the following:

- `aws ecs list-clusters`
- `aws ecs create-cluster`
- `aws ecs describe-clusters`
- `aws ecs list-container-instances`
- `aws ecs delete-cluster`

By default, you have one cluster in ECS, but until you have launched an instance in that cluster, it is not active. Try to describe the default cluster:

```
$ aws ecs describe-clusters
-----------------------------------------------------------------
|                     DescribeClusters                          |
+---------------------------------------------------------------+
||                       failures                              ||
|+-----------------------------------------------+-----------+|
||                     arn                        |  reason   ||
|+-----------------------------------------------+-----------+|
|| arn:aws:ecs:us-east-1:587534442583:cluster/default | MISSING ||
|+-----------------------------------------------+-----------+|
```

Currently you are limited to two ECS clusters.

To activate this cluster, launch an instance using Boto. The AMI used is specific to ECS and contains the ECS agent (*https://github.com/aws/amazon-ecs-agent*). You need to have created an SSH key pair to `ssh` into the instance, and you need an instance profile associated with a role that has the ECS policy (see Recipe 8.11):

```
$ python
...
>>> import boto
```

```
>>> c = boto.connect_ec2()
>>> c.run_instances('ami-34ddbe5c', \
                    key_name='ecs', \
                    instance_type='t2.micro', \
                    instance_profile_name='cookbook')
```

With one instance started, wait for it to run and register in the cluster. Then if you
describe the cluster again, you will see that the default cluster has switched to active
state. You can also list container instances:

```
$ aws ecs describe-clusters
---------------------------------------------------------------------------
|                            DescribeClusters                             |
+-------------------------------------------------------------------------+
||                               clusters                                ||
|+------------------------------------------------+-------------+-------+|
||                    clusterArn                   | clusterName | status ||
|+------------------------------------------------+-------------+-------+|
||  arn:aws:ecs:us-east-1:587432148683:cluster/default | default    | ACTIVE ||
|+------------------------------------------------+-------------+-------+|
$ aws ecs list-container-instances
---------------------------------------------------------------------------
|                          ListContainerInstances                         |
+-------------------------------------------------------------------------+
||                         containerInstanceArns                         ||
|+---------------------------------------------------------------------+|
||  arn:aws:ecs:us-east-1:541234428683:container-instance/ ...          ||
|+---------------------------------------------------------------------+|
```

Starting additional instances increases the size of the cluster:

```
$ aws ecs list-container-instances
---------------------------------------------------------------------------
|                          ListContainerInstances                         |
+-------------------------------------------------------------------+
||                         containerInstanceArns                     ||
|+---------------------------------------------------------------------+|
||  arn:aws:ecs:us-east-1:587342368683:container-instance/75738343-...  ||
||  arn:aws:ecs:us-east-1:587423448683:container-instance/b457e535-...  ||
||  arn:aws:ecs:us-east-1:584242468683:container-instance/e5c0be59-...  ||
||  arn:aws:ecs:us-east-1:587421468683:container-instance/e62d3d79-...  ||
|+---------------------------------------------------------------------+|
```

Since these container instances are regular EC2 instances, you will see them in your
EC2 console. If you have set up an SSH key properly and opened port 22 on the security group used, you can also ssh to them:

```
$ ssh -i ~/.ssh/id_rsa_ecs ec2-user@52.1.224.245
...

   _|  _|  _|
  _|  (  \_ \  Amazon ECS-Optimized Amazon Linux AMI
 ___|\__|___/
```

```
  Image created: Thu Dec 18 01:39:14 UTC 2014
  PREVIEW AMI

9 package(s) needed for security, out of 10 available
Run "sudo yum update" to apply all updates.
[ec2-user@ip-172-31-33-78 ~]$ docker ps
CONTAINER ID    IMAGE                              ...
4bc4d480a362    amazon/amazon-ecs-agent:latest     ...
[ec2-user@ip-172-31-33-78 ~]$ docker version
Client version: 1.6.2
Client API version: 1.18
Go version (client): go1.3.3
Git commit (client): 7c8fca2/1.6.2
OS/Arch (client): linux/amd64
Server version: 1.6.2
Server API version: 1.18
Go version (server): go1.3.3
Git commit (server): 7c8fca2/1.6.2
OS/Arch (server): linux/amd64
```

You see that the container instance is running Docker and that the ECS agent is a
container. The Docker version that you see will most likely be different, as Docker
releases a new version approximately every two months.

Discussion

Although you can use the default cluster, you can also create your own:

```
$ aws ecs create-cluster --cluster-name cookbook
-------------------------------------------------------------------------
|                            CreateCluster                              |
+---------------------------------------------------------------------+
||                             cluster                               | |
|+-----------------------------------------+-------------+---------+|
||                clusterArn                | clusterName | status ||
|+-----------------------------------------+-------------+---------+|
|| arn:aws:ecs:us-east-1:...:cluster/cookbook | cookbook  | ACTIVE ||
|+-----------------------------------------+-------------+---------+|
$ aws ecs list-clusters
-------------------------------------------------------------------------
|                            ListClusters                              |
+-----------------------------------------------------------+
||                          clusterArns                     | |
|+---------------------------------------------------------+|
|| arn:aws:ecs:us-east-1:587264368683:cluster/cookbook     ||
|| arn:aws:ecs:us-east-1:587264368683:cluster/default      ||
|+---------------------------------------------------------+|
```

To launch instances in that freshly created cluster instead of the default one, you need
to pass some user data (*http://docs.aws.amazon.com/AWSEC2/latest/UserGuide/user-*

data.html) during the instance creation step. Via Boto, this can be achieved with the following script:

```python
#!/usr/bin/env python

import boto
import base64

userdata="""
#!/bin/bash
echo ECS_CLUSTER=cookbook >> /etc/ecs/ecs.config
"""

c = boto.connect_ec2()
c.run_instances('ami-34ddbe5c', \
                key_name='ecs', \
                instance_type='t2.micro', \
                instance_profile_name='cookbook', \
                user_data=base64.b64encode(userdata))
```

Once you are done with the cluster, you can delete it entirely with the `aws ecs delete-cluster --cluster cookbook` command.

See Also

- The ECS (*https://github.com/aws/amazon-ecs-agent*) agent on GitHub

8.13 Starting Docker Containers on an ECS Cluster

Problem

You know how to create an ECS cluster on AWS (see Recipe 8.12), and now you are ready to start containers on the instances forming the cluster.

Solution

Define your containers or group of containers in a definition file in JSON format. This will be called a *task*. You will register this task and then run it; it is a two-step process. Once the task is running in the cluster, you can *list*, *stop*, and *start* it.

For example, to run Nginx in a container based on the *nginx* image from Docker Hub, you create the following task definition in JSON format:

```json
[
  {
    "environment": [],
    "name": "nginx",
    "image": "nginx",
```

```
    "cpu": 10,
    "portMappings": [
      {
        "containerPort": 80,
        "hostPort": 80
      }
    ],
    "memory": 10,
    "essential": true
  }
]
```

You can notice the similarities between this task definition, a Kubernetes Pod (Recipe 5.4) and a compose file (Recipe 7.1). To register this task, use the ECS `register-task-definition` call. Specify a *family* that groups the tasks and helps you keep revision history, which can be handy for rollback purposes:

```
$ aws ecs register-task-definition --family nginx \
                              --cli-input-json file://$PWD/nginx.json
$ aws ecs list-task-definitions
-----------------------------------------------------------------
|                      ListTaskDefinitions                      |
+---------------------------------------------------------------+
||                    taskDefinitionArns                      ||
|+-------------------------------------------------------------+|
||  arn:aws:ecs:us-east-1:584523528683:task-definition/nginx:1  ||
|+-------------------------------------------------------------+|
```

To start the container in this task definition, you use the `run-task` command and specify the number of containers you want running. To stop the container, you stop the task specifying it via its task UUID obtained from `list-tasks`, as shown here:

```
$ aws ecs run-task --task-definition nginx:1 --count 1
$ aws ecs stop-task --task 6223f2d3-3689-4b3b-a110-ea128350adb2
```

ECS schedules the task on one of the container instances in your cluster. The image is pulled from Docker Hub, and the container started using the options specified in the task definition. At this preview stage of ECS, finding the instance where the task is running and finding the associated IP address isn't straightforward. If you have multiple instances running, you will have to do a bit of guesswork. There does not seem to be a proxy service as in Kubernetes either.

Discussion

The Nginx example represents a task with a single container running, but you can also define a task with linked containers. The task definition reference (*http://docs.aws.amazon.com/AmazonECS/latest/developerguide/task_defintions.html*) describes all possible keys that can be used to define a task. To continue with our example of running WordPress with two containers (a *wordpress* one and a *mysql* one), you can define a *wordpress* task. It is similar to a Compose definition (see Recipe 7.1) file to AWS ECS task definition format. It will not go unnoticed that a standardization effort among *compose*, *pod*, and *task* would benefit the community.

```
[
  {
    "image": "wordpress",
    "name": "wordpress",
    "cpu": 10,
    "memory": 200,
    "essential": true,
    "links": [
      "mysql"
    ],
    "portMappings": [
      {
        "containerPort": 80,
        "hostPort": 80
      }
    ],
    "environment": [
      {
        "name": "WORDPRESS_DB_NAME",
        "value": "wordpress"
      },
      {
        "name": "WORDPRESS_DB_USER",
        "value": "wordpress"
      },
      {
        "name": "WORDPRESS_DB_PASSWORD",
        "value": "wordpresspwd"
      }
    ]
  },
  {
    "image": "mysql",
    "name": "mysql",
    "cpu": 10,
    "memory": 200,
    "essential": true,
    "environment": [
      {
        "name": "MYSQL_ROOT_PASSWORD",
        "value": "wordpressdocker"
      },
      {
        "name": "MYSQL_DATABASE",
        "value": "wordpress"
      },
      {
        "name": "MYSQL_USER",
```

```
      "value": "wordpress"
    },
    {
      "name": "MYSQL_PASSWORD",
      "value": "wordpresspwd"
    }
  ]
 }
]
```

The task is registered the same way as done previously with Nginx, but you specify a new *family*. But when the task is run, it could fail due to constraints not being met. In this example, my container instances are of type t2.micro with 1GB of memory. Since the task definition is asking for 500 MB for *wordpress* and 500 MB for *mysql*, there's not enough memory for the cluster scheduler to find an instance that matches the constraints and running the task fails:

```
$ aws ecs register-task-definition --family wordpress \
                          --cli-input-json file://$PWD/wordpress.json
$ aws ecs run-task --task-definition wordpress:1 --count 1
-------------------------------------------------------------------------
|                              RunTask                                  |
+---------------------------------------------------------------------+
||                            failures                               ||
|+-----------------------------------------------+-----------------+|
||                     arn                        |     reason      ||
|+-----------------------------------------------+-----------------+|
|| arn:aws:ecs:us-east-1:587264368683:container-instance/...|RESOURCE:MEMORY ||
|| arn:aws:ecs:us-east-1:587264368683:container-instance/...|RESOURCE:MEMORY ||
|| arn:aws:ecs:us-east-1:587264368683:container-instance/...|RESOURCE:MEMORY ||
|+---------------------------------------------------------------------+|
```

You can edit the task definition, relax the memory constraint, and register a new task in the same family (revision 2). It will successfully run. If you log in to the instance running this task, you will see the containers running alongside the ECS agent:

```
$ aws ecs run-task --task-definition wordpress:2 --count 1
$ ssh -i ~/.ssh/id_rsa_ecs ec2-user@54.152.108.134
...


   __|  __|  __|
   _|  (    \__ \   Amazon ECS-Optimized Amazon Linux AMI
 ____|\___|____/


...
[ec2-user@ip-172-31-36-83 ~]$ docker ps
CONTAINER ID  IMAGE            ... PORTS                 NAMES
36d590a206df  wordpress:4      ... 0.0.0.0:80->80/tcp    ecs-wordpress...
893d1bd24421  mysql:5          ... 3306/tcp              ecs-wordpress...
81023576f81e  amazon/amazon-ecs ... 127.0.0.1:51678->51678/tcp ecs-agent
```

Enjoy ECS and keep an eye on improvements and general availability.

See Also

- Task definition reference (*http://docs.aws.amazon.com/AmazonECS/latest/develo perguide/task_defintions.html*)

8.14 Starting an Application in the Cloud Using Docker Support in AWS Beanstalk

Problem

You would like to deploy a Docker-based application in the cloud by just *pushing* your Dockerfile. You want the cloud service to automatically spin up instances and configure possible load-balancers.

Solution

Use AWS Elastic Beanstalk (*http://aws.amazon.com/elasticbeanstalk/*). Beanstalk uses AWS EC2 instances, and can automatically create an elastic load-balancer, create a security group, and monitor the health of your application and resources. Docker support in Beanstalk was announced (*https://aws.amazon.com/blogs/aws/aws-elastic-beanstalk-for-docker/*) in April 2014. Originally, Beanstalk supported only single-container applications, but recently AWS announced a coupling (*http://docs.aws.amazon.com/elasticbeanstalk/latest/dg/create_deploy_docker_ecs.html*) between AWS ECS and Beanstalk. This coupling allows you to let Beanstalk use an ECS cluster as an environment for your application and run multiple containers per instances.

To illustrate Docker support in Beanstalk, you are going to set up a Beanstalk environment using AWS CLI tools, and deploy the 2048 game (*http://gabrielecir ulli.github.io/2048/*) using a single Dockerfile. This is a variant of the official Beanstalk documentation (*http://docs.aws.amazon.com/elasticbeanstalk/latest/dg/create_deploy_docker_image.html*).

To get started, you will need a few things:

- An AWS account (see Figure 8-1)
- The AWS CLI (see Recipe 8.2)
- Register for Beanstalk by accessing the console (*https://console.aws.amazon.com/elasticbeanstalk/*) and following the onscreen instructions

The application deployment consists of three steps:

1. Create a Beanstalk application with `awscli`.

2. Create a Beanstalk environment based on a Docker software stack (called a *solution stack* in Beanstalk).

3. Create your Dockerfile and deploy it using the `eb` CLI.

 All these steps can be done via the AWS console. This recipe shows a complete CLI-based deployment, but the output of the `awscli` calls are truncated.

With the AWS CLI, create an application `foobar`, list the solution stacks, and pick the Docker environment you need. Create a *configuration template* by using the solution stack of your choice, and finally, create an *environment*:

```
$ aws elasticbeanstalk create-application --application-name foobar
...
$ aws elasticbeanstalk list-available-solution-stacks
...
$ aws elasticbeanstalk create-configuration-template
                    --application-name foobar
                    --solution-stack-name="64bit Amazon Linux 2014.09 v1.2.1 \
                    running Docker 1.5.0"
                    --template-name foo
...
$ aws elasticbeanstalk create-environment
                    --application-name foobar
                    --environment-name cookbook
                    --template-name foo
```

At this point, if you head over to the AWS Beanstalk console, you will see a *foobar* application and a *cookbook* environment being created. Once Beanstalk has finished creating the environment, you can use the `describe-environments` API call and see that the environment is ready. In the console, you will also see that an EC2 instance, a security group, and an elastic load-balancer have been created. You can configure the load-balancers through the Beanstalk console.

Going back to our CLI steps, check that the environment is ready:

```
$ aws elasticbeanstalk describe-environments
---------------------------------------------------------------------------
|                            DescribeEnvironments                         |
+-------------------------------------------------------------------------+
||                              Environments                             ||
|+-----------------------+-----------------------------------------------+|
|| ApplicationName       | foobar                                        ||
|| CNAME                 | cookbook-pmpgzmx2e6.elasticbeanstalk.com      ||
```

```
|| DateCreated      | 2015-03-30T15:32:47.814Z                           ||
|| DateUpdated      | 2015-03-30T15:38:14.291Z                           ||
|| EndpointURL      | awseb-e-7-AWSEBLoa-CUXDVD6RL9R7-992275618.eu-west-1...||
|| EnvironmentId    | e-7hamntqqnw                                       ||
|| EnvironmentName  | cookbook                                           ||
|| Health           | Green                                              ||
|| SolutionStackName| 64bit Amazon Linux 2014.09 v1.2.1 running Docker 1.5.0||
|| Status           | Ready                                              ||
|+-----------------+----------------------------------------------------+|
|||                                Tier                                 |||
||+----------------------------------------+------------------------+||
|||  Name                                   | WebServer              |||
|||  Type                                   | Standard               |||
|||  Version                                |                        |||
||+----------------------------------------+------------------------+||
```

Once it is ready, you can push your Docker application to it. This is most easily done by using the eb CLI, which unfortunately is not included in the awscli. To finish the deployment, you will perform the following steps:

1. Install the awsebcli.

2. Create your Dockerfile.

3. Initialize the application *foobar* that you created earlier.

4. List the environment to make sure you are using the *cookbook* environment created previously.

5. Deploy the application.

Let's do this: install awsebcli, and create your application directory with our Dockerfile in it:

```
$ sudo pip install awsebcli
$ mkdir beanstalk
$ cd beanstalk
$ cat > Dockerfile
FROM ubuntu:12.04

RUN apt-get update
RUN apt-get install -y nginx zip curl

RUN echo "daemon off;" >> /etc/nginx/nginx.conf
RUN curl -o /usr/share/nginx/www/master.zip -L https://codeload.github.com/ \
gabrielecirulli/2048/zip/master
RUN cd /usr/share/nginx/www/ && unzip master.zip && mv 2048-master/* . && \
    rm -rf 2048-master master.zip

EXPOSE 80

CMD ["/usr/sbin/nginx", "-c", "/etc/nginx/nginx.conf"]
```

You can then use the eb CLI to initialize the application (using the application name used in the preceding steps—*foobar*) and deploy it with eb deploy:

```
$ eb init foobar
$ eb list
* cookbook
$ eb deploy
Creating application version archive "app-150331_181300".
Uploading foobar/app-150331_181300.zip to S3. This may take a while.
Upload Complete.
INFO: Environment update is starting.
...
INFO: Successfully built aws_beanstalk/staging-app
INFO: Docker container ba7e79c37c43 is running aws_beanstalk/current-app.
INFO: New application version was deployed to running EC2 instances.
INFO: Environment update completed successfully.
```

Your application is now deployed. Head over to the Beanstalk console (shown in Figure 8-12) and you will find the URL of the application. Click the URL and it will open the *2048 game*. This is fronted by an elastic load-balancer, which means that increased load on the game will trigger the creation of additional instances serving the game behind the load-balancer.

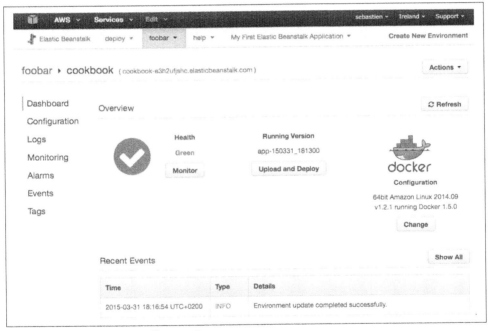

Figure 8-12. AWS Beanstalk console

Discussion

In the preceding example, our application is encapsulated in a single Dockerfile with no additional dependencies.

Monitoring Containers

9.0 Introduction

When operating distributed systems and distributed applications, you need access to as much information as possible. You will never need to monitor a large number of resources, extract trends, and trigger alerts. You will also need to collect logs from all processes running in containers and aggregate those logs in data stores for further indexing and searching. Finally, you will need to visualize all this information to quickly navigate your application and debug it if need be.

This chapter starts with some Docker commands that give you basic debugging tools that you can use in small-scale deployments or when you have to dive deeper into a specific container. Recipe 9.1 introduces the docker inspect method that gives you all the information about a container of an image. Recipe 9.2 shows you how to use docker stats to get a stream of resource usage for a specific container. Finally, Recipe 9.3 presents docker events, which listens to Docker events on a particular host. These capabilities are available through the Docker API and hence can be used through any Docker client that supports them.

As you build your application you will want to collect the logs of your services running in containers. This is not specifically monitoring, but logs can be used to derive new metrics that you need to monitor. Docker provides a simple mechanism to look at stdout of the foreground process running in a container, Recipe 9.4. You can also redirect those logs to a remote syslog server of another log aggregation system like Fluentd, which we show in Recipe 9.5. Prior to the log driver feature, a container was made famous for solving the logging challenge in Docker, logspout. In Recipe 9.6 we show you how logspout works. While it does not need to be used anymore it is still an interesting system worth your time. To wrap up this section we show you how to deploy an ELK stack using containers in Recipe 9.8. ELK stands for Elastic, Logstash, and Kibana. Logstash is a log aggregator system that can feed data to Elastic. Elastic is a distributed data store that provides efficient indexing and searching capability. Kibana is a dashboard system to visualize data stored in Elastic. If you want an alternative to ELK you might like Recipe 9.11, which lays the foundation for using InfluxDB (*https://influxdb.com*) as a data store and Grafana (*http://grafana.org*) as a dashboard.

While docker stats gives you single-container usage statistics, you might want to collect these metrics for multiple containers and aggregate them. Recipe 9.9 is an advanced recipe that brings together multiple concepts. It features a two-hosts setup. One host runs an ELK stack, and the other host runs logspout and collectd (*https://collectd.org*), which is the system statistics collection daemon. What this recipe shows is that the resource usage of all containers started on the second host will be collected by collectd via the docker stats API and further aggregated by logspout, which will send the data to the ELK setup. Certainly worth your time if you need to bring up your own monitoring solution. While this setup works perfectly, Recipe 9.10 introduces cAdvisor, a containerized solution to container monitoring. You can deploy cAdvisor on all your Docker hosts and it will monitor all the rescue usage of all the containers running on your hosts.

We finish this chapter with a look at Weave Scope in Recipe 9.12. This is a container infrastructure visualization tool. If you imagine thousands of containers composing your complete applications, having an interactive explorer for a distributed application is very appealing. Weave Scope has the potential to fulfill that promise and give you quick insight into your application.

9.1 Getting Detailed Information About a Container with docker inspect

Problem

You want to get detailed information about a container—such as when it was created, what command was passed to the container, what port mappings exist, what IP address the container has, and so forth.

Solution

Use the docker inspect command. For example, start an Nginx container and use inspect:

```
$ docker run -d -p 80:80 nginx
$ docker inspect kickass_babbage
[{
    "AppArmorProfile": "",
```

```
        "Args": [
            "-g",
            "daemon off;"
        ],
...
            "ExposedPorts": {
                "443/tcp": {},
                "80/tcp": {}
            },
...
        "NetworkSettings": {
...
            "IPAddress": "172.17.0.3",
...
```

The `inspect` command also works on an image:

```
$ docker inspect nginx
[{
    "Architecture": "amd64",
    "Author": "NGINX Docker Maintainers \"docker-maint@nginx.com\"",
    "Comment": "",
    "Config": {
        "AttachStderr": false,
        "AttachStdin": false,
        "AttachStdout": false,
        "Cmd": [
            "nginx",
            "-g",
            "daemon off;"
        ],
...
```

Discussion

The Docker `inspect` command takes a `format` option. You can use it to specify a Golang template and extract specific information about a container or image instead of getting the full JSON output:

```
$ docker inspect --help

Usage: docker inspect [OPTIONS] CONTAINER|IMAGE [CONTAINER|IMAGE...]

Return low-level information on a container or image

  -f, --format=""      Format the output using the given go template.
  --help=false         Print usage
```

For example, to get the IP address of a running container and check its state:

```
$ docker inspect -f '{{ .NetworkSettings.IPAddress }}' kickass_babbage
172.17.0.3
```

```
$ docker inspect -f '{{ .State.Running }}' kickass_babbage
true
```

If you prefer to use another Docker client such as docker-py (see Recipe 4.10), you can also access the detailed information about containers and images by using standard Python dictionary notation:

```
$ python
...
>>> from docker import Client
>>> c=Client(base_url="unix://var/run/docker.sock")
>>> c.inspect_container('kickass_babbage')['State']['Running']
True
>>> c.inspect_container('kickass_babbage')['NetworkSettings']['IPAddress']
u'172.17.0.3'
```

9.2 Obtaining Usage Statistics of a Running Container

Problem

You have a running container on one of your Docker hosts and would like to monitor its resource usage (e.g., memory, CPU, network).

Solution

Use the docker stats command. This new API endpoint was introduced on February 10, 2015 and is accessible in Docker 1.5. The usage syntax is simple: you pass the container name (or container ID) to it and receive a stream of statistics. Here you start a Flask application container and run stats on it:

```
$ docker run -d -p 5000:5000 runseb/flask
$ docker stats dreamy_mccarthy
CONTAINER        CPU %   MEM USAGE/LIMIT      MEM %    NET I/O
dreamy_mccarthy  0.03%   24.01 MiB/1.955 GiB  1.20%    648 B/648 B
```

Since you are receiving a stream, you will not press the Ctrl-C keys to kill the stream.

Discussion

Getting quick stats from the command line is useful for interactive debugging. However, you will most likely want to collect all these statistics and aggregate them with a log collector solution like Logstash (*http://logstash.net*) for futher visualization and analysis.

To prepare for such a monitoring framework, you can try to use the stats API via curl, by issuing TCP requests to the Docker daemon. First you will need to configure your local Docker daemon to listen on port 2375 over TCP. On Ubuntu systems, edit */etc/default/docker* to include the following:

```
DOCKER_OPTS="-H tcp://127.0.0.1:2375"
```

Restart your Docker daemon with `sudo service docker restart`. You are now ready to use `curl` and target the Docker remote API. The syntax (*http://bit.ly/container-stats*) is again simple: it is an HTTP GET request to the */containers/(id)/stats* URI. Try it like so:

```
$ $ docker -H tcp://127.0.0.1:2375 run -d -p 5001:5000 runseb/flask
$ curl http://127.0.0.1:2375/containers/agitated_albattani/stats
{"read":"2015-04-01T11:48:40.609469913Z",\
"network":{"rx_bytes":648,"rx_packets":8,"...
```

Do not forget to replace `agitated_albattani` with the name of your container. You will start receiving a stream of statistics that you can interrupt with Ctrl-C. For practical purposes, I truncated most of the results from the previous command. This is handy for trying things out, but if (like me) you like Python, you might want to access these statistics from a Python program. To do this, you can use `docker-py` (see Recipe 4.10). A Python script like the one here will put you on the right track:

```
#!/usr/bin/env python

import json
import docker
import sys

cli=docker.Client(base_url='tcp://127.0.0.1:2375')
stats=cli.stats(sys.argv[1])
print json.dumps(json.loads(next(stats).rstrip('\n')),indent=4)
```

 The `stats` object in this Python script is a *generator*, which yields results instead of the standard return behavior of functions. It is used to capture the statistics stream and pick up where it left off. `next(stats)` in the script is the way to yield the latest result from the stream.

See Also

- Original GitHub pull request (*https://github.com/docker/docker/pull/9984*) for `stats`
- API documentation (*http://bit.ly/container-stats*)

9.3 Listening to Docker Events on Your Docker Hosts

Problem

You want to monitor Docker events on your host. You are interested in image untagging and deletion and container life-cycle events (e.g., create, destroy, kill).

Solution

Use the `docker events` command. It will return a stream of events as they happen on your Docker host. The command takes a few optional arguments if you want to select events for a specific time range:

```
$ docker events --help

Usage: docker events [OPTIONS]

Get real time events from the server

  -f, --filter=[]     Provide filter values (i.e., 'event=stop')
  --help=false        Print usage
  --since=""          Show all events created since timestamp
  --until=""          Stream events until this timestamp
```

Although `docker events` will work and block until you Ctrl-C the stream, you can use the `--since` or `--until` options like so:

```
$ docker events --since 1427890602
2015-04-01T12:17:04....9393146cb55e5bc9f04e20eb5a0622b3e26aae7: untag
2015-04-01T12:17:09....d5266f8777bfba4974ac56e3270e7760f6f0a81: untag
2015-04-01T12:17:22....d5266f8777bfba4974ac56e3270e7760f6f0a85: untag
2015-04-01T12:17:23....66f8777bfba4974ac56e3270e7760f6f0a81253: delete
2015-04-01T12:17:23....e9b5a793523481a0a18645fc77ad53c4eadsfa2: delete
2015-04-01T12:17:23....878585defcc1bc6f79d2728a13957871b345345: delete
```

> Just as a reminder, you can get the current timestamp in Epoch with `date +"%s"`.

Discussion

This `events` command is also available as an API call, and you can use `curl` to access it (see Recipe 9.2). Let's leave this as an exercise and give an example of using `docker-py` to get the list of events.

Recipe 9.2 reconfigured the Docker daemon to access the remote API over TCP. You can also use `docker-py` to access the Unix Docker socket. A sample Python script that would do this and save you some time to reconfigure the Docker daemon looks like this:

```
#!/usr/bin/env python
import json
import docker
import sys

cli=docker.Client(base_url='unix://var/run/docker.sock')
events=cli.events(since=sys.argv[1],until=sys.argv[2])
for e in events:
    print e
```

This script takes two timestamps as arguments and returns the events between these two. An example output is as follows:

```
$ ./events.py 1427890602 1427891476
{"status":"untag","id":"967a84db1eff36cab6e77fe9c9393146c...","time":1427890624}
{"status":"untag","id":"4986bf8c15363d1c5d15512d5266f8777...","time":1427890629}
{"status":"untag","id":"4986bf8c15363d1c5d15512d5266f8777...","time":1427890642}
{"status":"delete","id":"4986bf8c15363d1c5d15512d5266f877...","time":1427890643}
{"status":"delete","id":"ea13149945cb6b1e746bf28032f02e9b...","time":1427890643}
{"status":"delete","id":"df7546f9f060a2268024c8a230d86398...","time":1427890643}
```

Event-based tools like StackStorm (*http://stackstorm.com*) take advantage of this to orchestrate various parts of a Docker base infrastructure.

See Also

- API documentation (*http://bit.ly/monitor-events*)

9.4 Getting the Logs of a Container with docker logs

Problem

You have a running container that runs a process in the foreground within the container. You would like to access the process logs from the host.

Solution

Use the docker logs command.

For example, start an Nginx container and open your browser on port 80 of the Docker host:

```
$ docker run -d -p 80:80 nginx
$ docker ps
CONTAINER ID    IMAGE          ...  PORTS                        NAMES
dd0e926c4015    nginx:latest   ...  443/tcp, 0.0.0.0:80->80/tcp  gloomy_mclean
```

```
$ docker logs gloomy_mclean
192.168.34.1 - - [10/Mar/2015:10:12:35 +0000] "GET / HTTP/1.1" 200 612 "-" ...
...
```

Discussion

You can get a continuous log stream by using the -f option:

```
$ docker logs -f gloomy_mclean
192.168.34.1 - - [10/Mar/2015:10:12:35 +0000] "GET / HTTP/1.1" 200 612 "-" ...
...
```

In addition, you can monitor the process running in the container with docker top:

```
$ docker top gloomy_mclean
UID         PID        PPID    ...  CMD
root        5605       4732    ...  nginx: master process nginx -g daemon off;
syslog      5632       5605    ...  nginx: worker process
```

9.5 Using a Different Logging Driver than the Docker Daemon

Problem

By default, Docker provides container logs through JSON files. The logs are available via the docker logs command (see Recipe 9.4). However, you would like to collect and aggregate your logs differently, potentially using systems like syslog or jour nald.

Solution

Start containers by using the --log-driver option and specify a logging driver. This feature was introduced in Docker 1.6, and various drivers are being added in new Docker releases. With the logging driver functionality, you can direct the Docker logs to syslog, journald, GELF (*https://www.graylog.org*) (Graylog Extended Log Format), and Fluentd (*http://www.fluentd.org*). You can also disable any logging entirely by setting the driver to none: --log-driver=none. Each driver and its options are well documented (*https://docs.docker.com/reference/logging/overview/*).

> When you define a logging driver different from the default json-file driver, the docker logs command will not work.

You can use the logging driver functionality to redirect your logs to local syslog or journald. But to illustrate this feature in a more advanced way, let's use Fluentd to collect all the logs of running containers. First you need to install the Fluentd packages on your Docker host. The easiest way to do this is to use the Treasure Data (*http://www.treasuredata.com*) distribution of Fluentd called td-agent. If you trust their installation procedure, you can get it via curl:

```
$ curl -L https://td-toolbelt.herokuapp.com/sh/\
         install-ubuntu-trusty-td-agent2.sh | sh
```

Once the package is installed, you need to configure td-agent, telling it to match certain events and redirect them to a specific *location*. For example, to match all Docker events (which by default are tagged with docker.<CONTAINER_ID>) and redirect them to *stdout*, edit the *td-agent* configuration file */etc/td-agent/td-agent.conf* and add the following line:

```
<match docker.**>
type stdout
</match>
```

Then restart the service:

```
$ sudo service td-agent restart
```

You are now ready to start using Fluentd to manage your Docker logs. Let's start an Nginx container and use this logging driver:

```
$ docker run -d -p 80:80 --name nginx --log-driver=fluentd nginx
```

Now if you access Nginx in your browser and then check the *td-agent* log file, you will see the Docker logs:

```
$ tail -n 3 /var/log/td-agent/td-agent.log
...
2015-08-17 13:41:10 docker.dc3a645abfaa: {"log":"192.168.33.1 ...,\
                                "container_id":"dc3a645abfaa...",\
                                "container_name":"/nginx",\
                                "source":"stdout"}
```

You see that the logs are prefixed with docker.<CONTAINER_ID>. If you wanted to prefix the logs with something else, you could specify a different Go template (currently {{.ID}}, {{.FullID}}, {{.Name}}). For example, to prefix the logs with the name of the container, use the log-opt option like so:

```
$ docker kill nginx
$ docker rm nginx
$ docker run -d -p 80:80 --name nginx \
                --log-driver=fluentd \
                --log-opt fluentd-tag=docker.{{.Name}} nginx
```

The logs will become similar to the following:

```
$ tail -n 3 /var/log/td-agent/td-agent.log
...
2015-08-17 13:43:45 docker./nginx: {"container_id":"e4152ad9bdba...",\
                                    "container_name":"/stupefied_franklin",\
                                    "source":"stdout",\
                                    "log":"192.168.33.1 ...}
```

In this example, you redirected the logs to only the Fluentd logs themselves. This is not extremely useful or practical. In a production deployment, you would redirect the logs to a remote data store like `elasticsearch`, `influxdb`, or `mongoDB`, for example.

Discussion

In the solution section, you ran *td-agent* as a local service on the Docker host. You could also run it in a local container. Let's write a configuration file in your working directory called *test.conf* that contains the following:

```
<source>
  type forward
</source>
<match docker.**>
  type stdout
</match>
```

Then let's start a *fluentd* container. You specify a volume mount to put your configuration file in the running container and specify an environment variable that points to this file:

```
$ docker run -it -d -p 24224:24224 -v /path/to/conf:/fluentd/etc \
-e FLUENTD_CONF=test.conf fluent/fluentd:latest
```

By default, the `fluentd` logging driver tries to reach a `fluentd` server on localhost at port 24224. Therefore, if you run another container with the `--log-driver=fluentd` option, it will automatically reach `fluentd` running in the container.

Now start an Nginx container as you did earlier and watch the logs on the Fluentd container with `docker logs`.

See Also

- Configuring logging drivers (*https://docs.docker.com/reference/logging/overview/*)
- Fluentd logging driver for Docker documentation (*https://github.com/docker/docker/blob/master/docs/reference/logging/fluentd.md*)

9.6 Using Logspout to Collect Container Logs

Problem

Container logs can be obtained from `docker logs`, as seen in Recipe 9.4, but you would like to collect these logs from containers running in multiple Docker hosts and aggregate them.

Solution

Use `logspout` (*https://github.com/gliderlabs/logspout*). Logspout can collect logs from all containers running on a host and route them to another host. It runs as a container and is purely stateless. You can use it to route logs to a syslog server or send it to Logstash (*http://logstash.net*) for processing. Logspout was created prior to the release of Docker 1.6, which introduced the logging driver (see Recipe 9.5) functionality. You can still use Logspout, but the logging driver also gives you a straightforward way to redirect your logs.

Let's install Logspout on one Docker host to collect logs from an Nginx container. You run `nginx` on port 80 of the host. Start `logspout`, mount the Docker Unix socket */var/run/docker.sock* in */tmp/docker.sock*, and specify a syslog endpoint (here you use another Docker host with the IP address of 192.168.34.11):

```
$ docker pull nginx
$ docker pull gliderlabs/logspout
$ docker run -d --name webserver -p 80:80 nginx
$ docker run -d --name logspout -v /var/run/docker.sock:/tmp/docker.sock \
        gliderlabs/logspout syslog://192.168.34.11:5000
```

To collect the logs, you'll use a Logstash container running at 192.168.34.11. To simplify things, it will listen for syslog input on UDP port 5000 and output everything to *stdout* on the same host. Start by pulling the *logstash* image. (This example uses the image *ehazlett/logstash*, but there are many Logstash images that you might want to consider.) After pulling the image, you'll build your own and specify a custom Logstash configuration file (this is based on the */etc/logstash.conf.sample* from the *ehazlett/logstash* image):

```
$ docker pull ehazlett/logstash
$ cat logstash.conf
input {
  tcp {
    port => 5000
    type => syslog
  }
}

filter {
  if [type] == "syslog" {
```

```
      grok {
        match => { "message" => "%{SYSLOGTIMESTAMP:syslog_timestamp} \
        %{SYSLOGHOST:syslog_hostname} \
        %{DATA:syslog_program}(?:\[%{POSINT:syslog_pid}\])?: \
        %{GREEDYDATA:syslog_message}" }
        add_field => [ "received_at", "%{@timestamp}" ]
        add_field => [ "received_from", "%{host}" ]
      }
      syslog_pri { }
      date {
        match => [ "syslog_timestamp", "MMM  d HH:mm:ss", "MMM dd HH:mm:ss" ]
      }
    }
  }
}

output {
  stdout { codec => rubydebug }
}
$ cat Dockerfile
FROM ehazlett/logstash

COPY logstash.conf /etc/logstash.conf
ENTRYPOINT ["/opt/logstash/bin/logstash"]
$ docker build -t logstash .
```

You are now ready to run the Logstash container, and bind port 5000 of the container to port 5000 of the host listening for UDP traffic:

```
$ docker run -d --name logstash -p 5000:5000/udp logstash -f /etc/logstash.conf
```

Once you open your browser to access Nginx running on the first Docker host you used, logs will appear in the Logstash container:

```
$ docker logs logstash
...
{
  "message" => "<14>2015-03-10T13:00:39Z 889bbf0753a8 nginx[1]: 192.168.34.1 - \
              - [10/Mar/2015:13:00:39 +0000] \"GET / HTTP/1.1\" 200 612 \"-\"
                \"Mozilla/5.0 \
              (Macintosh; Intel Mac OS X 10_8_5) \
              AppleWebKit/600.3.18 (KHTML, like Gecko) \
              Version/6.2.3 Safari/537.85.12\" \"-\"\n",
              "@version" => "1",
              "@timestamp" => "2015-03-10T13:00:36.241Z",
                  "type" => "syslog",
                  "host" => "192.168.34.10",
                  "tags" => [
  ...
```

Discussion

To simplify testing Logspout with Logstash, you can clone the repository accompanying this book and go to the *ch09/logspout* directory. A Vagrantfile will start two Docker hosts and pull the required Docker images on each host:

```
$ git clone https://github.com/how2dock/docbook.git
$ vagrant up
$ vagrant status
Current machine states:

w                       running (virtualbox)
elk                     running (virtualbox)
...
```

On the *web server* node, you can run Nginx and the Logspout container. On the *elk* node, you can run the Logstash container:

```
$ vagrant ssh w
$ docker run --name nginx -d -p 80:80 nginx
$ docker run -d --name logspout -v /var/run/docker.sock:/tmp/docker.sock \
             gliderlabs/logspout syslog://192.168.34.11:5000

$ vagrant ssh elk
$ cd /vagrant
$ docker build -t logstash .
$ docker run -d --name logstash -p 5000:5000/udp logstash -f /etc/logstash.conf
```

You should see your Nginx logs in the Logstash container. Experiment with more hosts and different containers, and play with the Logstash plug-ins to store your logs in different formats.

See Also

- Logstash (*http://logstash.net*) website
- Configuration of Logstash (*http://logstash.net/docs/1.4.2/configuration*)
- Plug-ins (*http://logstash.net/docs/1.4.2/index*) for Logstash inputs, outputs, codecs, and filters

9.7 Managing Logspout Routes to Store Container Logs

Problem

You are using Logspout to stream your logs to a remote server, but you would like to modify this endpoint. Specifically, you want to debug your containers by looking directly at Logspout, change the endpoint it uses, or add more endpoints.

Solution

In Recipe 9.6, you might have noticed that the Logspout container has port 8000 exposed. You can use this port to manage routes via a straightfoward HTTP API.

You can bind port 8000 to the host to access this API remotely, but as an exercise you are going to use a linked container to do it locally. Pull an image that contains `curl` and start a container interactively. Verify that you can ping the Logspout container (here I assume that you have the same setup as in Recipe 9.6). Then use `curl` to access the Logspout API at *http://logspout:8000*.

```
$ docker pull tutum/curl
$ docker run -ti --link logspout:logspout tutum/curl /bin/bash
root@c94a4eacb7cc:/# ping logspout
PING logspout (172.17.0.10) 56(84) bytes of data.
64 bytes from logspout (172.17.0.10): icmp_seq=1 ttl=64 time=0.075 ms
...
root@c94a4eacb7cc:/# curl http://logspout:8000/logs
       logspout|[martini] Started GET /logs for 172.17.0.12:38353
       nginx|192.168.34.1 [10/Mar/2015:13:57:38 +0000] "GET / HTTP/1.1" 200 ...
       nginx|192.168.34.1 [10/Mar/2015:13:57:43 +0000] "GET / HTTP/1.1" 200 ...
```

Discussion

To manage the log streams, the API exposes a */routes* route. The standard HTTP verbs `GET`, `DELETE`, and `POST` can be used to list, delete, and update the streaming endpoints, respectively:

```
root@1fbb2f9636a8:/# curl http://logspout:8000/routes
[
  {
    "id": "e508de0c9689",
    "target": {
      "type": "syslog",
      "addr": "192.168.34.11:5000"
    }
  }
]
root@1fbb2f9636a8:/# curl http://logspout:8000/routes/e508de0c9689
{
  "id": "e508de0c9689",
  "target": {
    "type": "syslog",
    "addr": "192.168.34.11:5000"
  }
}
root@1fbb2f9636a8:/# curl -X DELETE http://logspout:8000/routes/e508de0c9689
root@1fbb2f9636a8:/# curl http://logspout:8000/routes
[]
root@1fbb2f9636a8:/# curl -X POST \
                   -d '{"target": {"type": "syslog", \
```

```
                              "addr": "192.168.34.11:5000"}}' \
              http://logspout:8000/routes
{
  "id": "f60d30502654",
  "target": {
    "type": "syslog",
    "addr": "192.168.34.11:5000"
  }
}
root@1fbb2f9636a8:/# curl http://logspout:8000/routes
[
  {
    "id": "f60d30502654",
    "target": {
      "type": "syslog",
      "addr": "192.168.34.11:5000"
    }
  }
]
```

 You can create a route to Papertrail (*https://papertrailapp.com*) that provides automatic backup to Amazon S3.

9.8 Using Elasticsearch and Kibana to Store and Visualize Container Logs

Problem

Recipe 9.6 uses Logstash (*http://logstash.net*) to receive logs and send them to *stdout*. However, Logstash has many plug-ins (*http://logstash.net/docs/1.4.2/index*) that allow you to do much more. You would like to go further and use Elasticsearch (*http://www.elasticsearch.com*) to store your container logs.

Solution

Start an Elasticsearch and a Kibana container. Kibana (*http://www.elasticsearch.org/overview/kibana/*) is a dashboard that allows you to easily visualize and query your Elasticsearch indexes. Start a Logstash container by using the default configuration from the *ehazlett/logstash* image:

```
$ docker run --name es -d -p 9200:9200 -p 9300:9300 ehazlett/elasticsearch
$ docker run --name kibana -d -p 80:80 ehazlett/kibana
$ docker run -d --name logstash -p 5000:5000/udp \
             --link es:elasticsearch ehazlett/logstash \
             -f /etc/logstash.conf.sample
```

Notice that the Logstash container is linked to the Elasticsearch container. If you do not link it, Logstash will not be able to find the Elasticsearch server.

With the container running, you can open your browser on port 80 of the Docker host where you are running the Kibana container. You will see the Kibana default dashboard. Select Sample Dashboard to extract some information from your index and build a basic dashboard. You should see the logs obtained from hitting the Nginx server, as shown in Figure 9-1.

Figure 9-1. Snapshot of a Kibana dashboard obtained with this recipe

Discussion

In the solution, Elasticsearch is running on a single container. The index created when storing your logs streamed by Logspout will not persist if you kill and remove the Elasticsearch container. Consider mounting a volume and backing it up to persist your Elasticsearch data. In addition, if you need more storage and an efficient index, you should create an Elasticsearch cluster across multiple Docker hosts.

9.9 Using Collectd to Visualize Container Metrics

Problem

In addition to visualizing application logs (see Recipe 9.8), you would like to monitor container metrics such as CPU.

Solution

Use Collectd (*https://collectd.org*). Run it in a container on all hosts where you have running containers that you want to monitor. By mounting the */var/run/docker.sock* socket in a *collectd* container, you can use a Collectd plug-in that uses the Docker stats API (see Recipe 9.2) and sends metrics to a Graphite dashboard running in a different host.

This is an advanced recipe that uses several concepts covered earlier. Make sure to do Recipe 7.1 and Recipe 9.8 before doing this recipe.

To test this, you'll use the following setup, with two Docker hosts. One runs four containers: an Nginx container used to generate dummy logs to *stdout*, a Logspout container that will route all *stdout* logs to a Logstash instance, one that generates a synthetic load (i.e., *borja/unixbench*), and one Collectd container. These four containers can be started using Docker Compose.

The other host runs four containers as well: a Logstash container to collect the logs coming from Logspout, an Elasticsearch container to store the logs, a Kibana container to visualize those logs, and a Graphite container. The Graphite container also runs `carbon` to store the metrics.

Figure 9-2 illustrates this two-host, eight-container setup.

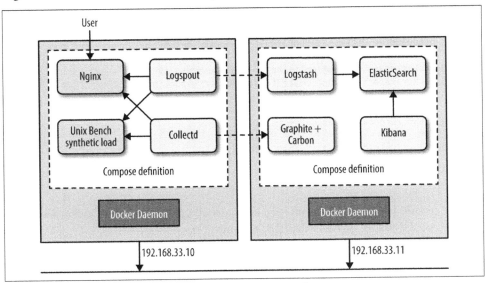

Figure 9-2. Two-host, Collectd, Logstash, Kibana, Graphite setup

On the first host (the worker), you can start all the containers with Docker Compose (see Recipe 7.1) using a YAML file like this one:

```
nginx:
  image: nginx
  ports:
    - 80:80
logspout:
  image: gliderlabs/logspout
```

```
    volumes:
      - /var/run/docker.sock:/tmp/docker.sock
    command: syslog://192.168.33.11:5000
  collectd:
    build: .
    volumes:
      - /var/run/docker.sock:/var/run/docker.sock
  load:
    image: borja/unixbench
```

The Logspout container uses a command that specifies your Logstash endpoint.
Change the IP if you are running in a different networking environment. The Collectd container is built by Docker Compose and based on the following Dockerfile:

```
FROM debian:jessie

RUN apt-get update && apt-get -y install \
    collectd \
    python \
    python-pip
RUN apt-get clean
RUN pip install docker-py

RUN groupadd -r docker && useradd -r -g docker docker

ADD docker-stats.py /opt/collectd/bin/docker-stats.py
ADD docker-report.py /opt/collectd/bin/docker-report.py
ADD collectd.conf /etc/collectd/collectd.conf

RUN chown -R docker /opt/collectd/bin

CMD ["/usr/sbin/collectd","-f"]
```

In the discussion section of this recipe, you will go over the scripts used in this Dockerfile.

On the second host (the monitor), you can start all containers with Docker Compose
(see Recipe 7.1) using a YAML file like this one:

```
es:
  image: ehazlett/elasticsearch
  ports:
    - 9300:9300
    - 9200:9200
kibana:
  image: ehazlett/kibana
  ports:
    - 8080:80
graphite:
  image: hopsoft/graphite-statsd
  ports:
    - 80:80
    - 2003:2003
```

```
  - 8125:8125/udp
logstash:
  image: ehazlett/logstash
  ports:
  - 5000:5000
  - 5000:5000/udp
  volumes:
  - /root/docbook/ch09/collectd/logstash.conf:/etc/logstash.conf
  links:
  - es:elasticsearch
  command: -f /etc/logstash.conf
```

 Several nonofficial images are used in this setup: *gliderlabs/logsp-out*, *borja/unixbench*, *ehazlett/elasticsearch*, *ehazlett/kibana*, *ehazlett/logstash*, and *hopsoft/graphite-statsd*. Check the Dockerfile of these images on Docker Hub or build your own images if you do not trust them.

Once all the containers are up on the two hosts, and assuming that you set up the networking and any firewall that may exist properly (open ports on security groups if you are using cloud instances), you will be able to access the Nginx container on port 80 of the worker host, the Kibana dashboard on port 8080 of the monitor host, and the Graphite dashboard on port 80 of the monitor host.

The Graphite dashboard will show you basic CPU metrics coming from all the containers running on the worker host. See Figure 9-3 for what you should see.

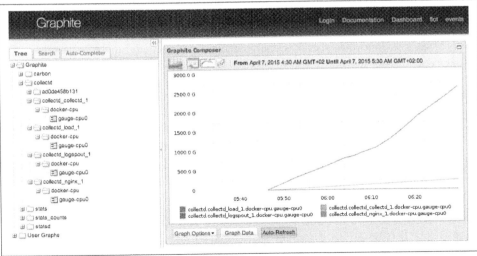

Figure 9-3. The Graphite dashboard showing CPU metrics for all containers

Discussion

You can get all the scripts used in this recipe by using the online material that comes with this book. Clone the repository if you have not done so already and head over to the *docbook/ch09/collectd* directory:

```
$ git clone https://github.com/how2dock/docbook.git
$ cd docbook/ch09/collectd
$ tree
.
├── Dockerfile
├── README.md
├── Vagrantfile
├── collectd.conf
├── docker-report.py
├── docker-stats.py
├── logstash.conf
├── monitor.yml
└── worker.yml
```

The Vagrantfile allows you to start two Docker hosts on your local machine to experiment with this setup. However, you can clone this repository in two cloud instances that have Docker and Docker Compose installed and then start all the containers. If you use Vagrant, do the following:

```
$ vagrant up
$ vagrant ssh monitor
$ vagrant ssh worker
```

 While using Vagrant for this recipe, I encountered several intermittent errors as well as delays when downloading the images. Using cloud instances with better network connectivity might be more enjoyable.

The two YAML files are used to easily start all containers on the two hosts. Do not run them on the same host:

```
$ docker-compose -f monitor.yml up -d
$ docker-compose -f worker.yml up -d
```

The *logstash.conf* file was discussed in Recipe 9.6. Go back to this recipe if you do not understand this configuration file.

The Dockerfile is used to build a Collectd image and was shown in the solution section earlier. It is based on a Debian Jessie image and installs docker-py (see Recipe 4.10) and a few other scripts.

Collectd uses plug-ins (*https://collectd.org/wiki/index.php/Table_of_Plugins*) to collect metrics and send them to a data store (e.g., Carbon with Graphite). In this setup, you use the simplest form of Collectd plug-in, which is called an exec plug-in. This is defined in the *collectd.conf* file in the following section:

```
<Plugin exec>
    Exec "docker" "/opt/collectd/bin/docker-stats.py"
    NotificationExec "docker" "/opt/collectd/bin/docker-report.py"
</Plugin>
```

The Collectd process running in the foreground in the Collectd container will routinely execute the two Python scripts defined in the configuration file. This is also why you copy them in the Dockerfile. The *docker-report.py* script outputs values to syslog. This has the benefit that you will also collect them via your Logspout container and see them in your Kibana dashboard. The *docker-stats.py* script uses the Docker stats API (see Recipe 9.2) and the docker-py Python package. This script lists all the running containers, and obtains the statistics for them. For the stats called cpu_stats, it writes a *PUTVAL* string to *stdout*. This string is understood by Collectd and sent to the Graphite data store (a.k.a Carbon) for storage and visualization. The *PUTVAL* string follows the Collectd exec plug-in syntax:

```
#!/usr/bin/env python

import random
import json
import docker
import sys

cli=docker.Client(base_url='unix://var/run/docker.sock')

types = ["gauge-cpu0"]

for h in cli.containers():
    if not h["Status"].startswith("Up"):
        continue
    stats = json.loads(cli.stats(h["Id"]).next())
    for k, v in stats.items():
        if k == "cpu_stats":
            print("PUTVAL %s/%s/%s N:%s" % (h['Names'][0].lstrip('/'), \
                                 'docker-cpu', types[0], \
                                 v['cpu_usage']['total_usage']))
```

The example plug-in in this recipe is minimal, and the statistics need to be processed further. You might want to consider using this (*https://github.com/cloudwatt/docker-collectd-plugin*) Python-based plug-in instead.

See Also

- Collectd website (*https://collectd.org*)

- Collectd Exec plug-in (*http://collectd.org/documentation/manpages/collectd-exec. 5.shtml*)
- Graphite website (*http://graphite.wikidot.com*)
- Logstash website (*http://logstash.net*)
- Collectd Docker plug-in (*https://github.com/cloudwatt/docker-collectd-plugin*)

9.10 Using cAdvisor to Monitor Resource Usage in Containers

Problem

Although Logspout (see Recipe 9.6) allows you to stream application logs to remote endpoints, you need a resource utilization monitoring system.

Solution

Use *cAdvisor* (*https://github.com/google/cadvisor*), created by Google to monitor resource usage and performance of its lcmtfy (*https://github.com/google/lmctfy*) containers. cAdvisor runs as a container on your Docker hosts. By mounting local volumes, it can monitor the performance of all other running containers on that same host. It provides a local web UI, exposes an API (*https://github.com/google/cadvisor/blob/master/docs/api.md*), and can stream data to InfluxDB (*http://influxdb.com*). Streaming data from running containers to a remote InfluxDB cluster allows you to aggregate performance metrics for all your containers running in a cluster.

To get started, let's use a single host. Download the *cAdvisor* image as well as *borja/unixbench*, an image that enables you to simulate a workload inside a container:

```
$ docker pull google/cadvisor:latest
$ docker pull borja/unixbench
$ docker run -v /var/run:/var/run:rw\
             -v /sys:/sys:ro \
             -v /var/lib/docker/:/var/lib/docker:ro \
             -p 8080:8080 \
             -d \
             --name cadvisor \
             google/cadvisor:latest
$ docker run -d borja/unixbench
```

With the two containers running, you can open your browser at *http://<IP_DOCKER_HOST>:8080* and you will enjoy the cAdvisor UI (see Figure 9-4). You will be able to browse the running containers and access metrics for each of them.

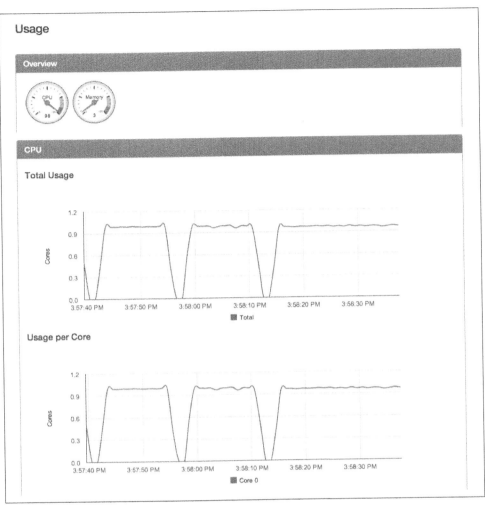

Figure 9-4. The cAdvisor UI

See Also

- cAdvisor API documentation (*https://github.com/google/cadvisor/blob/master/docs/api.md*)

9.11 Monitoring Container Metrics with InfluxDB, Grafana, and cAdvisor

Problem

You would like to use an alternative to Elastic/Logstash/Kibana for your logging and monitoring stack.

Solution

Consider using cAdvisor (see Recipe 9.10) in conjunction with InfluxDB (*https://influxdb.com*) for storing the time-series data, and Grafana (*http://grafana.org*) for visualizing the information. cAdvisor collects good metrics from the containers running on your Docker host, and has an InfluxDB storage driver that enables you to store all the metrics as a time series in InfluxDB (a distributed database for time-series data). Visualizing the data from InfluxDB can be done with Grafana, an equivalent to Kibana.

The following is the basic setup for a single node. You would run cAdvisor, configured to send data to an InfluxDB host, and you would run InfluxDB and Grafana. All of these come as containers:

```
$ docker run -d -p 8083:8083 -p 8086:8086 \
              -e PRE_CREATE_DB="db" \
              --name influxdb \
              tutum/influxdb:0.8.8
$ docker run -d -p 80:80 \
              --link=influxdb:influxdb \
              -e HTTP_USER=admin \
              -e HTTP_PASS=root \
              -e INFLUXDB_HOST=influxdb \
              -e INFLUXDB_NAME=db \
              --name=grafana \
              tutum/grafana
$ docker run -v /var/run:/var/run:rw \
              -v /sys:/sys:ro \
              -v /var/lib/docker/:/var/lib/docker:ro \
              -p 8080:8080 \
              --link=influxdb:influxdb \
              -d --name=cadvisor \
              google/cadvisor:latest \
              -storage_driver=influxdb \
              -storage_driver_host=influxdb:8086 \
              -storage_driver_db=db
```

In a multiple hosts setup, you would run only cAdvisor on all your nodes. InfluxDB would be running in a distributed manner on several hosts, and Grafana might be behind an Nginx proxy for load-balancing. Considering the fast pace of development

---

of these systems and the changes going on in the images, you might have to adjust the `docker run` commands shown previously to get a working system.

9.12 Gaining Visibility into Your Containers' Layout with Weave Scope

Problem

Building a distributed application based on a microservices architecture (*http://martinfowler.com/articles/microservices.html*) leads to hundreds of (and potentially more) containers running in your data center. Visibility into that application and all the containers that it's made of is crucial and a key part of your overall infrastructure.

Solution

Weave Scope from Weaveworks (*http://weave.works*) provides a simple yet powerful way of probing your infrastructure and dynamically creating a map of all your containers. It gives you multiple views—per container, per image, per host, and per application—allowing you to group containers and drill down on their characteristics.

It is open source and available on GitHub (*https://github.com/weaveworks/scope*).

To facilitate testing, I prepared a Vagrant box, similar to many other recipes in this book. Clone the repository with Git and launch the Vagrant box:

```
$ git clone https://github.com/how2dock/docbook.git
$ cd how2dock/ch09/weavescope
$ vagrant up
```

The Vagrant box installs the latest Docker version (i.e., 1.6.2 as of this writing) and installs Docker Compose (see Recipe 7.1). In the */vagrant* folder, you will find a *compose* file that gives you a synthetic three-tiered application made of two load-balancers, two application containers, and three database containers. This is a toy application meant to illustrate Weave Scope. Once the VM has booted, `ssh` into it, go to the */vagrant* folder, and launch Compose and the Weave Scope script (i.e., `scope`) like so:

```
$ vagrant ssh
$ cd /vagrant
$ docker-compose up -d
$ ./scope launch
```

You will end up with eight containers running: seven for the tiered toy application and one for Weave Scope. The toy application is accessible at *http://192.168.33.10:8001* or *http://192.168.33.10:8002*. Of course, the most interesting part is the Weave Scope dashboard. Open your browser at *http://192.168.33.10:4040* and you will see something similar to Figure 9-5.

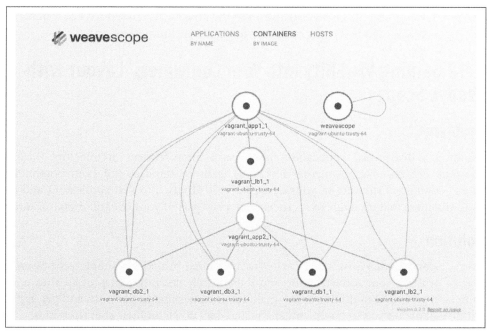

Figure 9-5. The Weave Scope dashboard

Navigate through the UI, explore the various grouping capabilities, and explore the information of each container.

Discussion

Weave Scope is still in early development and considered pre-alpha as of this writing. You should expect more features to be added to this open source product. Keeping an eye on this visibility solution for Docker containers is definitely worthwhile.

Building from source is straightforward with a Makefile that builds a Docker image.

See Also

- Detect, Map, and Monitor Docker Containers with Weave Scope (*http://bit.ly/dmm-weave*)

## CHAPTER 10

Application Use Cases

10.0 Introduction

To finish this book, I will argue that Docker makes building distributed applications painless. You now have all the tools in your arsenal to build a microservices application that will scale within and outside of your datacenter. At the very least, deploying existing distributed systems/frameworks is made easier because you need to only launch a few containers. Docker Hub (*https://hub.docker.com*) is full of MongoDB, Elastic, and Cassandra images, and more. Assuming that you like what is inside those images, you can grab them and run one or multiple containers, and you are done.

This last chapter presents a few use-cases that are meant as teasers and put you on your way to building your own application. First in Recipe 10.1, Pini Reznik shows you how to build a continuous integration pipeline with Docker and Jenkins. He then shows you how to extend it and build a continuous deployment pipeline using Mesos in Recipe 10.2.

In Recipe 10.3, we present an advanced recipe that show you how to build a dynamic load-balancing setup. It leverages `registrator` with a `consul` key-value store and `confd`. `confd` is a system to manage configuration templates. It watches keys in your key-value store and upon modification of the values of those keys automatically re-writes a configuration file based on a template. Using this setup you can, for example, automatically reconfigure a load-balancer when new backends are added. This is key to building an elastic load-balancer.

With Recipe 10.4, we build an S3-compatible object store, based on Cassandra running in Kubernetes and a software called pithos (*http://pithos.io*), which exposes an S3 API and manages buckets in Cassandra. It scales automatically through the use of Kubernetes replication controllers.

In Recipe 10.5 and Recipe 10.6 we build a MySQL Galera cluster using Docker Network. Docker network is still experimental at the time of writing but this recipe will give you a great insight into what will be possible with it. With automatic container linking, nodes of a MySQL Galera cluster can discover themselves on a multihost network and build a cluster as if the containers were on a single host. This is extremely powerful and will simplify distributed application design.

We finish with a Big Data example by deploying Spark (*http://spark.apache.org*), a large-scale data processing system. You can run a Spark on a Kubernetes cluster but you can also run it on a Docker Network–based infrastructure extremely easily. This last recipe shows you how.

Enjoy this last chapter and hopefully it will spark your interest.

10.1 CI/CD: Setting Up a Development Environment

Contributed by Pini Reznik

Problem

You need a consistent and reproducible development environment for your Node.js application. You don't want to rebuild the Docker image every time you make small changes to the Node.js sources.

Solution

Create a Docker image that includes all the required dependencies. Mount external volumes during the development and use the ADD instruction in the Dockerfile for distributing the image with the application to other developers.

First you need a Node.js Hello World application that includes two files:

app.js:

```
// Load the http module to create an http server.
var http = require('http');

// Configure our HTTP server to respond with Hello World to all requests.
var server = http.createServer(function (request, response) {
  response.writeHead(200, {"Content-Type": "text/plain"});
  response.end("Hello World");
});

// Listen on port 8000, IP defaults to "0.0.0.0"
server.listen(8000);

// Put a friendly message on the terminal
console.log("Server running at http://127.0.0.1:8000/");
```

package.json:

```
{
  "name": "hello-world",
  "description": "hello world",
  "version": "0.0.1",
  "private": true,
  "dependencies": {
    "express": "3.x"
  },
  "scripts": {"start": "node app.js"}
}
```

To create the Docker image, you can use the following Dockerfile:

```
FROM google/nodejs

WORKDIR /app
ADD package.json /app/
RUN npm install
ADD . /app

EXPOSE 8000
CMD []
ENTRYPOINT ["/nodejs/bin/npm", "start"]
```

This Dockerfile installs all the application dependencies and adds the application to the image, ready to be started by using the ENTRYPOINT instruction.

 The order of the instructions in the Dockerfile is important. Adding *package.json* and installing dependencies before the addition of the rest of the application will help to shorten the build time in all cases when the application changes but dependencies remain the same. This is because the ADD instruction invalidates the Docker cache when any of copied files have been changed, and this leads to the repetitive execution of all the commands that follow.

When you have your three files, you can build the Docker image and run a container:

```
$ docker build -t my_nodejs_image .
$ docker run -p 8000:8000 my_nodejs_image
```

This starts a container with the application built into the image by the ADD instruction. To be able to test your application changes, you can mount a volume with the source into the container by using the following command:

```
$ docker run -p 8000:8000 -v "$PWD":/app my_nodejs_image
```

This mounts the current folder with the latest sources inside the container as the application folder. This way, you can inject the latest sources during the development without rebuilding the image.

To share the images between the developers and push the images to alternative testing environments, you can use a Docker registry. The following commands build and push the image to the specified Docker registry:

```
$ docker build -t <docker registry URL>:<docker registry port> \
/containersol/nodejs_app:<image tag>
$ docker push <docker registry URL>:<docker registry port>\
/containersol/nodejs_app:<image tag>
```

To simplify the work with the development environment and ease the future integration into a centralized testing environment, you can use the following three scripts: *build.sh*, *test.sh*, and *push.sh*. These scripts will become a single command interface for every common operation you are required to perform during the development.

build.sh:

```
#!/bin/bash

# The first parameter passed to this script will be used as an image version.
# If none is passed, latest will be used as a tag.
if [ -z "${1}" ]; then
    version="latest"
else
    version="${1}"
fi

cd nodejs_app
docker build -t localhost:5000/containersol/nodejs_app:${version} .
cd ..
```

test.sh:

```
#!/bin/bash

# The first parameter passed to this script will be used as an image version.
# If none is passed, latest will be used as a tag.
if [ -z "${1}" ]; then
    version="latest"
else
    version="${1}"
fi
docker run -d --name node_app_test -p 8000:8000 -v "$PWD":/app localhost:5000/ \
containersol/nodejs_app:${version}

echo "Testing image: localhost:5000/containersol/nodejs_app:${version}"

# Allow the webserver to start up
sleep 1

# Test will be successful if the webpage at the
# following URL includes the word "success"
curl -s GET http://localhost:8000 | grep success
status=$?
```

```
# Clean up the testing container
docker kill node_app_test
docker rm node_app_test

if [ $status -eq 0 ] ; then
    echo "Test succeeded"
else
    echo "Test failed"
fi

exit $status
```

push.sh:

```
#!/bin/bash

# The first parameter passed to this script will be used as an image version.
# If none is passed, latest will be used as a tag.
if [ -z "${1}" ]; then
    version="latest"
else
    version="${1}"
fi

docker push localhost:5000/containersol/nodejs_app:"${version}"
```

Now you can build, test, and push the resulting image to a Docker registry by using the following commands:

```
$ ./build.sh <version>
$ ./test.sh <version>
$ ./push.sh <version>
```

Discussion

It is generally a good practice to have a consistent set of build, test, and deployment commands that can be executed in any environment, including development machines. This way, developers can test the application in exactly the same way as it is going to be tested in the continuous integration environment and catch the problems related to the environment itself at earlier stages.

This example uses simple shell scripts, but a more common way to achieve the same results is to use build systems such as Maven or Gradle. Both systems have Docker plug-ins and can be easily used to build and push the images, using the same build interface already used for compiling and packaging the code.

Our current testing environment has only a single container, but in case you need a multicontainer setup, you can use docker-compose to set up the environment as well as replace a simple curl/grep combination with more-appropriate testing systems such as Selenium. Selenium is also available in a Docker container and can be deployed together with the rest of the application containers by using docker-compose.

10.2 CI/CD: Building a Continuous Delivery Pipeline with Jenkins and Apache Mesos

Contributed by Pini Reznik

Problem

You would like to set up a continuous delivery pipeline for an application packaged using Docker containers.

Solution

Set up a Jenkins continuous integration server to deploy an application to a Mesos cluster in case the tests are passing.

Figure 10-1 gives a graphical representation of the environment you are going to use at the end of this recipe. The goal is to take an application from a development environment, package it into a Docker container, push it to the Docker registry in case the tests are passing, and tell Marathon to schedule the application on Mesos.

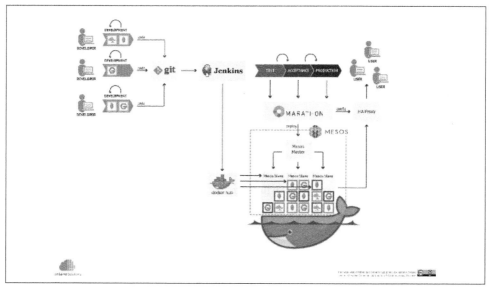

Figure 10-1. Continuous delivery pipeline using Jenkins and Apache Mesos

This recipe uses the previous example in Recipe 10.1. You can also see a way to set up a Mesos cluster for development purposes in Recipe 7.2.

First you need to set up a Jenkins server. The easiest way is to use the following Docker Compose configuration:

```
jenkins:
  image: jenkins
  volumes:
  - jenkins-home:/var/jenkins_home
ports:
    - "8080:8080"
```

The volumes defined in the preceding Compose file act as persistent storage to avoid losing your build configurations and data every time you restart your Jenkins container. It is the responsibility of the owner to back up and maintain those folders outside Docker containers.

Start Docker Compose with the following command:

```
$ docker-compose up
```

You get a functional Jenkins server running on the following address: *http://localhost: 8080*.

This was an easy task, but unfortunately not useful because you need to build an image that includes your application and also need to start containers using the newly built image to test your application. This is not possible in a standard Docker container.

To solve this, you can add two more lines to *docker-compose.yml*:

```
jenkins:
  image: jenkins
  volumes:
  - jenkins-home:/var/jenkins_home
  - /var/run/docker.sock:/var/run/docker.sock
  - /usr/bin/docker:/usr/bin/docker
  ports:
  - "8080:8080"
```

Two new volumes will mount the socket used for the communication between Docker client and server and add the Docker binary itself to act as a client. This way, you can run Docker commands inside the Jenkins container, and they will be executed on the host in parallel to the Jenkins container itself.

Another hurdle on the way toward a fully functional Jenkins server capable of running Docker commands is permissions. By default, */var/run/docker.sock* is accessible to root or anyone in the group called docker. The default Jenkins container is using a user called jenkins to start the server. The Jenkins server does not belong to the docker group, but even if it was in such a group inside the container, it still would not get the access to the Docker socket, as groups' and users' IDs differ between the host and the containers running on it (with exception of `root`, which always has ID 0). To solve this, you can use `root` to start the Jenkins server.

For this, you need to add a new `user` instruction to *docker-compose.yml*:

```
jenkins:
  image: Jenkins
  user: root
  volumes:
  - jenkins-home:/var/jenkins_home
  - /var/run/docker.sock:/var/run/docker.sock
  - /usr/bin/docker:/usr/bin/docker
  ports:
  - "8080:8080"
```

Now, when you have a functional Jenkins server, you can deploy the Node.js application described in Recipe 10.1.

In the Node.js recipe, you already have scripts to build, test, and push the image to a Docker registry. You need to add a configuration file to schedule the application on Mesos, using Marathon and another script to deploy the application.

You call the application configuration for Marathon `app_marathon.json`:

```
{
  "id": "app",
  "container": {
    "docker": {
      "image": "localhost:5000/containersol/nodejs_app:latest",
      "network": "BRIDGE",
      "portMappings": [
          {"containerPort": 8000, "servicePort": 8000}
      ]
    }
  },
  "cpus": 0.2,
  "mem": 512.0,
  "instances": 1
}
```

This configuration uses our application Docker image that you are going to build using Jenkins and deploy it on Mesos by using Marathon. This file also defines the resources needed for your application and can also include a health check.

The last piece of the configuration is the deployment script that you are going to run from Jenkins.

deploy.sh:

```
#!/bin/bash

marathon=<Marathon URL>
```

```
if [ -z "${1}" ]; then
    version="latest"
else
    version="${1}"

fi

# destroy old application
curl -X DELETE -H "Content-Type: application/json" \
    http://${marathon}:8080/v2/apps/app

# At this point we can query Marathon until the application is down.
sleep 1

# these lines will create a copy of app_marathon.json and update the image
# version. This is required for sing the cottect image tag, as the marathon
# configuration file does not support variables.
cp -f app_marathon.json app_marathon.json.tmp
sed -i "s/latest/${version}/g" app_marathon.json.tmp

# post the application to Marathon
curl -X POST -H "Content-Type: application/json" \
    http://${marathon}:8080/v2/apps \
    -d@app_marathon.json.tmp
```

Now you can start the Jenkins server by using docker-compose and define the execution steps in the Jenkins job configuration. Figure 10-2 shows the UI where this configuration can be done.

Figure 10-2. The Jenkins UI

Discussion

There are multiple ways to solve the problem of starting containers from within a container. Mounting a socket used by Docker for communication between the server and client is one of them. Additional methods may include running a container directly within a container using a privileged container. Another way is to configure the Docker server to receive remote API calls and configure the Docker client within the Jenkins container to communicate with it using a full URL. This requires configuring networking to allow communication between the server and the client.

10.3 ELB: Creating a Dynamic Load-Balancer with Confd and Registrator

Problem

You want to build a dynamic load-balancer that gets dynamically reconfigured when containers come and go.

Solution

The solution is based on `registrator` (see Recipe 7.13), which acts as a service-discovery mechanism, and `confd` (*https://github.com/kelseyhightower/confd*), which gets information from the key-value store used by `registrator` and writes configuration files based on templates.

To illustrate this, you will build a simple one-node setup. A simple *hostname* application will run in multiple containers. An Nginx load-balancer will front these containers to distribute the load among the containers. These containers will get automatically registered in a Consul key-value store, thanks to `registrator`. Then `confd` will pull information from Consul to write an Nginx configuration file. The load-balancer (i.e., Nginx) will then get restarted using the new configuration. Figure 10-3 illustrates this example.

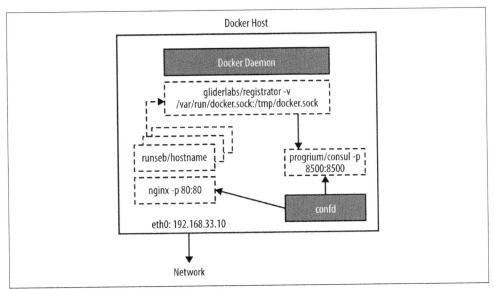

Docker Host

Docker Daemon

gliderlabs/registrator -v
/var/run/docker.sock:/tmp/docker.sock

runseb/hostname

progrium/consul -p
8500:8500

nginx -p 80:80

confd

eth0: 192.168.33.10

Network

Figure 10-3. Dynamic load-balancing schematic

To get started, you will reproduce the steps explained in Recipe 7.13. You will start a Consul-based key-value store via a single container.

In production deployments, you will want to use a multinode key-value store running separately from the nodes running your application.

This is done easily with the Docker image *progrium/consul*, like so:

```
$ docker run -d -p 8400:8400 -p 8500:8500 -p 8600:53/udp
             -h cookbook progrium/consul -server
             -bootstrap -ui-dir /ui
```

Then you will start the *registrator* container and set the registry URI to *consul:// 192.168.33.10:8500/elb*. The IP address of your Docker host will be different.

```
$ docker run -d -v /var/run/docker.sock:/tmp/docker.sock
             -h 192.168.33.10 gliderlabs/registrator
             -ip 192.168.33.10 consul://192.168.33.10:8500/elb
```

Next you will start your toy application. You can use your own and pull `runseb/host name`, which is a simple application that returns the container ID. Start two of them at first:

```
$ docker run -d -p 5001:5000 runseb/hostname
$ docker run -d -p 5002:5000 runseb/hostname
```

If you check the Consul UI, you will see that the two containers are properly registered, thanks to `registrator`, as shown in Figure 10-4.

Figure 10-4. Consul dynamic load-balancing nodes

Create an Nginx configuration file that acts as a load-balancer for these two applications. Assuming your Docker host is `192.168.33.10`, the following example will work:

```
events {
    worker_connections  1024;
}

http {
    upstream elb {
      server 192.168.33.10:5001;
      server 192.168.33.10:5002;
    }

    server {
        listen 80;
        location / {
            proxy_pass http://elb;
        }
```

```
        }
    }
```

Next start your Nginx container, binding port 80 of the container to port 80 of the host, and mount your configuration file inside the container. Give your container a name that will prove handy later:

```
$ docker run -d -p 80:80 -v /home/vagrant/nginx.conf:/etc/nginx/nginx.conf
            --name elb nginx
```

At this stage, you have a basic load-balancing setup. The Nginx container exposes port 80 on the host, and load balances two application containers. If you use `curl` to send an HTTP request to your Nginx container, you will get the container ID of the two application containers. It will look like this:

```
$ curl http://192.168.33.10
8eaab9c31e1a
$ curl http://192.168.33.10
a970ec6274ca
$ curl http://192.168.33.10
8eaab9c31e1a
$ curl http://192.168.33.10
a970ec6274ca
```

Up to now, there is nothing dynamic except the registration of the containers. To be able to reconfigure Nginx when containers come and go, you need a system that will watch keys in Consul and write a new Nginx configuration file when the values change. That is where `confd` (*https://github.com/kelseyhightower/confd*) comes into play. Download a *confd* binary from the GitHub release page (*https://github.com/ kelseyhightower/confd/releases*).

The quick start guide (*https://github.com/kelseyhightower/confd/blob/master/docs/ quick-start-guide.md*) is good. But we will go over the basic steps. First let's create the directories that will hold your configuration templates:

```
sudo mkdir -p /etc/confd/{conf.d,templates}
```

Next create a resource template, *resource config*. This file basically tells `confd` where the configuration template is that you want to be managed and tells where to write the configuration file after the values have been replaced. In */etc/confd/conf.d/ config.toml* write:

```
[template]
src = "config.conf.tmpl"
dest = "/home/vagrant/nginx.conf"
keys = [
    "/elb/hostname",
]
```

Now let's write our Nginx template file in */etc/confd/templates/config.conf.tmpl*. These templates are Golang text templates (*http://golang.org/pkg/text/template/#pkg-*

---

overview), so anything that you can do in a Golang template, you can do in this template:

```
events {
    worker_connections  1024;
}

http {
    upstream elb {
      {{range getvs "/elb/hostname/*"}}
       server {{.}};
      {{end}}
    }

    server {
        listen 80;

        location / {
            proxy_pass http://elb;
        }
    }
}
```

This template is a minimal Nginx load-balancing configuration file. You see that the *upstream* defined as elb will have a set of servers that will be extracted from the */elb/hostname/* keys stored in Consul.

Now that your templates are in place, let's try confd in a one-time shot mode. This means that you will call confd manually, you will specify the type of backend (i.e., in our case, Consul), and it will write the file */home/vagrant/nginx.conf* (this was defined as the *dest* key in the *config.toml* file):

```
$ ./confd -onetime -backend consul -node 192.168.33.10:8500
```

Since you have already written your *nginx.conf* file when you started the Nginx container, the configuration file written by confd should be exactly the same. Now let's start a new application container and rerun the confd command:

```
$ docker run -d -p 5003:5000 runseb/hostname
$ ./confd -onetime -backend consul -node 192.168.33.10:8500
... ./confd[832]: WARNING Skipping confd config file.
... ./confd[832]: INFO /home/vagrant/nginx.conf has md5sum \
acf6552d92cb9eb79b1068cf40b8ec0f should be 001894b713827404d0c5e72e2a66844d
... ./confd[832]: INFO Target config /home/vagrant/nginx.conf out of sync
... ./confd[832]: INFO Target config /home/vagrant/nginx.conf has been updated
```

You see that confd detects that the configuration has changed and it writes a new configuration file. When we start the new application container, registrator automatically registers it in consul, and confd is able to detect this and write the new configuration. Now since you did this as a one-time command, let's restart the Nginx container, and you will see that it will use the new configuration (which is accessible via a volume mount in the Nginx container):

```
$ docker restart elb
$ curl http://192.168.33.10
a970ec6274ca
$ curl http://192.168.33.10
8eaab9c31e1a
$ curl http://192.168.33.10
71d8297c1538
```

The only thing left to do now is to run `confd` in a daemon mode, and instruct it to stop and restart the Nginx container when changes to the configuration are done. To do this, edit */etc/confd/conf.d/config.toml* and add a `reload_cmd` to restart Nginx like so (this assumes you named your Nginx container *elb* as indicated earlier):

```
[template]
src = "config.conf.tmpl"
dest = "/home/vagrant/nginx.conf"
keys = [
    "/elb/hostname",
]
reload_cmd = "docker restart elb"
```

Finally, run `confd` in daemon mode, and for testing, set a short interval for when it will poll Consul. Then have fun starting and stopping your application container. You will see that every time you start or stop/kill an application container, `confd` will dynamically update your configuration and restart the *elb* container:

```
$ ./confd -backend consul -interval 5 -node 192.168.33.10:8500
... ./confd[1463]: WARNING Skipping confd config file.
... ./confd[1463]: INFO /home/vagrant/nginx.conf has md5sum \
acf6552d92cb9eb79b1068cf40b8ec0f should be 001894b713827404d0c5e72e2a66844d
... ./confd[1463]: INFO Target config /home/vagrant/nginx.conf out of sync
... ./confd[1463]: INFO Target config /home/vagrant/nginx.conf has been updated
... ./confd[1463]: INFO /home/vagrant/nginx.conf has md5sum \
001894b713827404d0c5e72e2a66844d should be cecb5ddc469ba3ef17f9861cde9d529a
... ./confd[1463]: INFO Target config /home/vagrant/nginx.conf out of sync
... ./confd[1463]: INFO Target config /home/vagrant/nginx.conf has been updated
... ./confd[1463]: INFO /home/vagrant/nginx.conf has md5sum \
cecb5ddc469ba3ef17f9861cde9d529a should be 0b97f157f437083ffba43f93a426d28f
... ./confd[1463]: INFO Target config /home/vagrant/nginx.conf out of sync
... ./confd[1463]: INFO Target config /home/vagrant/nginx.conf has been updated
```

This is dynamic load balancing with Docker. To make it elastic, you would need to monitor the load and automatically start a new application container, which would trigger a reconfiguration of the *elb* configuration.

Discussion

This recipe is quite long and has many steps. To facilitate the testing, I prepared a Vagrant box, as always; try this:

```
$ git clone https://github.com/how2dock/dockbook.git
$ cd docbook/ch10/confd
$ vagrant up
$ vagrant ssh
```

You will have all the images downloaded and ready to go:

```
$ docker images
REPOSITORY              TAG      IMAGE ID       CREATED        VIRTUAL SIZE
progrium/consul         latest   e66fb6787628   10 days ago    69.43 MB
nginx                   latest   319d2015d149   3 weeks ago    132.8 MB
runseb/hostname         latest   7c9d1ddd2ceb   3 months ago   349.3 MB
gliderlabs/registrator  latest   b1c29d1a74a9   4 months ago   11.79 MB
```

And the confd configuration files will be already set in */etc/confd/conf.d/config.toml* and */etc/confd/templates/config.conf.tmp*.

Just start the containers:

```
$ docker run -d -p 8400:8400 -p 8500:8500 -p 8600:53/udp
             -h cookbook progrium/consul -server
             -bootstrap -ui-dir /ui
$ docker run -d -v /var/run/docker.sock:/tmp/docker.sock
             -h 192.168.33.10 gliderlabs/registrator
             -ip 192.168.33.10 consul://192.168.33.10:8500/elb
$ docker run -d -p 80:80 -v /home/vagrant/nginx.conf:/etc/nginx/nginx.conf
             --name elb nginx
$ docker run -d -p 5001:5000 runseb/hostname
$ docker run -d -p 5002:5000 runseb/hostname
```

 You can start those containers via Docker Compose (see Recipe 7.1).

And run confd:

```
$ ./confd -backend consul -interval 5 -node 192.168.33.10:8500
```

See Also

- Quick Start guide for confd (*https://github.com/kelseyhightower/confd/blob/master/docs/quick-start-guide.md*)

10.4 DATA: Building an S3-Compatible Object Store with Cassandra on Kubernetes

Problem

You would like to build your own S3-like (*http://aws.amazon.com/s3/*) object store.

Solution

Amazon S3 is the leading cloud-based object storage service. Since it came online, several storage backends have developed an S3-compatible API frontend to their distributed storage system: RiakCS (*http://docs.basho.com/riakcs/latest/*), GlusterFS (*http://www.gluster.org*), and Ceph (*http://ceph.com*). The Apache Cassandra (*http://cassandra.apache.org*) distributed database is also a good choice, and recently a project called Pithos (*http://pithos.io*) has started that builds an S3-compatible object store on top of Cassandra.

This is particularly interesting because Cassandra is widely used in the enterprise. However, for Docker this might be challenging as you would need to build a Cassandra cluster using Docker containers. Thankfully, with a cluster manager/container orchestration system like Kubernetes, it is relatively painless to run a Docker-based Cassandra cluster. The Kubernetes documentation has an example (*https://github.com/GoogleCloudPlatform/kubernetes/tree/master/examples/cassandra*) of how to do it.

Therefore, to build our S3 object store, you are going to run a Cassandra cluster on Kubernetes and run a Pithos frontend that will expose an S3-compatible API.

 It is possible to do the same with Docker Swarm.

To start, you need to have access to a Kubernetes cluster. The easiest way is to use Google Container Engine (*https://cloud.google.com/container-engine/*) (see Recipe 8.10). If you do not want to use Google Container Engine or need to learn about Kubernetes, check Chapter 5 and you will learn how to deploy your own cluster. Whatever technique you use, before proceeding, you should be able to use the *kubectl* client and list the nodes in your cluster. For example:

```
$ ./kubectl get nodes
NAME                              LABELS                                STATUS
k8s-cookbook-935a6530-node-hsdb   kubernetes.io/hostname=...-node-hsdb  Ready
k8s-cookbook-935a6530-node-mukh   kubernetes.io/hostname=...-node-mukh  Ready
```

```
k8s-cookbook-935a6530-node-t9p8    kubernetes.io/hostname=...-node-t9p8    Ready
k8s-cookbook-935a6530-node-ugp4    kubernetes.io/hostname=...-node-ugp4    Ready
```

You are now ready to start a Cassandra cluster. You can use the Kubernetes example (*https://github.com/GoogleCloudPlatform/kubernetes/tree/master/examples/cassandra*) directly or clone my own repo:

```
$ git clone https://github.com/how2dock/dockbook.git
$ cd ch05/examples
```

 Since Kubernetes is a fast evolving software, the API is changing quickly. The *pod*, *replication controller*, and *service* specification files may need to be adapted to the latest API version.

Then launch the Cassandra replication controller, increase the number of replicas, and launch the service:

```
$ kubectl create -f ./cassandra/cassandra-controller.yaml
$ kubectl scale --replicas=4 rc cassandra
$ kubectl create -f ./cassandra/cassandra-service.yaml
```

Once the image is downloaded, you will have your Kubernetes pods in a running state. Note that the image currently used comes from the Google registry. That's because this image contains a discovery class specified in the Cassandra configuration. You could use the Cassandra image from Docker Hub but would have to put that Java class in there to allow all Cassandra nodes to discover each other. Changing the number of replicas allows you to scale your Cassandra cluster, and starting a service allows you to expose a DNS endpoint for it.

Check that the specified number of pods is running:

```
$ kubectl get pods --selector="name=cassandra"
```

Once Cassandra discovers all nodes and rebalances the database storage, you will get something like this (it will depend on the number of replicas you set, and the IDs will change):

```
$ ./kubectl exec cassandra-5f709 -c cassandra nodetool status
Datacenter: datacenter1
=========================
Status=Up/Down
|/ State=Normal/Leaving/Joining/Moving
--  Address     Load       Tokens  Owns (effective)  Host ID               Rack
UN  10.16.2.4   84.32 KB   256     46.0%             8a0c8663-074f-4987... rack1
UN  10.16.1.3   67.81 KB   256     53.7%             784c8f4d-7722-4d16... rack1
UN  10.16.0.3   51.37 KB   256     49.7%             2f551b3e-9314-4f12... rack1
UN  10.16.3.3   65.67 KB   256     50.6%             a746b8b3-984f-4b1e... rack1
```

You can access the logs of a container in a pod with the handy
`kubectl logs` command.

Now that you have a fully functioning Cassandra cluster, you can move on to launching Pithos, which will provide the S3 API and use Cassandra as the object store.

Pithos (*http://pithos.io*) is a daemon that "provides an S3-compatible frontend to a Cassandra cluster." So if you run Pithos in your Kubernetes cluster and point it to your running Cassandra cluster, you can expose an S3-compatible interface.

To that end, I created a Docker image for Pithos, *runseb/pithos*, on Docker Hub. It's an automated build, so you can check out the Dockerfile there. The image contains the default configuration file. You will want to change it to edit your access keys and bucket store definitions.

You will now launch Pithos as a Kubernetes replication controller and expose a service with an external load-balancer created on GCE. The Cassandra service that you launched allows Pithos to find Cassandra by using DNS resolution.

However, you need to set up the proper database schema for the object store. This is done through a bootstrapping process. To do it, you need to run a nonrestarting pod that installs the Pithos schema in Cassandra. Use the YAML file from the example directory that you cloned earlier:

```
$ kubectl create -f ./pithos/pithos-bootstrap.yaml
```

Wait for the bootstrap to happen (i.e., for the pod to get in *succeed* state). Then launch the replication controller. For now, you will launch only one replica. Using a replication controller makes it easy to attach a service and expose it via a public IP address.

```
$ kubectl create -f ./pithos/pithos-rc.yaml
$ kubectl create -f ./pithos/spithos.yaml
$ ./kubectl get services --selector="name=pithos"
NAME     LABELS       SELECTOR     IP(S)          PORT(S)
pithos   name=pithos  name=pithos  10.19.251.29   8080/TCP
                                   104.197.27.250
```

Since Pithos will serve on port 8080 by default, make sure that you open the firewall for the public IP of the load-balancer. Once the Pithos pod is in its running state, you are done and have built an S3-compatible object store backed by Cassandra running in Docker containers managed by Kubernetes. Congratulations!

Discussion

The setup is interesting, but you need to be able to use it and confirm that it is indeed S3 compatible. To do this, you can try the well-known S3 utilities like *s3cmd* or *boto*.

For example, start by installing s3cmd (*http://s3tools.org/s3cmd*) and create a configuration file:

```
$ cat ~/.s3cfg
[default]
access_key = AKIAIOSFODNN7EXAMPLE
secret_key = wJalrXUtnFEMI/K7MDENG/bPxRfiCYEXAMPLEKEY
check_ssl_certificate = False
enable_multipart = True
encoding = UTF-8
encrypt = False
host_base = s3.example.com
host_bucket = %(bucket)s.s3.example.com
proxy_host = 104.197.27.250
proxy_port = 8080
server_side_encryption = True
signature_v2 = True
use_https = False
verbosity = WARNING
```

Replace the *proxy_host* with the IP that you obtained from the Pithos service external load-balancer.

 This example uses an unencrypted proxy. Moreover, the access and secret keys are the default stored in the Dockerfile (*https://github.com/runseb/pithos*); change them.

With this configuration in place, you are ready to use s3cmd and create buckets to store content:

```
$ s3cmd mb s3://foobar
Bucket 's3://foobar/' created
$ s3cmd ls
2015-06-09 11:19  s3://foobar
```

If you wanted to use Boto (*https://github.com/boto/boto3*) in Python, this would work as well:

```
#!/usr/bin/env python

from boto.s3.key import Key
from boto.s3.connection import S3Connection
from boto.s3.connection import OrdinaryCallingFormat

apikey='AKIAIOSFODNN7EXAMPLE'
secretkey='wJalrXUtnFEMI/K7MDENG/bPxRfiCYEXAMPLEKEY'

cf=OrdinaryCallingFormat()

conn=S3Connection(aws_access_key_id=apikey,
```

```
        aws_secret_access_key=secretkey,
        is_secure=False,host='104.197.27.250',
        port=8080,
        calling_format=cf)

conn.create_bucket('foobar')
```

And that's it. All of these steps may sound like a lot, but it has never been that easy to run an S3 object store. Docker truly makes running distributed applications a breeze.

10.5 DATA: Building a MySQL Galera Cluster on a Docker Network

Problem

You would like to deploy a MySQL Galera cluster on two Docker hosts, taking advantage of the new Docker Network feature (see Recipe 3.14). Galera is a multimaster high-availability MySQL database solution.

Solution

Docker Network, which you saw in Recipe 3.14, can be used to build a network overlay using the VXLAN protocol across multiple Docker hosts. The overlay is useful as it gives containers IP addresses in the same routable subnet and also manages name resolution by updating */etc/hosts* on each container. Therefore, every container started in the same overlay can reach the other ones by using their container names.

This significantly simplifies networking across hosts, and makes a lot of solutions that have been built for single hosts also valid for a multiple-hosts setup.

 At time of this writing Docker Network is in preview in the experimental Docker binaries (i.e., 1.8.0-dev). It should be available in Docker 1.9. The use of a Consul server may not be needed in the future.

To build your Galera (*http://galeracluster.com*) cluster on two Docker hosts, you will start by setting up the hosts with the experimental Docker binary. You will then follow the instructions described in a blog post (*http://galeracluster.com/2015/05/getting-started-galera-with-docker-part-1/*). The setup of this recipe is the same as the one depicted in Recipe 3.14. You will start several containers on each node by using the *erkules/galera:basic* image from Docker Hub.

As always, let's use a Vagrant box from the repository accompanying this book:

```
$ git clone https://github.com/how2dock/dockbook.git
$ cd dockbook/ch10/mysqlgalera
$ vagrant up
$ vagrant status
Current machine states:

consul-server          running (virtualbox)
mysql-1                running (virtualbox)
mysql-2                running (virtualbox)
```

The consul-server machine is currently used by Docker Network, but this may change. Currently we use this Consul server as a key-value store; the Docker engine on each host uses it to store information about each host. As a reminder, check the Vagrantfile and see the DOCKER_OPTS specified at start-up; you will see that we also define a default overlay network called multihost.

Once the machines are up, ssh to the first one and start the first node of your Galera cluster by using the image *erkules/galera:basic*. You can check the reference (*http://galeracluster.com/2015/05/getting-started-galera-with-docker-part-1/*) to see what is in the Dockerfile used to build this image.

Let's do it:

```
$ vagrant ssh mysql-1
$ docker run -d --name node1 -h node1 erkules/galera:basic \
            --wsrep-cluster-name=local-test \
        --wsrep-cluster-address=gcomm://
```

Get on host mysql-2 and start two additional Galera nodes. Note that you use the node name node1 for the cluster address. This will work because Docker Network will automatically properly define the */etc/hosts* file and it will contain the IP address of node1, node2, and node3. Since the three containers are in the same overlay, they will be able to reach one another without any port mapping, container linking, or other more complex network setup:

```
$ vagrant ssh mysql-2
$ docker run --detach=true --name node2 -h node2 erkules/galera:basic \
            --wsrep-cluster-name=local-test \
        --wsrep-cluster-address=gcomm://node1
$ docker run --detach=true --name node3 -h node3 erkules/galera:basic \
            --wsrep-cluster-name=local-test \
        --wsrep-cluster-address=gcomm://node1
```

Back on mysql-1, you will see that after a short time, the two nodes started on mysql-2 have automatically joined the cluster:

```
$ docker exec -ti node1 mysql -e 'show status like "wsrep_cluster_size"'
+--------------------+-------+
| Variable_name      | Value |
+--------------------+-------+
```

```
| wsrep_cluster_size | 3      |
+--------------------+------+
```

And indeed the */etc/hosts* file on the node1 container has the IP address of the other two nodes:

```
$ docker exec -ti node1 cat /etc/hosts
...
172.21.0.6   node1.multihost
172.21.0.6   node1
172.21.0.8   node2
172.21.0.8   node2.multihost
172.21.0.9   node3
172.21.0.9   node3.multihost
```

This recipe is interesting because using Docker Network allows you to use the exact same deployment methodology that you would have used on a single Docker host.

Discussion

Try adding more Galera nodes, killing some, and you will see that the cluster size varies.

See Also

- Blog post on building a Galera cluster on a single Docker host (*http://galeraclus ter.com/2015/05/getting-started-galera-with-docker-part-1/*)
- Blog post on building a Galera cluster on multiple Docker hosts (*http://galeraclus ter.com/2015/05/getting-started-galera-with-docker-part-2-2/*)

10.6 DATA: Dynamically Configuring a Load-Balancer for a MySQL Galera Cluster

Problem

Recipe 10.5 created a multinode Galera cluster on two Docker hosts, taking advantage of the Docker Network capability to create a network overlay. Now you would like to automatically configure a load-balancer to share the load among all the nodes of this Galera cluster.

Solution

Use the setup described in Recipe 10.3. Use registrator to dynamically register the MySQL nodes in a key-value store like Consul, and use confd to manage an nginx template that will balance the load among the Galera cluster nodes. Figure 10-5 depicts a two-node setup in which Docker Network is used across the nodes, `regis trator` runs to publish the services running on each node, and Nginx runs on one of the nodes to provide load-balancing between these nodes.

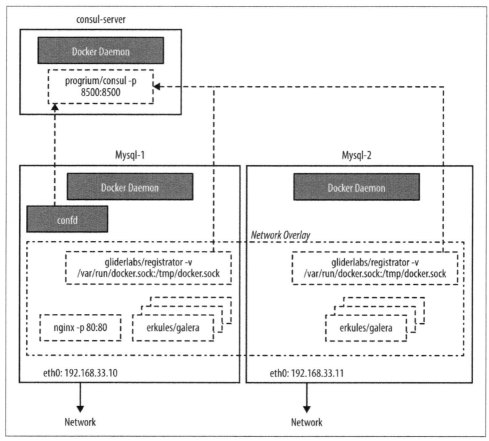

Figure 10-5. Dynamic load balancing of a Galera cluster

Run `registrator` on each host, pointing to the consul-server running on the separate VM at `192.168.33.10` and start the first two nodes of the Galera cluster using the image *erkules/galera:basic*.

On `mysql-1` at `192.168.33.11` run the following:

```
$ docker run -d -v /var/run/docker.sock:/tmp/docker.sock
          gliderlabs/registrator
          -ip 192.168.33.11 consul://192.168.33.10:8500/galera
$ docker run -d --name node1
          -h node1 erkules/galera:basic
          --wsrep-cluster-name=local-test --wsrep-cluster-address=gcomm://
```

On `mysql-2` at `192.168.33.12` use this:

```
$ docker run -d -v /var/run/docker.sock:/tmp/docker.sock
            gliderlabs/registrator
            -ip 192.168.33.12 consul://192.168.33.10:8500/galera
$ docker run -d --name node2
            -h node2 erkules/galera:basic
            --wsrep-cluster-name=local-test --wsrep-cluster-address=gcomm://node1
```

Create an Nginx configuration file that acts as a load-balancer for these two applications. Assuming you decide to run the load-balancer on the Docker host with IP `192.168.33.11`, the following example will work:

```
events {
    worker_connections  1024;
}

http {
    upstream galera {
      server 192.168.33.11:3306;
      server 192.168.33.12:3306;
    }

    server {
        listen 80;
        location / {
            proxy_pass http://galera;
        }
    }
}
```

Next start your Nginx container, binding port 80 of the container to port 80 of the host, and mount your configuration file inside the container. Give your container a name, as this will prove handy later:

```
$ docker run -d -p 3306:3306 -v /home/vagrant/nginx.conf:/etc/nginx/nginx.conf
            --name galera nginx
```

Test that your load-balancing works. Then head back to Recipe 10.3 and use the same steps presented there. Use `confd` to automatically reconfigure your nginx configuration template when you add MySQL containers.

10.7 DATA: Creating a Spark Cluster

Problem

You are looking for a data-processing engine that can work in parallel for fast computation and access to large datasets. You have settled on Apache Spark (*http://spark.apache.org*) and would like to deploy it using containers.

Solution

Apache Spark (*http://spark.apache.org*) is an extremely fast data-processing engine that works at large scale (for a large number of worker nodes) and that can also handle a large amount of data. With Java, Scala, Python, and R interfaces, Spark is a great tool to program complex data-processing problems.

A Spark cluster can be deployed in Kubernetes (*https://github.com/GoogleCloudPlatform/kubernetes/tree/master/examples/spark*), but with the development of Docker Network, the Kubernetes deployment scenario can be used almost as is. Indeed, Docker Network (see Recipe 3.14) builds isolated networks across multiple Docker hosts, manages simple name resolution, and exposes services.

Hence to deploy a Spark cluster, you are going to use a Docker network and then do the following:

- Start a Spark master by using the image available on the Google registry and used by the Kubernetes example.
- Start a set of Spark workers by using a slightly modified image (*https://registry.hub.docker.com/u/runseb/spark-worker/*) from the Google registry.

The worker image uses a start-up script that hardcodes the Spark master port to 7077 instead of using an environment variable set by Kubernetes. The image is available on Docker Hub (*https://registry.hub.docker.com/u/runseb/spark-worker/*) and you can see the start-up script on GitHub (*https://github.com/runseb/spark-docker*).

Let's start a master, making sure that you define the hostname spark-master:

```
$ docker run -d -p 8080:8080 --name spark-master -h spark-master gcr.io/ \
google_containers/spark-master
```

Now let's create three Spark workers. You could create more and create them on any hosts that are on the same Docker network:

 To avoid crashing your nodes and/or containers, limit the memory allocated to each Spark worker container. You do this with the -m option of docker run.

```
$ docker run -d -p 8081:8081 -m 256m --name worker-1 runseb/spark-worker
$ docker run -d -p 8082:8081 -m 256m --name worker-2 runseb/spark-worker
$ docker run -d -p 8083:8081 -m 256m --name worker-3 runseb/spark-worker
```

You might have noticed that you exposed port 8080 of the Spark master container on the host. This gives you access to the Spark master web interface. As soon as the

Spark master container is running, you can access this UI. After the workers come online, you will see them appear in the dashboard, as shown in Figure 10-6.

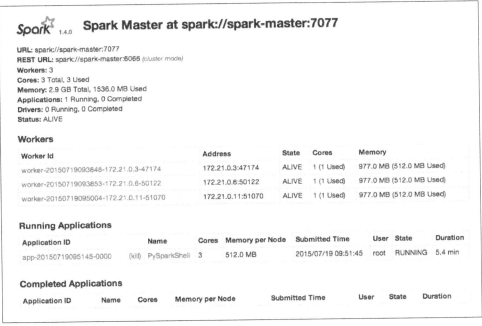

Figure 10-6. The Spark master UI

This is it. The ease of deployment comes from the fact that the Spark workers try to reach the master node with the hostname `spark-master`. Because the Docker Network manages name resolution, each container automatically knows the IP of the master and can reach it.

Discussion

If you check the network services that have been published, you see your four containers on the multihost network (i.e., `spark-master`, `worker-1`, `worker-2`, `worker-3`). But since you also published the ports for the UI, each container was also attached to the bridge network. In the following example, you see only the worker nodes on the bridge because this lists the services on the node that is not running the master. If you check the Docker host that is running the master, you will see that the `spark-master` is also on the bridge network:

```
$ docker service ls
SERVICE ID         NAME          NETWORK       CONTAINER
92e90b6556b5       worker-1      bridge        ba80b36e5abc
1831b9378d37       worker-2      bridge        c1c8bec01a2a
bc64584793df       worker-3      bridge        f7be3797affb
```

```
2bbe00afc559      worker-1      multihost      ba80b36e5abc
7be77369a0ac      worker-2      multihost      c1c8bec01a2a
3a576b7233b6      worker-3      multihost      f7be3797affb
e3c75728c402      spark-master   multihost      fa44cce982df
```

Since you exposed the Spark worker's web interface port, you can access the UI.
Figure 10-7 shows a snapshot of a task that has already completed on this worker.

Figure 10-7. The Spark worker UI

The task shown in the dashboard is the result of running the Spark shell (*https://spark.apache.org/docs/latest/quick-start.html*), which is a quick way to start learning Spark and running tasks on your containerized Spark cluster. You can run the Spark shell via another interactive container as shown here:

```
$ docker run -it gcr.io/google_containers/spark-base
root@ac912dd21619:/# . ./setup_client.sh spark-master 7077
root@ac912dd21619:/# pyspark
Python 2.7.9 (default, Mar  1 2015, 12:57:24)
...
Welcome to


      ____              __
     / __/__  ___ _____/ /__
    _\ \/ _ \/ _ `/ __/  '_/
   /__ / .__/\_,_/_/ /_/\_\   version 1.4.0
      /_/

...
>>>
```

Because `libnetwork` is changing rapidly, the network connectivity between the Spark master and the workers might be unreliable. The service publication mechanism might also change. Treat this example as a work in progress of what could be done, but not as a production deployment scenario. If you experience problems, remember to check the logs of each container with `docker logs -f <container_id>`.

See Also

- The Kubernetes Spark example (*https://github.com/GoogleCloudPlatform/kuber netes/tree/master/examples/spark*) that inspired this recipe

Index

Symbols

--net=host, 81
.dockerignore, 46

A

Amazon Linux AMI, 241
Amazon S3, 321
Amazon Web Services (see AWS)
Another Union File System (AUFS), 129
Ansible, 54, 214-216
Ansible Docker module, 214-216, 229
Apache Libcloud, 190
Apache Mesos (see Mesos)
Apache Spark cluster, 329-333
application programming interface (API)
    Docker remote, 121-123
    Kubernetes, 160-163
application use cases, 305-333
    continuous delivery pipeline with Jenkins
      and Apache Mesos, 310-314
    dynamic load balancer with confd and reg-
      istrator, 314-320
    dynamically configuring a load-balancer for
      a MySQL Galera cluster, 327-329
    MySQL Galera cluster on Docker Network,
      325-327
    S3-compatible object store with Cassandra
      on Kubernetes, 321
    setting up development environment,
      306-310
    Spark cluster, 329-333
Atomic, 185, 186
AUFS (Another Union File System), 129
authentication, 167

automated builds, 62
AWS (Amazon Web Services), 192
    account creation, 237
    CLI, 240-243
    ECS (see EC2 container service)
    Elastic Beanstalk, 274-278
    principles, 239
    running Weave Net, 99
    starting a Docker host with Docker
      Machine, 248-250
    starting Atomic instance to use Docker, 186
    starting Docker host on AWS EC2, 240-243
    Ubuntu Core Snappy instance on AWS EC2,
      190-193
AWS EC2
    Docker host on, 240-243
    Ubuntu Core Snappy instance on, 190-193
Azure, 192, 237, 245-247, 250-252

B

background, running service in, 22
Bash, xiii
Beanstalk, 274-278
binary (see Docker binary)
Bitbucket, 63-67
Boot2Docker
    and GCE CLI, 252
    docker-py integration with, 127
    for getting Docker host on OS X, 9-13
    on Windows 8.1 desktop, 13-15
Borg, 131
Boto, 266, 270, 324
bridge, custom, 91
build trigger, 66

builds, automated, 62-69

C

CA (certificate authority), 124
cAdvisor
    container metrics monitoring, 302
    resource usage monitoring, 300
Canonical, 188
cases, application (see application cases)
Cassandra, 321
CentOS 6.5, 3
CentOS 7, 4
CentOS project, 42
certificate authority (CA), 124
child image, 58
CI/CD (continuous integration/continuous
    deployment)
    development environment, 306-310
    pipeline with Jenkins and Apache Mesos,
      310-314
CLI (see command line interface)
cloud
    accessing public clouds to run Docker,
      237-239
    application using Docker support in AWS
      Beanstalk, 274-278
    cloud provider CLI in a Docker container,
      252-254
    Docker containers on an ECS cluster,
      270-273
    Docker host on AWS EC2, 240-243
    Docker host on AWS with Docker Machine,
      248-250
    Docker host on Azure with Docker
      Machine, 250-252
    Docker host on Google GCE, 243-245
    Docker host on Microsoft Azure, 245-247
    Docker in, 235-278
    Docker in GCE Google-container instances,
      257-259
    Docker Machine to start Docker host in,
      15-19
    EC2 container service, 264-266
    ECS cluster, 267-270
    GCR to store Docker images, 254-257
    Kubernetes via GCE, 259-263
cloud-init
    configuring cloud instances, 242
    starting container on CoreOS, 175

cluster IP services, 148-152
cluster(s)
    configuring authentication to, 167
    configuring client to access remote, 169
    CoreOS, 177-180
    creating with Docker Compose, 153-156
    Docker Machine to create, 206
    ECS, 267-270
    fleet to start containers on, 180
    Kubernetes, with Pods, 141-142
    Lattice for running containers on, 221-223
    load-balancer for MySQL Galera cluster,
      327-329
    Mesos Docker containerizer on, 228
    multinode, 137-140
    on Docker Network, 325-327
    Rancher to manage containers on, 217-220
    Spark, 329-333
    starting containers on, with Docker Swarm,
      203-205
CMD instruction, 42
Collectd, 294-299
command line interface (CLI)
    AWS, 240-243
    cloud provider, 252-254
    GCE, 252
    gcloud CLI, 261
Conduit, 68
confd, 317-320
config.rb, 173
configuring, 120-130
    (see also development)
    changing storage driver, 129-130
    Docker daemon, 110, 120, 123-125
    docker-py, 126-128, 128
    Kubernetes, 167, 169
consul, 232
container images (see images)
container linking
    alternatives for large-scale systems, 76
    and networking, 75-77
container logs
    docker logs for obtaining, 285
    managing Logspout routes to store, 291
    using Elasticsearch and Kibana to store and
      visualize, 293
    using Logspout to collect, 289-291
container metrics

About the Author

Sébastien Goasguen built his first compute cluster in the late 90s (when they were still called Beowulf clusters) while working on his PhD; he has been working on making computing a utility since then. He has done research in grid computing and high-performance computing, and with the advent of virtualization moved to cloud computing in the mid-2000s when he was a professor at Clemson University.

He is currently a senior open source solutions architect at Citrix, where he works primarily on the Apache CloudStack project helping develop the CloudStack ecosystem. He was elected vice president of the Apache CloudStack project in March 2015. He is also a member of the project management committee (PMC) of Apache libcloud, and a member of the Apache Software Foundation. Sébastien focuses on the cloud ecosystem and has contributed to dozens of open source projects.

Colophon

The animal on the cover of *Docker Cookbook* is a beluga whale (*Delphinapterus leucas*), which along with the narwhal is one of two members of the family Monodontidae.

Because it is adapted to life in the Arctic, the beluga whale is anatomically different from most other types of whales. It is all white in color, does not have a dorsal fin, has the highest percentage of blubber, and has a very large protuberance on its forehead that houses its echolocation organ (called the "melon"). The melon is very important because it not only allows the whale to hunt, but it also enables it to find blowholes among shifting ice sheets.

Belugas are very gregarious creatures, and usually live in groups of around 10 individuals. During the summer, these groups gather in coastal areas for breeding, meaning that there can be hundreds or even thousands of belugas in one place. The worldwide population has been estimated at 150,000, with the majority living in the seas off of North America, Russia, and Greenland.

The native peoples of North America and Russia have hunted belugas for centuries, but the whales were also hunted commercially during the 19th and early 20th centuries. Since whale hunting came under international regulation in the 1970s, only certain Inuit and Alaska Native tribes are allowed to continue the practice today.

Belugas in the wild can live for 70 to 80 years, but they are a popular species of whale for aquarium display, where the lifespan is significantly less. Currently the beluga is considered to be a "near threatened" species because of population loss due to changing habitat, polluted water, and infectious disease.

Many of the animals on O'Reilly covers are endangered; all of them are important to the world. To learn more about how you can help, go to *animals.oreilly.com*.

The cover image is from *A History of British Quadrupeds*. The cover fonts are URW Typewriter and Guardian Sans. The text font is Adobe Minion Pro; the heading font is Adobe Myriad Condensed; and the code font is Dalton Maag's Ubuntu Mono.

Get even more for your money.

Join the O'Reilly Community, and register the O'Reilly books you own. It's free, and you'll get:

- $4.99 ebook upgrade offer
- 40% upgrade offer on O'Reilly print books
- Membership discounts on books and events
- Free lifetime updates to ebooks and videos
- Multiple ebook formats, DRM FREE
- Participation in the O'Reilly community
- Newsletters
- Account management
- 100% Satisfaction Guarantee

Signing up is easy:

1. Go to: oreilly.com/go/register
2. Create an O'Reilly login.
3. Provide your address.
4. Register your books.

Note: English-language books only

To order books online:
oreilly.com/store

For questions about products or an order:
orders@oreilly.com

To sign up to get topic-specific email announcements and/or news about upcoming books, conferences, special offers, and new technologies:
elists@oreilly.com

For technical questions about book content:
booktech@oreilly.com

To submit new book proposals to our editors:
proposals@oreilly.com

O'Reilly books are available in multiple DRM-free ebook formats. For more information:
oreilly.com/ebooks

O'REILLY®

Have it your way.

Lightning Source UK Ltd.
Milton Keynes UK
UKOW05f0753211115

263208UK00001B/1/P